CONDUCTING MUSIC TODAY

Bruce Hangen

To access video visit:
www.halleonard.com/mylibrary

Enter Code
4644-7293-0184-0759

Berklee Press

BERKLEE PRESS
Editor in Chief: Jonathan Feist
Senior Vice President of Online Learning and Continuing Education/CEO of Berklee Online: Debbie Cavalier
Vice President of Enrollment Marketing and Management: Mike King
Vice President of Academic Strategy: Carin Nuernberg
Editorial Assistants: Emily Jones, Megan Richardson

ISBN 978-1-4950-9791-1

Berklee Press

1140 Boylston Street
Boston, MA 02215-3693 USA
(617) 747-2146

Visit Berklee Press Online at
www.berkleepress.com

Berklee Online

Study music online at
online.berklee.edu

DISTRIBUTED BY

HAL•LEONARD®

7777 W. BLUEMOUND RD. P.O. BOX 13819
MILWAUKEE, WISCONSIN 53213

Visit Hal Leonard Online
www.halleonard.com

Berklee Press, a publishing activity of Berklee College of Music, is a not-for-profit educational publisher.
Available proceeds from the sales of our products are contributed to the scholarship funds of the college.

CONTENTS

ACKNOWLEDGMENTS

I gratefully acknowledge all the musicians in all the orchestras I've conducted, as each and every one of them has taught me—often unknowingly—something invaluable in the art of conducting. While professional musicians can be bluntly critical, they are nevertheless the best teachers.

I also acknowledge Editor-in-Chief Jonathan Feist, for his unwavering patience in coaching me through the experience of writing my first book. He and our Berklee colleagues—particularly Joe Bennett, Carin Nuernberg, Emily Jones, Brittany McCorriston, Megan Richardson, and the Hal Leonard team—have been such supportive guides and helpers through the entire process.

Ultimately, I want to thank my wife, Anabelle, for her constant love and support. Her presence as friend, sounding board, advisor, and partner has helped me in more ways than one can imagine.

INTRODUCTION

In the last half century, the profession of orchestral conducting has expanded into areas that the likes of Arturo Toscanini, Wilhelm Furtwängler, and Fritz Reiner could never have predicted. Even conducting textbooks today tend to concentrate almost exclusively on the intricacies of old-world masterpieces by Beethoven, Mozart, or Brahms.

But today's conductor is as likely to be seen doing his or her thing in a music theater pit, on stage accompanying video games or full-screen movies, or in the sound studio, recording everything imaginable!

Gone, then, are the days of studying the scores *only* of one's favorite symphonies, operas, and ballets. Conductors now are responsible for learning the repertoires of the latest pop, jazz, and country stars, not to mention having to accompany a film screen in live or recorded performance. Those who choose these more contemporary avenues as a career find themselves never looking at a Richard Strauss tone poem but instead must decipher the computer-generated scores accompanying a video game, a George Lucas film, or the scratchy manuscript of a pop arranger.

This book is an attempt to introduce the emerging conductor to the essential gestural techniques appropriate for all career paths, not just the [stereo]-typical maestro in front of a hundred-piece symphony orchestra and two thousand adoring patrons. Actually, conducting technique is rather simple, but it's the application of the technique in a meaningful and effective way that gets complicated.

Today's symphonic conductor often is busy putting together new and interesting programs pretty much on the fly, with minimal, if any, rehearsal time; unusual and unfamiliar repertoire that's not necessarily sight-readable; scores requiring new playing techniques by the musicians; and the need to be creatively subservient to musical and non-musical impulses (classical and pops soloists and groups, film scores, click tracks, etc.).

As a conducting major at the Eastman School of Music, I can remember studying a Haydn symphony or two, seemingly forever, maybe some Beethoven, and then for variety(!), Stravinsky's *Rite of Spring*. But my earliest experiences at actually conducting in performance were baroque string music and contemporary chamber ensembles with ad hoc student ensembles. There had to have been some kind of relation between my conducting studies of the classical, orchestral repertoire and my conducting activities in the baroque and pre-baroque and twentieth-century smaller ensembles, though certainly at the time, I wouldn't have seen it.

After graduation, I became assistant conductor to a major regional U.S. orchestra, and were my conducting assignments in the repertoire with which I was already familiar and most comfortable? No! Full orchestra youth concerts for which the parameters were: 46 minutes of music total, no one piece longer than 6 minutes, all repertoire had to be from the orchestra's library (i.e., no rental and no new purchases), each selection had to be "interesting" to fourth- to sixth-grader audiences, no hiring of extra musicians outside the regular, full-time personnel, *and* the entire program had to be acceptable to/approved by a committee of community volunteers, all of whom had different ideas about what music education should be!

In my opinion, most conducting programs still concentrate only on the most basic, standard orchestral repertoire without sufficiently addressing the other repertoires into which most of today's emerging conductors will be engaged. While the specific examples contained herein are also from the orchestral repertoire as prime examples of the challenges to be found in all styles, I hope to at least introduce other responsibilities and career areas that require effective conducting talent. Assuming you can *apply creatively* what you read here, my wish for you is to be truly *effective* at what you do, no matter who or what you're conducting.

In this book, I will first provide you with what I believe are the essentials for conducting *anything*! It doesn't matter where or who your musicians are; if you're the one on the podium, there are certain universally-accepted principles of musical leadership. Secondly, I will introduce several of the different professional avenues requiring a conductor today, drawing both from my own experiences and the input garnered from many friends and associates. And finally, I will introduce a series of interviews with acknowledged leaders in those particular fields: conductors who have contributed so much to America's music, dealing with executive directors, stage directors, production managers, editors, and other related professionals.

This text is divided into three parts:

Part I. Conducting Technique

Section A. All the basics of what it takes to be a conductor. I address everything from posture to holding the baton to how to move the baton and how to prepare the printed score. Photos and video links are there to help your understanding of what I describe.

Section B. Several lessons on how to employ musically the technical principles learned in sections A and B, how to relate to the musicians you're guiding, and suggestions of best practices in podium demeanor.

Section C. Here is a collection of many thoughts and principles garnered from more than a decade's worth of teaching conducting at the Boston Conservatory at Berklee, as well as from my personal experience leading as music director and guest conducting many of this country's symphony orchestras.

Part II. Technical Suggestions in Standard Repertoire

Guidance to particular moments in specific orchestral repertoire that demonstrate many of the most particular conducting challenges that can be found in many different styles of music. I have also provided video links with music to more clearly describe the issues and solutions for each of the excerpts.

Part III. Interviews

Each one of these conductors is highly accomplished, experienced, and accustomed to speaking about their profession in ways that are both comprehensive and lucid. You will enjoy all of their comments. For the emerging conductor/reader, there are many gems of wisdom to remember.

Conducting Mahler symphonies with "my" orchestras of Omaha, or Portland (Maine), or Indian Hill, as well as having conducted literally hundreds of concerts with the Boston Pops and others, has given me a broad range of experience at conducting and leading ensembles of all kinds, in all situations, and for all kinds of audiences. All those experiences have proven remarkably valuable now with my teaching at the Boston Conservatory at Berklee, teaching some incredibly talented emerging conductors who themselves have given me the gift of understanding what it takes to teach this wildly abstract, subjective, diffuse topic of instrumental conducting.

ABOUT THE VIDEOS/EXCERPTS

To access the accompanying videos and notation for the orchestral excerpts, go to www.halleonard.com/mylibrary and enter the code found on the first page of this book. This will grant you instant access to every example. Examples with accompanying videos and notation are marked with icons.

Video

Notation

PART I
Conducting Technique

Section A. The Basics

Like any other artistic discipline, the art of conducting involves certain techniques, principles, and rules to learning the art before attempting creativity of motion and interpretation. The pianist learns proper posture, hand placement, and early technique to develop all the right muscles; the cellist learns the most advantageous setup for controlling the bow and managing the myriad left-hand positions. With any creative endeavor, the basics must first be absorbed before embarking on one's own style by bending or accommodating the basic rules in developing a personal, unique approach that works for you only. No clearer example of the adage that you need to know the rules before you can break them could be found than the learning and developing of a conducting technique.

Regardless of your ultimate goal, the basics as presented first in this book—along with the support of the accompanying videos—should help you establish at the very least a clear understanding of *why* the basics are indeed so...basic.

1

Posture

Stand up straight, face the ensemble straight ahead, and have the *tip* of your baton directly in front of your navel, though slightly higher. The baton should feel to you, and look to others, as centered. Feet should be spaced comfortably apart, parallel to each other, and neither foot should be ahead of the other. Your weight should be evenly divided on both the balls and heels of both feet for proper balance. Relax your shoulders and position them back, opening your front posture.

The music stand should be placed directly in front of you, with the music at a height where you can conveniently turn pages without having to move your body to accommodate the page turn. The higher the music is, relative to your waist, the more you risk creating a psychological barrier between you and the musicians. The lower the music is, the more you risk interfering with your line of communication with the musicians by having to bend, or reach out, or even turn your torso to reach the page you wish to turn.

I have found that some conductors have a difficult time allowing their downbeats to extend as low as their waist. Rather, the area of their field of motion is placed quite higher, extending perhaps only to slightly below shoulder level. This is uncomfortable, not only for the conductor in the long run, but also for ensemble musicians located in close proximity, forced to raise their normal playing position in order to see the conducting gestures. Allowing your field of motion to reside mostly in front of your torso allows for very effective, constant, and important eye contact with your ensemble. There is a direct line of sight you will eventually maintain, from your eyes to the musician or section you're addressing, and without interfering in that line, the expressive baton will still be within the field of vision you are establishing with the musician/section.

Stand tall when on the podium. If you're not using a podium for a smaller ensemble, still stand tall! Correct, beneficial, and healthy posture is just as important for you as it is any performing musician.

Investigate the principles of Alexander Technique (there are basic resources online, and Alexander Technique teachers are everywhere) to get the feel of proper spine, shoulder, neck, head, and knee alignment that, in the long run, will make you much more comfortable both to be, and to be seen by others. You'll be grateful for the training when you find yourself conducting three- or four-hour operas, or two or three rehearsals or recording sessions in a day. Take a year's course in the technique, engage a personal coach or, at the very least, follow the basic steps online. It will make a world of difference.

FIG. 1.1. Basic Posture: Side View. Please note the straight back, eyes directly into the orchestra, hands together and centered, music stand at an angle, straight-line relationship between eyes, through hands, to music.

FIG. 1.2. Music Stand. The basic posture does not need to change when reaching to turn the score page.

FIG. 1.3. Feet Position. A simple, balanced approach to feet placement gives the conductor a solid foundation for all conducting movement.

1. Posture

2

The Baton

The baton is your *instrument.* Like any instrument, it can be either expressive or just another inanimate object. But an expressive baton is directly related to your ability to manipulate your wrist so as to give much more flexibility (i.e., expression) to the conducting gesture. Remember that the effectiveness of your gestures will determine the sound your ensemble returns to you. Your ensemble is *responding* to your conducting technique, purely and simply. The sound they make is in direct correlation to what they see and feel from your gestures. It behooves you, then, to be impeccably clean, articulate, and clear with your gestures so your ensemble may respond in kind.

The following should be your earliest, default position, from which (years later) you will find yourself wanting to grow. If you can first grasp the baton in this described manner, it is more likely than not your baton will become the expressive instrument that you eventually will want it to be.

Hold the baton as if it is an extension of your arm. The key point of contact will be between the *tip* of your thumb and the first knuckle of your index fingers. All other fingers will wrap gently around the baton's handle, which itself should be unseen, and folded into the palm of your hand! Imagining that your palm and underside of your forearm are parallel to, and facing the floor (flat, as if resting on a tabletop), the wrist angled sideways to the right, in order to maintain a relatively straight line from your forearm through the *tip* of the stick. Your elbow should be relaxed, though not touching your torso, and extended slightly in front of you to put the baton itself in the space over your music stand. The point of the baton, in your default position, should be directly in front of your navel, though perhaps a couple inches higher. When you give a solid downbeat, you should feel like the underside of your forearm and the palm of your hand (while holding the baton) are actually facing the floor, and your forearm is actually parallel to the floor.

The baton passes through the tip of the thumb and the first knuckle of the index finger, which form a "T" as the primary contact point for holding it.

FIG. 2.1. Grasping the Baton

Given the primary contact point shown in figure 2.1, your remaining fingers gently fold around the handle of the baton.

FIG. 2.2. Grasping the Baton: View from Underneath

Here's another view of the hand grasping the baton, this time elevated to show the underside more clearly.

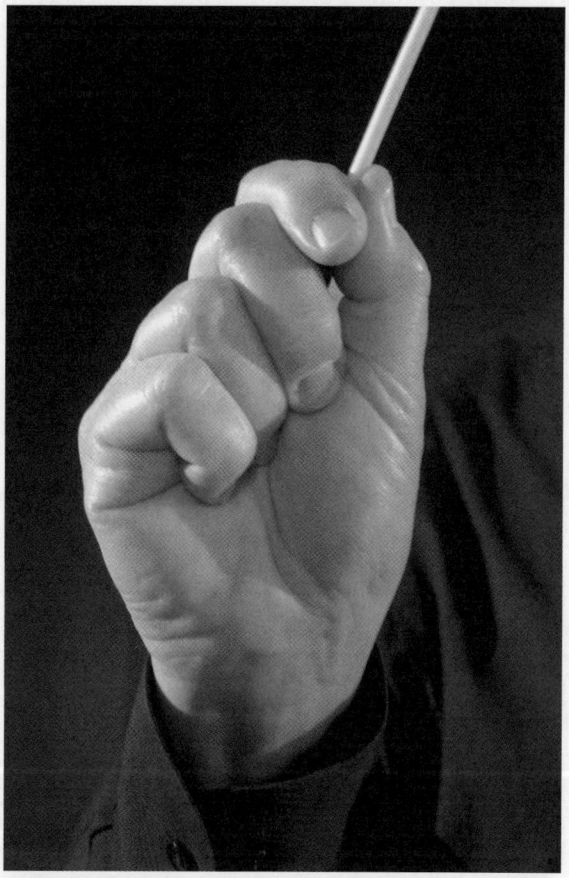

FIG. 2.3. Grasping the Baton: Another View

Note the downbeat is pointing down, the hand remains clasped around the handle as indicated before, the arm is projecting toward the ensemble, and the baton is centered over the music and in front of the body.

FIG. 2.4. Frontal View

2. Baton

When you conduct, it should be the *tip* of the baton, not your hand, that's the focus of attention. Some conductors, even well-established professionals, disagree with this concept. For them, the baton is not an expressive instrument, only a stick that elongates the conductor's arm for greater visibility. But I believe that, if in fact the baton is considered to be not just an extension, but actually becomes an additional part of your arm (upper arm, forearm, "baton-arm"), then the wrist must play an integral role in having the baton behave expressively. So, your wrist becomes the fulcrum manifesting the pivoting action you want to create. Allow the wrist to manipulate the baton, not so much as if it were operating independently, but rather in an organic fashion, the movement of which begins with the shoulder, continues through the elbow to the wrist and the baton, ultimately to the very *tip* of the baton! My conducting students have all seen me demonstrate thinking of the baton as a writing instrument that you are using in space, dotting your i's, crossing your t's, and managing your musical cutoffs.

To continue the analogy, draw a rhythmic and dynamic picture with your baton that the orchestra can follow. Keep your focus on the *tip*, not on your hand. *Lead* the orchestra by making your wrist more active than any other part of your body, so they can actually read what you're expressing! This is so much more effective (and energy-saving!) a method than to pound away using the whole arm holding on to a baton as if it were a club.

While left-handed conductors do exist, professional musicians almost always are far more comfortable following a right-handed leader. I have come across several left-handed conductors and left-handed wannabe conductors, and it has yet to make sense to me why (1) emerging conductors want to insist—at their own risk of resistance by ensembles—on conducting left-handed, and (2) they feel they cannot learn how to "play" this baton-instrument in the traditional way. After all, how many left-handed violinists are in the world, who actually bow using their left hand? To date, I am familiar with only one who had a long orchestral career despite the fact that her bow moved in the opposite direction from all others in her section!

Think about it, with extremely rare exceptions, classical music instruments are all held one way, regardless of whether one is right- or left-handed. To begin your early instruction in conducting by insisting on holding the baton in your left hand only shows an unwillingness to learn. And besides, if you're early in your career, why would you want to set yourself up as the extremely rare exception to the norm when ensembles have so many right-handed conductors with whom they'd more comfortably play?

It is all in the wrist! is a mantra easier said than done. Finding the right balance of wrist movement as compared to the elbow and the shoulder can be difficult, if the emerging conductor does not already play an instrument requiring a flexible wrist. Emerging conductors tend to conduct either with a stiff, rigid wrist, or such a loose wrist as to indicate a flippant approach to the task of conducting.

3

The Other Hand

With your right hand holding the baton, what is it you should be doing with your left hand? Observing even the legendary Fritz Reiner conducting mostly single-handedly (literally!) with the right hand and baton would be an extremely rare occurrence with practically any conductor today. Conducting with both hands mirroring themselves feels just so "normal" that it takes real concentration to practice doing otherwise. I can attest to the real discomfort my own conducting students feel when trying to conduct—even by themselves in a private studio lesson—with the left hand and arm not in total, equal engagement! And with orchestra? It's a given: both hands are almost always in constant motion. Otherwise, it would feel just so…awkward!

Unfortunately, having both hands equally engaged in motion leads to an inevitable "mirroring," where the left hand is simply mimicking in the opposite direction what the leading, baton hand is doing. This is a huge trap for emerging conductors, depriving them from a desired independence of motion and therefore adding to their inability to express multiple communications to multiple sections of the ensemble simultaneously. Obviously, there will be times when the conductor will wish (consciously or subconsciously) to employ the mirroring technique. This can be important, for instance, when conducting a relatively complicated passage with a large ensemble in which both sides of the ensemble would benefit from the closer proximity of each conductor's hand.

Back in the day, conducting textbooks would admonish those learning the craft to employ the baton hand as the utilitarian one: i.e., dictating the tempo, beat, dynamic, and basic character, whereas the left hand was to be reserved for expression: i.e., phrasing, cueing, subtle characterizations, and dynamics. While perhaps somewhat outdated, this is still a good concept to follow. What this means, however, is that the emerging conductor should strive to achieve complete independence of hands so that at any musical moment in time, s/he can physically respond with a leading or corrective gesture to any member or section of the ensemble without interfering with the basic process of beating time for the ensemble overall.

If you have practiced and created a truly flexible wrist, you can conduct absolutely everything you want clearly, cleanly, and effectively without the mooching effect caused by a mirroring left hand. And no, the left hand/arm does not need to lifelessly hang at one's side. While there's absolutely nothing wrong with that, most conductors will feel more comfortable with the left hand held passively (but ready!) waist high, in front of one's torso.

Later chapters in this book purposely avoid speaking more specifically about actions and gestures for the left, non-baton hand. Pay attention to a traffic cop, sometime. You'll rarely see both hands moving together. Rather, one hand motions to a portion of the traffic to stop ("softer"), or to others, to go ("louder"). The cop points to some to get attention (a "cue"); he or she might indicate a slowing down (a "diminuendo"). And so on, and so on. The variety of gestures is as unlimited as the musical circumstances that require action. I believe that if one develops a solid baton technique that truly can serve every intent found in any music, and if one maintains the complete independence of hands, then finding something to do with the left hand will become both obvious and easy… and, more effectively communicating to the ensemble.

Ultimately, what all conductors should attempt to avoid is the continuous flopping of both hands in total mirror fashion, seen in so many career conductors who haven't stopped to think what they're doing or what they look like to their musicians or audiences. It just doesn't make any sense to conduct like that, and it's just not effective. Put the left hand down, and see how compelling you can be by gesturing only with the baton in hand! Use your wrist to manage that baton as if it truly is an expressive instrument capable of communicating every little desire on your part, while still giving the beats!

4

Field of Motion

Your basic field of motion when conducting should be within an ellipse touching vertically from waist to eyes, and horizontally by extending your arms almost to the point of the elbows being straight, both right and left. Yes, there will be musical moments when it makes sense to go beyond this ellipse, but your basic, default area of conducting will be directly in front of your torso.

Developing a strong sense of ellipse that ranges from slightly above your waist on the bottom, to slightly above your eyes at the top, and almost as far as you can reach both left and right will be most comfortable for your musicians. Think of this area not as a circle, but as an ellipse that extends more to the right and left than it does higher or lower.

Certainly, there will be loud and/or dramatic and/or special musical circumstances in which your baton naturally will extend beyond the ellipse, but like any good recording meter, peaking beyond the normal range of motion should happen only rarely. Also, directing your right-hand pattern beyond your normal, default torso position can be helpful. With an orchestra, raising your pattern higher can communicate with the brass and percussion, at times. Directing to the left can help the violins in tricky passages. Moving directly forward into the ensemble can create the immediate need for everyone to be attentive.

Figure 4.1 is your best basic, default position for conducting. Hands are low enough to establish eye contact with your players. Each hand attracts equal attention, and they are close enough to each other for you to send multiple messages. Both hands are directly in front of the torso, allowing the musicians to focus on the entire you—your baton, left hand, eyes, and overall facial expression.

FIG. 4.1. The Conducting Ellipse: Correct

While the extended field of motion in figure 4.2 might be used on rare occasions as a default position, it is not so good. Both hands extend beyond the acceptable ellipse, causing fractured focus on the part of the musicians. In a quick instant, where should the musicians look? To the baton, to you, to the left hand? Save going beyond your ellipse like this for rare moments only, when the focus doesn't need to be on the specific technique you're indicating but instead on that most important, large, musical effect.

FIG. 4.2. Both Hands High, Outside the Ellipse

Figure 4.3 is an exaggeration of figure 4.2. The focus of any of your musicians is totally fractured with not knowing where to look for direction. Neither hand is contained within the ellipse, the baton isn't giving any direction, and the left hand seems stuck—almost removed from any kind of expression you might be trying to indicate.

FIG. 4.3. Both Hands Outside the Ellipse

Figure 4.4 is a good position, but note how your eye is drawn to my left hand, not so much the baton. Both hands are elevated, encouraging a larger sound, but the left hand seems to be making a stronger message than the baton is. With the baton pointed up, it contributes to the focus on the left hand because it is directed up, away from establishing communication with any musicians.

Figure 4.5 shows an exaggerated version of Figure 4.4 The baton is far enough outside the ellipse rendering it out of sight for most musicians. Holding it such would be appropriate only during, say, a fermata or some similar situation in which a beat is not being given. And with the left hand in this position, it appears as if it is about to indicate with a downward motion a long diminuando.

FIG. 4.4. Left Hand High

FIG. 4.5. Left Hand High, Right Hand Low

Imagine your torso, behind your ellipse, is the backdrop for the overwhelming majority of your conducting motions. When in performance, your dark apparel will provide an appropriate background to your white or natural wood baton. This is extremely helpful with large ensembles and in rooms (pits!) where lighting might not be ideal. An expressive, white baton can be so much more communicative when contrasted to your torso, dressed in black.

3. Field of Motion

5

The Podium

How high should your podium be? It may not even be appropriate to use a podium at all! The reason for having a podium is to be visible to all, especially conducting a large ensemble. Also, the additional elevation allows conductors to conduct for lengthy periods of time without their arms raised uncomfortably high. Shorter conductors might want a slightly higher podium. I know a taller conductor (he's over 7 feet tall) who doesn't use a podium at all! And if you're conducting a symphony concert that includes a smaller, say, baroque ensemble, as well as a romantic, full orchestra composition, I suggest using the orchestra's normal podium for the full orchestra and have stage management remove the podium for the smaller group. It is silly seeing a conductor standing on a normal orchestra-sized podium conducting an ensemble of less than full orchestral proportions. Be sensible in your approach; it's not about how you look to your audience.

Factory-made podiums come in standard heights, usually in 6- or 8-inch increments. Obviously, any custom-made podium can be any size or shape. Generally speaking, the emerging conductor will have very little choice of podiums at all, let alone being able to choose different heights.

Just remember the overriding principle that podiums came into being for the express purpose of musicians needing to see the conductor's gestures. If your ensemble can see you plainly while you're not elevated, then that's what you should do. If your ensemble is, say, thirty to forty musicians, you might want to be raised 6 inches to help accommodate your physical and visual communication with them. If your ensemble has seventy or more musicians, you'll likely want to be anywhere from 8 to 12 inches, even!

This is only a simple guideline. Most important to remember is that when you are conducting, your eyes should be able to meet all your musicians' eyes directly, and your conducting field of motion should be clearly visible to all musicians in a more-or-less direct line from their eyes to their music to you.

6

Beat Patterns

Besides the over-arching principle that any beat pattern is a physical depiction of each beat in the same measure of music that the ensemble is playing, the whole reason for conducting beat patterns is to show your ensemble *both* the exact point of the beat (to which their playing is supposed to connect) *and* the speed with which they're going to get to the next one. There are a few generally understood rules of movement, however, that virtually every instrumental ensemble expects to see in order for the players to feel comfortably together. I say "instrumental" because in an instrumental ensemble, the individual musicians have, of course, only their single line of music, without any regard for the other individual parts. Therefore, beating time in regular patterns per measure helps all individual parts keep their place in the composition overall. Each musician is counting and playing their own part throughout the composition, and the only other musicians who are doing exactly the same thing are those in the same section playing the same part (any of the string sections, for instance). The beat becomes, therefore, incredibly important in keeping the ensemble together.

Choral music, on the other hand, is generally printed with all parts in the same score, usually from which all individual choristers read. So, whether their music is homophonic or polyphonic, they almost always are able to follow the other parts in the event their single part is resting for a time. This allows a choral conductor much greater freedom of expression, without being bound to always giving beat patterns for each and every measure.

(a) Two Pattern: Down/Up

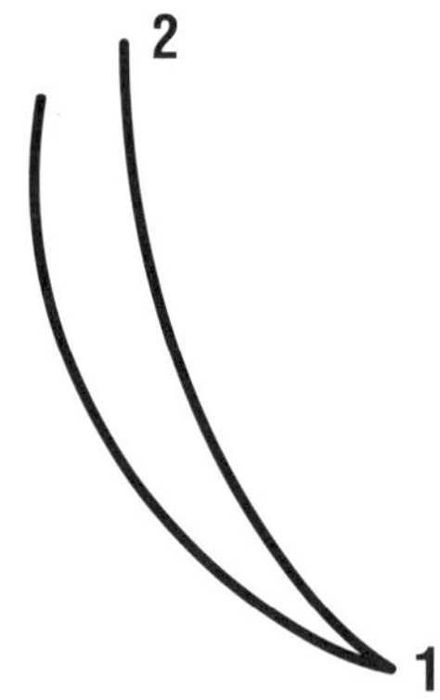

(b) Three Pattern: Down/Right/Up

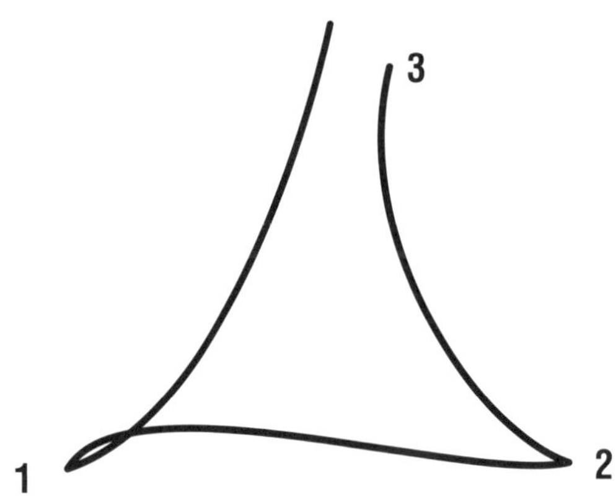

(c) Four Pattern: Down/Left/Right/Up

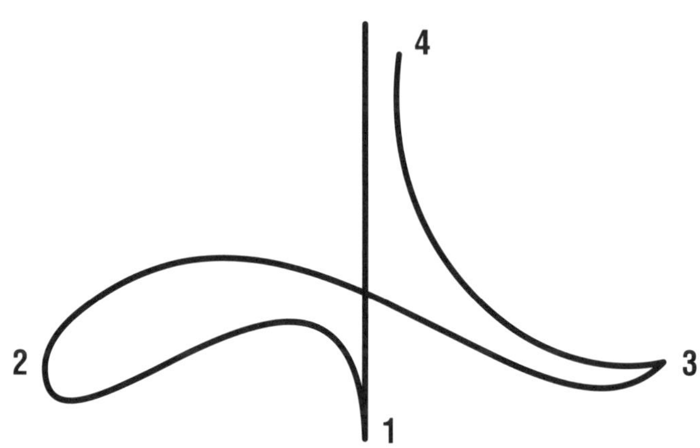

FIG. 6.1. Beat Patterns: (a) Two (b) Three (c) Four

4. Basic Patterns:
2, 3, 4, 5

There are some who call the simple, non-expressive beat pattern "truth." Conducting the pattern expressively, however, then "truth" becomes "music." It is the "music" of course that we all strive for, when the entire ensemble is generally moving along within a singular rhythmic pulse and the conductor has the freedom to allow the ensemble to progress, while maintaining a more expressive series of gestures.

It's the connecting distance, then, that in some ways is even more important than the beat itself, because it goes beyond "truth" to "expression." In other words, let's say you've just indicated the downbeat, but now your concentration, your motion, your baton, your *leadership* must now indicate the pacing and character toward the *next* beat, which in turn *leads* to the continuing *next* beat.

Joseph A. Labuta, in his very popular and successful textbook, describes this motion as the "and...now" gesture. Very simply put, this is what the technique of conducting is: the "and..." is the *preparation* for an arrival/departure of the next beat, and the "now" is the ultimate arrival. At that very "now" instant, you are immediately preparing the next beat, and the next, and so on, until the very end of the piece when you *still* make a preparation move for the final release, or cutoff.

Too many conductors concentrate so much on the *arrival* of the beat (or, as I mentioned above, "truth") that they forget the preparation motion ("expression") involved in getting to "music."

5. Patterns: Connectors

My conducting students over the years have become intensely aware of my very simple Four Rules of Conducting:

Rule 1: The first beat must go down.
Rule 2: The last beat must go up.
Rule 3: All other beats alternate more or less on a horizontal plane in-between.
Rule 4: Show the music!

RULE 1: THE FIRST BEAT MUST GO DOWN.

I know it sounds so simple, but I have seen too many emerging conductors who don't realize or haven't internalized the incredible importance that a professional large ensemble places on seeing downbeats. Why? As I mentioned earlier in the chapter, in the orchestral world there are too many individual parts progressing simultaneously, and each musician reads only his/her part.

For example, in the case of symphony orchestras, there can be as many as thirty different instrumental parts. Theoretically, no one has a clue as to what the others are doing, because they don't have each other's parts. This requires all performers to *count*—both rests and notes, requiring the conductor's *beat* as the primary organizing factor in putting the music together. What all this means is that your musicians are *counting measures of rest, and often not the same numbers of measures as even the person sitting next to them.* The clarity of your beat patterns, beginning with the all-important downbeat is therefore crucial to your musicians' musical security and comfort. Be there for them.

Any observer of even the most professional orchestras in the world can easily see musicians using their fingers to keep track of extended measures of rest. It's a simple but effective way, especially in relatively complex music, for musicians to keep their place while counting extended measures of rest. Making an incorrect entrance is a huge fear for even the most experienced of professionals. Consequently, make the upbeat-downbeat gesture in *any* time signature the most prominent so the musicians are more comfortable with where they are in the music. You are helping them by organizing the beats of music you're conducting into manageable segments (measures) of rest they're counting.

Naturally, there are exceptions to the rule, so in no way am I suggesting that your conducting technique ought to follow the rules so dogmatically that you ultimately lose the point of leading your musicians effectively. One obvious exception has to do with music in which everyone is playing most of the time. Another would be in music that has so regular a rhythmic pulse that counting rests becomes almost natural. Then you, the conductor, can spend time and energy concentrating on phrasing, cues, and balances without having to think so consciously about giving those dreaded beat patterns.

RULE 2: THE LAST BEAT (OF THE MEASURE) MUST GO UP.

For all reasons mentioned in Rule 1, it is equally important for the last beat of each measure to be attention-gettingly larger than the previous, middle beat(s), as a preparation for the larger downbeat. It is often helpful and comforting to the musicians when the upbeat goes obviously higher than the other beats in the pattern, setting up the next, most important downbeat.

There is an exception here as well. Obviously, one needn't emphasize the first and last beats when the music and musicians are moving along in unison motion. Then it is really just a matter of the conductor maintaining a pulse as the primary responsibility, regardless of beat pattern itself.

RULE 3: ALL OTHER BEATS GO ROUGHLY BACK AND FORTH ON A HORIZONTAL PLANE IN BETWEEN DOWNBEAT AND UPBEAT.

Over the years, I've seen far too many emerging conductors obsess over the direction of their beat patterns for all beats between the first and last beats. *It's not that important!...really!* Once you get your ensemble started, they're pretty much on their own until you arrive at a musical "corner" or transition when something different—a tempo, a dynamic, a meter change—happens. The best conductors I've seen also use the opportunity in the middle of measures to be particularly creative and musical with their gestures, emphasizing therefore their expression rather than time-beating.

What's important to remember here is that the *primary* responsibility of the conductor is to *lead*—to *inspire* and to *motivate*—the ensemble in synch with each other, pursuing a collective vision of what the composition is all about. If one were to conduct only the "truth," there would be a lot of miscommunication and lost musical "expression." Watch practically any professional conductor today, and while you'll see the *essence* of exactly these beat patterns I've described, you'll also notice that the conducting is not about the beat patterns, but really all about the music.

There's also an important sub-rule to this, which is that professional musicians accustomed to playing under a conductor also generally are more comfortable seeing the *penultimate* beat off to the right of your body, in preparation for the upbeat motion.

Many conductors are shy about conducting truly horizontal beats. Emerging conductors *think* they're going to the left and to the right, but generally speaking the rebounds they express after each beat have an upward direction, which means their next beat goes *downward*. This of course is very confusing, especially in non-familiar music and any series of mixed meters.

In complex music with a large ensemble, if your "sideways" beats (2 and 3, in a 4-meter) rebound vertically instead of continuing their sideways direction, players off to your sides (in an orchestra, your most important string players) will see your next motion as a downward beat, which can be confusing. Be sure to maintain the integrity of your overall pattern for cleanliness, togetherness, and comfort of all players. Doing so will only help them as they concentrate on making music, playing the notes, and otherwise managing their own part.

6. Side View

RULE 4: SHOW THE MUSIC!

This, of course, is the most difficult, both to understand as well as accomplish. What it really means is that all conducting must *portray* the character of the music and *in advance* of any—and every—given moment.

I strongly encourage you to hold the baton as if it's an expressive instrument. The wrist must allow the baton to draw out the qualities inherent in the music. Beyond staccato, legato, or simple dynamics, showing the music means indicating phrase lengths, managing the emotions, and carrying the ensemble through the large structures, all the while maintaining proper pulse and tempo.

Many emerging conductors feel the need to *be* the music, almost as if choreographed. This is over-conducting, which means the conductor is ignoring the need to be *preparing* the ensemble for each next musical moment. If you're so involved in dancing to the music, how do you expect to *lead* them into the next beat, the next measure, the next phrase, or even the next movement?

Also, if you're conducting so emotionally (i.e., *distractedly*), you're probably working too hard. Rule of thumb: the harder you conduct, the less you listen. All conducting *must* begin with listening. It's cyclical: what you *hear* determines what you *show*, which results in the next musical moment that you *hear*, determining your next *show* moment, and so on.

THE SIX-PATTERN

I am not a big fan of the (so-called) "German six" pattern. Many years ago, my mentor at Tanglewood, Joseph Silverstein (then concertmaster of the Boston Symphony Orchestra), insisted that I and other conducting fellows conduct the six pattern as if it were a subdivided two—the so-called "Italian six pattern." The entire pattern sits completely on your right side, and is totally more freeing, flexible and musical.

(a) Italian Six

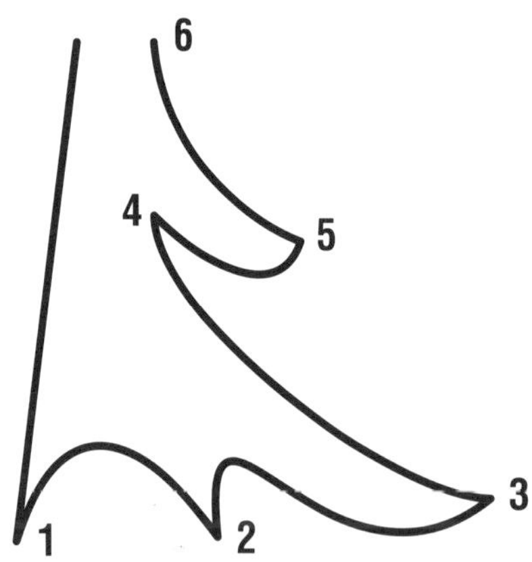

(b) German Six

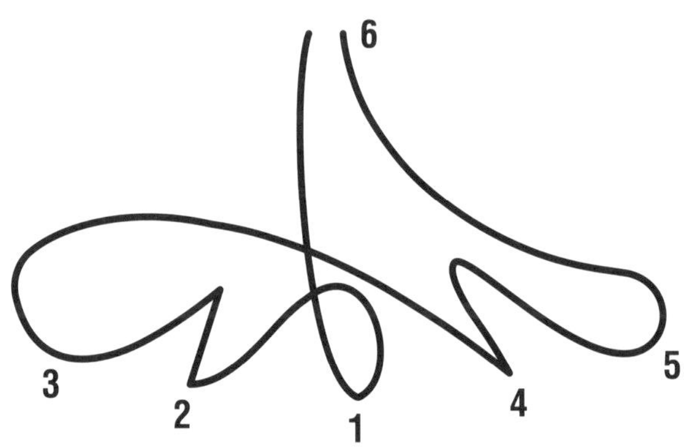

FIG. 6.2. Six Pattern: (a) Italian (b) German

7. Six Patterns: Italian (and German)

For a long time, I resisted Mr. Silverstein's mandate, but now I am totally convinced that it is so much more convenient to transform the Italian six pattern into a two pattern when making an accelerando, or vice-versa when making a ritardando.

THE FIVE PATTERN

Conducting five beats to a bar raises several issues you need to decide. Based on tempo, musical flow and pulse, and general comfort for your ensemble, you have several options for indicating this to an orchestra:

1. Divide your five beats into a 3+2 pattern. You will give one primary downbeat in the 3-pattern, followed by a smaller, subordinate downbeat and the 2-pattern.

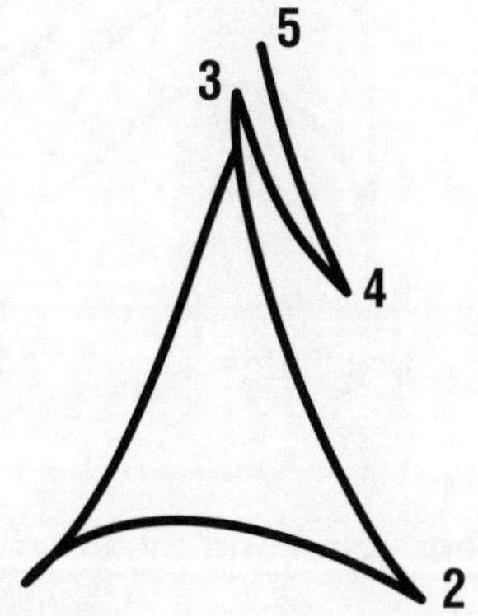

FIG. 6.3. Five Pattern: 3+2. Down/Right/Up/Partial Down/Up

2. Divide your five beats into a 2+3 pattern. You will give one primary downbeat in the 2-pattern, followed by a smaller, subordinate downbeat in the 3-pattern.

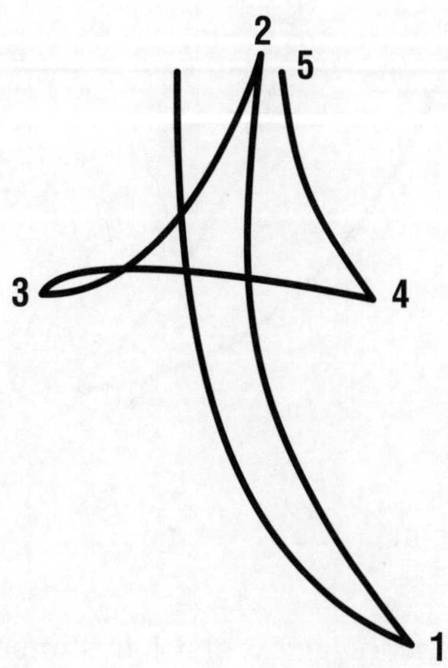

FIG. 6.4. Five Pattern: 2+3. Down/Up/Partial Down/Right/Up

3. Conduct five equal beats. You will give one downbeat and one upbeat with beats 2, 3, and 4 going roughly back and forth horizontally (Rule 3).

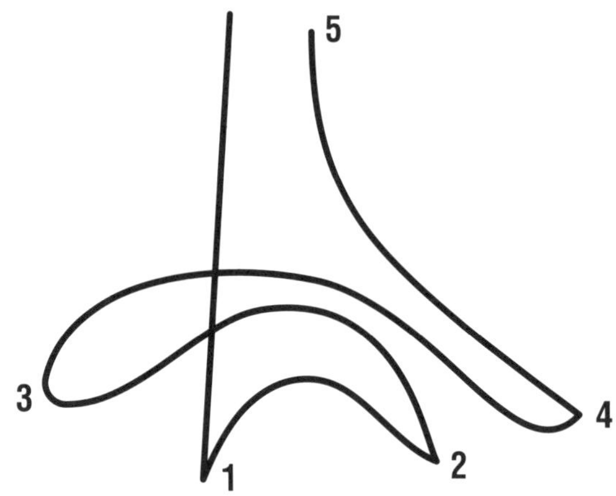

FIG. 6.5. Five Pattern: Equal Beats. Down/Right/Left/Right/Up

4. If the tempo is quick enough, conduct a two-pattern. You will give just one downbeat and one upbeat of unequal length, with one consisting of two parts and the other, three parts.

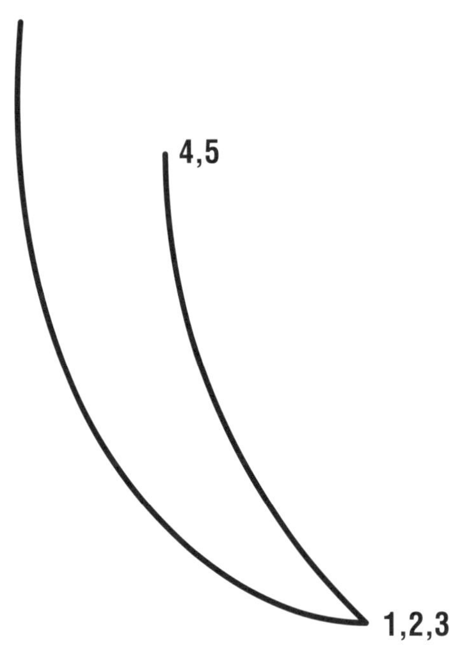

FIG. 6.6. Five Pattern: In Two

When choosing either figure 6.3 or 6.4, it is important to make the subordinate downbeat in the middle of the measure not as prominent nor as low as the primary downbeat of each measure.

Do *not* make your decision based only on your own comfort or convenience, or by analyzing only one part in the orchestration. Consider every part in the orchestration to see what's best, and what can be brought off successfully with the utmost clarity. Every move you make must be made for the right musical *and communicative* reasons for your ensemble!

When conducting five equal beats, I have found success at conducting basically a four-pattern, but the additional beat is a repeat of the downbeat, followed by left for beat 3, right for beat 4, and up for beat 5.

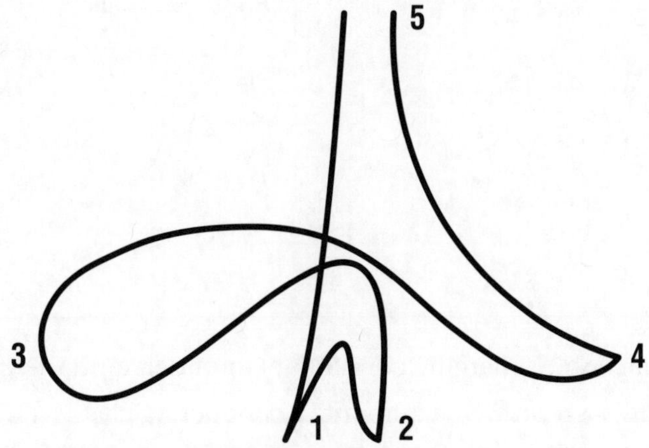

FIG. 6.7. Conducting a 5-Pattern When All Beats Are Equal. Down/Down/Left/Right/Up

COMPOUND METERS

Conducting seven or nine beats in a bar is simply a combination of two different, smaller beat patterns where you still conduct the two's and three's as you would any stand-alone two or three, but the *subsidiary* downbeats wouldn't reach the same, lower base level as the main, first, downbeat of each measure. This way, your orchestra still sees the largest beat you give as the real downbeat of each printed measure.

8. Compound Meters

Subdividing the Beat

The determination for when to subdivide the beat is based on both the slowness of the tempo itself and also the note values being expressed. For example, if you are conducting very slowly, where the note values are quarter and half notes, there is no need to subdivide. But if in that same example, sixteenth or thirty-second notes occur, then you will want to divide each quarter. Most importantly, always maintain the overall larger beat pattern.

How do you do this, technically speaking? When giving your downbeat, simply do a gentle rebound, and "tap" the same downbeat an additional time. Then, musically move your baton to the second large beat, and tap gently at that same place as many times as there are subdivisions.

9. Subdivisions

7

The Ictus

It is difficult for some emerging conductors to understand the physical motion that is the *ictus*—a term we hear about in conducting classes and nowhere else. Physically, the ictus is a very slight flick of the wrist that allows the tip (*only* the tip!) of the baton to give a visual "click," allowing the ensemble to see the exact definition of the beat.

The ictus really indicates an arrival point that has been led up to from the previous beat. This is obviously more helpful in slower tempos, but musicians appreciate this "click" in just about every tempo. It is *not* a musical gesture! Rather, it really is a tiny flick of the wrist, intended to have the tip of the baton visually define the precise moment when you expect your ensemble to attack, enter, or play together. The flick always will look the same, no matter what the tempo or dynamic, because it's always the same physical gesture—a tiny but visible flick of the wrist. Better yet, think of yourself going to a hotel and needing to ring the customer service bell for assistance. You ring the bell with your wrist only, with no involvement of any other parts of your arm. It's exactly the same gesture while holding a baton.

When conducting, many emerging conductors attempt to create the ictus by moving the arm, not the wrist. I'll repeat here: the ictus is *not* a musical gesture. Let your arms and hands move in the direction you wish, but when you want the beat itself to be clearly defined, then give each beat a flick of the wrist, a tap of the baton's *tip*, to visually mark the precise moment of the beat. If the tip of your baton actually moves more than an inch (really!) when manifesting the flick/ictus, then it's a too obvious, too nonsensical a gesture.

10. Ictus

8

The Preparation for Any Beat

Give a clear preparation beat when starting a piece or a section. Always! The preparation beat must indicate the tempo, the musical quality of the entrance, and the dynamic.

It is most important to understand that a preparation is a breath. Every instrumentalist and vocalist breathes before making an entrance; conductors should be no exception. So, every mention of a preparation beat is best described as a breathing arm-motion designed to get everyone in your ensemble to enter together, and in the same style that you indicate.

WHEN THE MUSIC BEGINS ON THE BEAT

Whichever beat your music begins on, your baton must start at least from the beat before. For example, if the music begins on beat 3, your preparation motion starts from beat 2. And since every beat you give is a preparation for the next beat, your beat 2 preparation must indicate the proper tempo, dynamic, and character of the music you want the ensemble to express.

It also helps to define beat 2 with an ictus as you begin the preparation motion. The ictus gives an indication to your ensemble the exact definition of where beat 2 lies, making the timing of the ensemble's entrance on beat 3 that much more obvious.

If the music is loud and staccato, then your preparation should be in that style. This is often fairly uncomfortable for an emerging conductor, as it necessarily means making a large, emphatic preparation gesture before any sound is made. It must be done if you want to be effective.

WHEN THE MUSIC BEGINS INSIDE (AFTER, NOT ON) THE BEAT

In slow and moderate tempos, you should give the ensemble only the beat before which they enter. If the tempo is fast enough, or if the musical language requires a certain additional moment for catching the tempo, then it is acceptable for the conductor to give an additional "dead" beat preparation that helps the musicians understand the tempo in advance. A dead beat can be thought of as the "ready" in "ready, set, go!" You don't prepare this "ready" beat. Rather, the technique is to drop it, with a clear ictus as a *beginning* reference point for the musicians. How you connect that "dead" beat to the next, actual preparation beat will give significant support to the musicians for a together entrance.

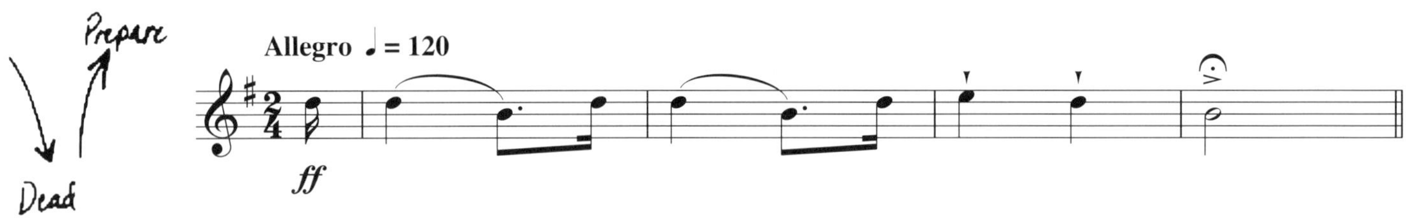

FIG. 8.1. Dead Beat Required

This "dead" beat technique can be done as well with music that begins *on* the beat, but in a tempo so quick as to render a single preparation beat as insufficient. In rehearsal, when you might be stopping and starting frequently, giving an extra beat or two is perfectly acceptable. It's appreciated by your musicians after having spent time talking, rehearsing under tempo, or otherwise getting off the desired normal tempo. Some conductors in rehearsal—and only if it's helpful to the ensemble at that point in their progress—will say something like "a measure for nothing," then conduct and even verbally count off the beats for that length of time as preparation.

Without a preparation, drop the tip of the baton into the downbeat position to define the dead beat. Then in tempo, give the preparation upbeat to achieve greater clarity and understanding for a clean downbeat entrance.

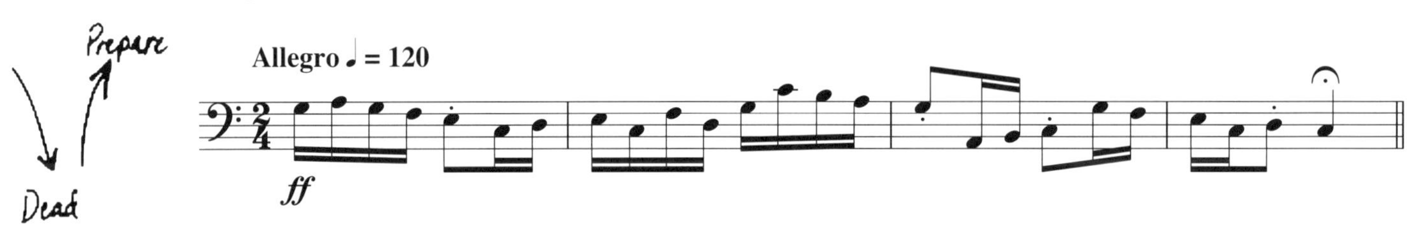

FIG. 8.2. Downbeat Entrance with Dead Beat

Another example of counting off can be when you are about to begin a piece for a recording session. Since precision of ensemble becomes of utmost importance in this situation, it is possible to verbally but quietly count off a measure or two for your ensemble. Leave out the last couple beats verbally, but continue conducting the beat pattern so the recording can begin in silence. Doing this can eliminate even the slightest misinterpretation of your tempo for a large ensemble when beginning a precious recording session.

11. Preparations

GESTURE OF SYNCOPATION

You make the music happen! Just as every preparation you give for an on-the-beat entrance must be in the tempo, style, and dynamic of the music, so too should the gesture of syncopation be equally matched to the music which enters *after* your beat.

Some after-beat entrances happen in such a way that simply giving one beat preceding the entrance is not really comfortable enough for the musicians to feel precisely what your tempo is. Here is where you give an additional *pre*-preparation dead beat, as mentioned above. This helps put the ensemble in the correct tempo frame of mind for them to enter properly and comfortably.

It can take a bit of practice to get the feel of how to create that extra dead beat. The beat has no preparation itself, and has no ictus. But even without the ictus, the dead beat must have a specific placement, a defining point to it. Using the "set-go" phrase I introduced earlier, it's easier to understand how the "set" is only a starting point from which you proceed in tempo to the gesture of syncopation, which in turn is what the musicians respond to with their entrance.

Let's say you have a section entering on the "and" of beat 4 (in 4/4) in a moderate tempo. With your baton starting from the beat 2 position, you move to beat 3 without preparing it, stop dead at beat 3 to establish it as the jumping-off point, then proceed to beat 4 as you always would to initiate the music, which in this case enters after beat 4, not on it.

The gesture of syncopation can be difficult to master. It requires (1) your knowledge of the score in knowing that an entrance or a group dynamic is coming up *inside* a given beat, and (2) an understanding that you are showing the *beat inside which* your ensemble is to make their entrance. This is what gives its name, a *syncopation* that the ensemble players manifest after seeing your beat.

12. Dead Beat

9

Cutoffs and Rests

A cutoff is required most frequently on notes being held by a fermata. Another common occurrence is a passage in which sections of your ensemble play consecutive chords that require releasing together. A third instance is a passage with no fermata but a release nevertheless (Mahler's *Luftpause* or breath) for unison separation. A final instance would be cutting off a chord while a soloist continues on their own.

Cutoffs can be facilitated by either your left hand or the baton, depending on the circumstances. If the music doesn't continue, the cutoff for a final, large dynamic chord might best be accomplished with the baton. But if it's a long, soft chord, the left hand can more gently express the culmination of the sound. In the middle of a work, determining how to cut off will be decided on what happens next after the fermata. If you need the baton to further conduct beats and measures, then likely, a left-hand cutoff is desirable.

PREPARE THE CUTOFF!

In releasing a fermata, your cutoff gesture—like any other preparation—should be in the style and dynamic of the note being released. If your motion is abrupt, so will the sound be. If your preparation shows hesitancy, the ensemble likely will not cut off together. But if the release is well prepared—generally, with some kind of loop or other preparatory motion—the cutoff should be perfect.

Here are some examples:

1. **No fermata.** A circular gesture, starting from a dead placement is the most common of cutoffs. It is the most clear, well-defined motion. Use the penultimate beat as the starting point of a loop that will indicate the final cutoff beat. Clockwise or counter-clockwise, it really doesn't matter so long as the loop is preparatory.
2. **Fermata, full ensemble at a loud dynamic.** Hold the fermata for as long as necessary. Do not beat time. Actually, freeze the baton with the same intensity you desire from the players. When you move the baton, it should be the beginning of the cutoff loop. It's an "and...now!" kind of gesture.

3. **Fermata, any size ensemble, *diminuendo al niente*.** You can indicate a very slow whole-arm loop, which will be helpful to musicians but still requires an extra gesture ("and…now") to make the final stopping point exceptionally clear. Depending on the musical circumstance, I have also done a long diminuendo with the left hand (in full view, of course, to all musicians), indicating the diminuendo by gently closing the fingers to the thumb. This can work well if your intent is to have the sound die away imperceptibly, and not have everyone stopping at precisely the same moment.

WHEN NOT TO CUT OFF

Sometimes, the score plays up to a rest or to a non-existent downbeat, where your conducting up to that [silent] beat doesn't require an actual cutoff. If the ensemble can see that you've conducted up to a point where they have a rest in their music, then they will stop automatically.

Further, don't assume that all fermatas need to be cut off. A great example is in the last movement of Beethoven's Third Symphony, measure 105, where you hold the downbeat fermata, and the second beat becomes both the preparation for the violins to continue to the A-natural as well as the cutoff for everyone else in the orchestra.

13. Cutoffs and Countoffs

WHEN TO CONDUCT RESTS

If there are rests in the music, then the well-trained musician is expecting to see you conduct both the beat *and* rest that each individual has in his/her own part. A rest is the absence of musical gesture, but it does represent the passage of time in the music. Conduct a rest in a clear but usually uninvolved way, paying attention to the *timing* as well as the time.

Sometimes, the beginning of a work is indicated by one or more rests even before a sound is made. A conductor can handle this in two different ways:

1. Rhythmically, but not musically, mark with the baton in the indicated tempo, using the final beat rest as the preparation for the ensemble's entrance.
2. To avoid any musician expecting to hear a sound on any of the initial silent beats, announce to the ensemble which beat you are going to begin conducting. Give them time to mark their parts accordingly, then conduct them beginning with your announced beat.

10

Preparing the Score

Every conductor approaches the marking of a score differently, depending on its familiarity and technique required. The ultimate goal, of course, should be to study and really know any score so well that there is no need to mark it up at all. But the reality of life is such that, for various reasons it makes sense to mark a score with anything from cues, to tempo markings, to bowings or breath marks, to phrase lengths, to balance or articulations.

It only makes sense that the more times you conduct a composition, the more it becomes a part of you, and in the words of my mentor Joseph Silverstein, the more you memorize the music "by heart" rather than just intellectually at your desk, the less you need to pay attention to the score in real time when you're on the podium.

So, the converse is also true: let's say you're conducting a work for the very first time. Obviously, your dependency on the score as you rehearse and perform will be greater. But all markings should be done to highlight, or draw one's attention to, what's already there in the print. Do not mark up a score so heavily that, in real time, you're conducting only your own notations!

What's required first is to spend the necessary time to actually *learn* the score, without having to mark it up! Then develop a simple, shorthand approach to writing essential reminders to yourself that will help guide your viewing of the music so that you can conduct it musically.

Clearly, there will be times in your life when you don't have all the time necessary to study appropriately. The top priority, then, is to pay primary attention to the "road map," *identifying the **ensemble** needs of your musicians at every critical moment.* Fermatas, meters, tempo changes, entrances, releases, important cues, and dynamic changes are all prime targets for your attention. Remember, you are the only person in the room given the responsibility of keeping all the musicians together. Acknowledge that responsibility by being fully prepared with the road map, regardless of all the musical basics or subtleties.

Everyone develops their own unique shorthand system of notation to help guide viewing a score. My guidance is to *not* mark anything that's not necessary. For instance, if you're completely aware of a given tempo or change of tempo, don't mark it. But if, in the study of a new composition, you've found yourself unsure of a tempo, tempo change, or other musical moment, write a reminder to yourself.

Do Not Mark Any Rental Scores that have been entrusted to you! It only adds to the degradation of the print material. But a rental score can be used effectively, thanks to supplies such as Post-it® and other such brands. Many choices of color, size, and transparency are available if you spend some time at your favorite retail office supply store investigating what's there.

Formally, given sufficient time, it is most important that you understand the overall structure of a piece. Whatever analytic method you may use, be sure you are comfortable with the piece's overarching form as well as the combination of phrase lengths that comprise the architecture. This is the basis for your own conception of the piece—important structural, harmonic, and melodic milestones all contribute to your overall understanding and successful performance. Remember, the musicians are really only concerned about their own specific details. The form will *not* be obvious to them if you are unable to convey it to them.

Orchestrationally, if you're not clearly aware of the orchestration tools the composer/arranger uses, you will fail in conducting the music overall. How the composer/arranger treats all the instruments in your ensemble should influence how you conduct—and balance—your own ensemble. How does the composer/arranger utilize doublings and leading voices? Are there inherent balance challenges where the composer may not have been specific? Are there issues related to your own ensemble's strengths?

Stylistically, look to make decisions in these categories:

- Tempo: Define tempo indications that are appropriate for your venue and ensemble. What is the composer's musical *intent,* and does that match what's in print?
- Style: Do all notes get played rhythmically the same, or shorter, longer? Are they "swung" as in a pops chart? Are three- and four-note chords in string instruments to be played divisi? Should harp chords be arpeggiated, cracked, or straight? Do the brass and woodwinds need to breathe in synch? Do the strings play on or off the string?
- Proofreading: Does the score accurately indicate issues of mutes? Are there notes outside the range of any instruments, and what's your plan for fixing them? Does the score clearly indicate to winds and brass when to bring their bells back down after a bells-up indication? Are you familiar with all the composer's terms, and does your ensemble need teaching?
- Timing: If you need to conduct any tempo changes, fermatas, ritards, or accelerandos, what do you need to know for what's stylistically appropriate?

Develop your own systems and shorthand for marking in such a way that's meaningful and helpful to you each time you glance at the page, always maintaining the integrity of the print, and make no markings that will hinder your reading of the score!

Highlighters can work really well, if you don't mind their markings being indelible. I use them very sparingly, and usually only with large-size, contemporary works where my eye normally might not take me. My highlights are generally saved for specific tempo changes and metronome marks.

Colored pencils can be helpful, too. I have favored erasable, blue lead pencils for years, which I will use for any conducting issues. The blue is different enough from the black print to get my attention, but not so overwhelming as to take my attention away from the music itself. I use the blue for cueing instruments at important times that I particularly want to remember.

Figure 10.2 is a chart of some of my own markings I frequently use in marking a score when I feel I need to make any at all. Some of the most important and common markings are these:

- **Phrase lengths**, indicated sometimes by a diagonal stroke emanating from the top barline on the page, sometimes by a vertical barline drawn from top to bottom system. I may also indicate at my lines the number of measures in that next phrase (see "Phrase Length Indication" in figure 10.2).
- **Short, curved arrows** pointing to an instrument or section entrance, to attract my attention in advance of the entrance (see "cue" in figure 10.2).
- **Lines and triangles**, indicating how to conduct mixed meters when they're not consistent (see "2-part beat followed by 3-part beat" in figure 10.2).

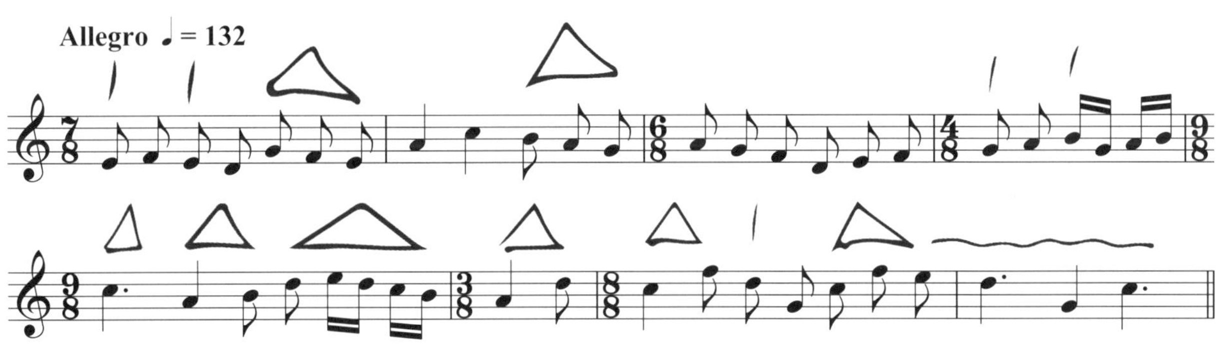

FIG. 10.1. Lines and Triangles

- The two most essential pieces of information for the conductor are: (1) the number of beats in a bar (see "four beats in a bar" in figure 10.2), which I will indicate wherever on the page I believe my eye will travel in real time, and (2) the speed (tempo) at which those beats have to be given (see "tempo reminder" in figure 10.2).
- Occasionally, I use diagonal, curved, long lines when I want to remember the orchestrational flow from one part to another.

- Metric modulation notations (e.g., ♩ = ♩.; 𝅗𝅥 = ♩.; ♩. = 𝅗𝅥), again, used only as a reminder, placed directly over the barline where the change happens.
- Notations of any important event (e.g., a dynamic, an instrumental entrance, a tempo change, a fermata) made in the end-of-page margin if the event occurs immediately after the page turn. I have made such quick notations when confronted with brand-new pops arrangements given to me only minutes before rehearsal!

The following shorthand is my own. You should feel free to develop your own unique shorthand symbols that you will recognize instantaneously while reading and conducting the score.

	**Glasses.** A generic symbol to catch my attention, particularly when something isn't easily visible in the published score. It could be a reminder for a specific entrance, or for a tempo/dynamic indication.
!	**Exclamation point.** A generic reminder, similar to the glasses, and again, often following an entrance cue or tempo/dynamic indication. Generally used when addressing an event that may seem surprising or unexpected, as well as being unnoticed in the score, or it might be a cue I promised to make.
	**Dead beat followed by the preparation beat.** This pattern reminder happens most frequently after a fermata in the body of the piece, but sometimes also at the very beginning of a piece. This is especially important as a reminder to yourself when you've made a point of telling your ensemble you're going to give two beats as a preparation.
//	**Tutti cutoff.** Used most often to end a fermata (often difficult to see) over a bar line, a *Luftpause* (breath), or any other time I wish to have the entire ensemble stop when it isn't obvious in the printed score. Usually, the notation will be at an angle over the bar line, drawn right across it, set at two or three places up and down the score.
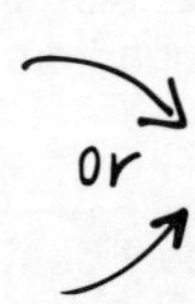	**Cue.** This curved, short arrow (in blue) is a helpful reminder to cue an individual musician.
FL Ob Cl Fg Tpt Trb Tu Hp Cel/Pf Timp VI VII VA Vc CB Gtr S, S1, S2 A T B Brass WW Perc Stgs Hpsd	**Instrument reminder.** I have developed unique, easily identifiable reminders for each instrument, as shown.

	**Section or chair indications**, such as for violins or horns. This indication clarifies which part requires a cue, which can be confusing in some scores. (You don't want to accidentally cue horn I when it's a horn III entrance.) For violins, a Roman numeral with a bracket can be especially helpful when there are multiple divisi parts. If I indicate a Roman numeral in the middle of the page, I'll automatically know it's an indication for horn(s).
	**Section brackets.** Helpful for clarifying multiple string divisi, or in combination with an instrumental section cue—especially on large orchestral scores. Contemporary scores printed through common music print software often print each individual part on its own music line, by default. Bracketing, say, all six clarinet lines in this way helps the eye sort the various lines into sections. This is especially true of string sections, each of which are divided into multiple parts.
	**Chorus stand/sit.** Before the beginning or after the end of a work, when there is no sound, I'll usually add the indication "CHOR" to the arrow. When it occurs within the body of the music. I indicate this in the choral parts only, at the exact beat where they are to move one way or the other. Some choral directors have the chorus mark these directions in their scores. I've found it helpful to indicate these reminders in my own score.
	**Phrase length indication.** The number represents how many measures are in the form, for the upcoming phrase. It may be multiple numbers: 8+2, or 4+4+4 for example. I draw the vertical line in black pencil over the bar line for the entire page, and then the angled line pointing to the number.
	**Four beats in a bar.** I always put the number in a circle. Especially helpful when there are many meter changes, a particularly large number of staves, and/or when the score's engraving of the printed meters is difficult to read.
	**Divided beat.** Used during ritards in the middle of a measure, to indicate the need to subdivide a beat pattern. I place this directly over the beats where I need to pay attention as I change from whole beats to subdivided beats.
	**2-part beat followed by a 3-part beat.** In more complicated, less familiar, and/or newer compositions. I tend to set this notation in one or two locations in the score, usually above the violin I line, between the woodwinds and brass section, and sometimes at the very top of the page. See figure 10.1.
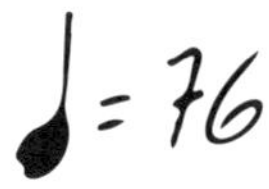	**Tempo reminder.** Helpful when the tempo indication in the score is difficult to read. This has nothing to do with beat patterns.

	**Accelerando.** In the case of an extended, poco a poco accelerando I'll use multiple iterations of the arrow until I get to the destination. Usually placed either at the top of the score page or somewhere in the middle.
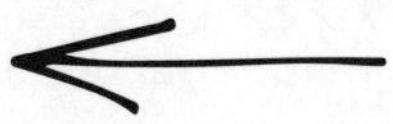	**Rallentando.** In the case of an extended slowing down, I'll use multiple iterations, as with the accelerando.
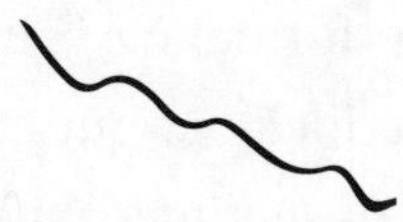	**Ritardando.** Usually located directly over the leading voice at the time, but I may write in rather large wavy lines over multiple staves in the score when it seems appropriate. Usually, it is a momentary, not an extended, end-of-phrase slowing down.
easy! Go!	**Various reminders.** Used especially if I've found that I need to change what I may have just done (not so successfully) in an actual rehearsal. "Easy" and "Go" both relate to tempo, and by the time I decide to write such words in, I'm already well-acquainted with what they mean to me qualitatively.

FIG. 10.2. Shorthand Symbols

Every conductor dreams of studying a Mahler symphony in advance of an extended rehearsal cycle in which every little detail they imagined will be perfected. Alas, that truly is a dream world, in which even a Mahler symphony likely will be rehearsed with insufficient time. Therefore, score study of this kind needs a different approach. More than structure or shape or phrasing, the conductor must pay attention to the specific physical moves that will be required, making shorthand symbols such as I show above all the more important. Very careful attention must be paid to tempos, tempo changes/relationships, important cues, the composer's dynamic map and relationships, fermatas and continuations, cutoffs, ensemble beginnings, and overall rhythmic ensemble. In short, always ask yourself, "What must I do to keep my ensemble comfortably together?"

11

Cueing/Serving the Musicians

Ideally, your goal is not to have to give any cues at all. In performance, you should concentrate on the music's flow, pacing, and expression. Ideally, your cues will indicate to your ensemble how the music fits one player or section to the next.

Conventional textbook training specifies that cueing is to be done with the left hand, while the right hand holding the baton does the "business" of time beating. In reality, one can make any gesture one wants with either hand. Cueing can be done even with the baton, requiring your leaving your default elliptical field of motion. It is okay to turn in the direction of a section or player with the baton, establish eye contact, then acknowledge the cue by making the previous beat in your pattern an actual welcoming, breathing preparation beat.

Speaking of which, cueing can be done with only a glance, a smile, or even with the eyebrows! If you have created a culture in which eye contact between you and all ensemble musicians happens as a matter of course, cueing with a knowing glance, a smile or raising of the eyebrows can be very effective. Think of these physical gestures as preparation beats in and of themselves, so the timing of a wink or a smile should be in the previous beat. Experience has shown that a smile or glance or eyebrow preparation works even better if eye contact has been established in the previous measure or several beats ahead.

Cueing can be done with a mere turn of the body in the direction of the intended cue-ee. This works best when cueing a large section (e.g., first violins) within a larger ensemble. Conducting an important first violin entrance in a large symphonic work can be very meaningful if you turn to face and address them as a group. As with the other gestures, doing so requires the same timing as any other preparation beat.

Whatever cueing you choose to make, do so in an authentic, non-choreographed gesture rising out of the musical moment at hand. As conductor, feel free to be creative and in the moment, allowing your gestures to be spontaneous and direct. But the specific gesture should be both stylistically appropriate and create the desired musical effect, all within the continuously successful musical flow.

Cueing should be done according to what's musically necessary. One doesn't need to cue, say, the harpist, if you notice in advance that s/he's all ready to make the entrance (though a smiling acknowledgement before or after the entrance is nice). One doesn't need to cue, say, the brass section in their fortissimo entrance just because it's there. But if that moment is one in which the brass section leads the entire ensemble in a particularly momentous climax, your attention to them helps all others understand their role! Finally, don't cue a guest soloist unless s/he requests, or needs it. You are there to accompany the soloist's rendition, not to dictate it.

Ultimately, the conductor is conducting the overall shape of the music's totality. Successful conducting involves directing what *is most important* to the overall flow of the music and togetherness of the ensemble. If the important line alternates between, say, first violin and the woodwind section, then first encourage and *lead* the violins, turning your attention to the woodwinds. On the other hand, if the proper synchronization of the ensemble means paying attention to sections with delicate or tricky rhythms while the melodic elements can play themselves, then pay attention to the tricky elements.

Too many conductors *display* the music through their gestures, rather than *lead* the ensemble in manifesting a combined interpretation. A conducting gesture should not be a choreographed moment; it should be a combination of inspiration, prevention, preparation, and confirmation of what you expect for the ultimate musical result.

Remain aware of *all* your players' needs, not just the leading line. There are many situations in which the primary line will take care of itself while you pay attention to the accompanying parts, harmonies, and rhythms. Ultimately, your job is to create and maintain the integrity of the ensemble as an ensemble: (1) impose your direction when the ensemble is looking to you for clarity, (2) guide the melodic phraseology of the moment at hand, (3) back off and hold the reins when the ensemble maintains its own momentum, and, in the pit (4) channel the pit musicians with those on stage, acting simultaneously as leader and follower.

Serving your musicians requires a unique combination-cycle of anticipation, preparation, leading the moment, and ultimately evaluating the immediate past moment. This is a constant process occurring simultaneously with your making gestures both specific to that musical moment as well as how that moment fits within the overall scheme/structure of the work.

PREVENTIVE CONDUCTING

The bottom line is, be there for your ensemble. Help them! Think of the music in *their* terms and needs! Be a servant leader, leading by serving. Think in advance what their needs might be, then give them the most helpful direction.

Emerging conductors often develop particular gestures to use to choreograph their musical ideas. This is a sure setup for failure, as it doesn't allow for being in the musical moment. Rather, gestures must come directly as a result of how the ensemble is playing at any time compared to how you want them to sound. Make your gestures always a combination of *predictive, preventive*, and *reactive. Predictive* because you're showing the ensemble what you want from them; *preventive* because you have anticipated the pitfalls any musicians might experience; and *reactive* because musicians might need even more (or better yet, *less*) attention from you!

14. Cueing

12

Recitative/Narration/ Open Measures

Opera is a complicated art form to conduct, and while the conductor may be the apparent musician-in-chief, in reality, it's more like being collaborator-in-chief. Sometimes, you are the lead; sometimes, you're only supporting the lead; sometimes, you need to adjust the music to agree with the stage direction; sometimes you're dealing with pits with awkward setups. But the single most difficult task is conducting the orchestral recitative. One or more singers are reciting (singing) mouthfuls of text, at conversational speed, and with no attention being paid to you in the pit, while you're panicking over the timing and gestural requirements for the orchestral interpolations.

Most importantly, the conductor must be completely familiar with the singer's text as well as how the text and subtext are illustrated in the actual notes. The conductor should be able to sing the recitative with the same inflections and tempo as the trained singer, even if not so beautifully.

Next, your ensemble must know how time is passing by your marking downbeats, especially for multiple measures of rest. Your accompanying instrumentalists are only counting measures, so give your silent, marked downbeats within an appropriate timing and speed to make your ensemble most comfortable with where they are in *their* music! A common occurrence in opera is the conductor giving downbeats in fairly rapid succession, without regard for where the singer is, in order to have the ensemble completely ready for their next entrance. Doing so can be very helpful, especially because singers approach their music texturally, not rhythmically in the metronomic sense. But I caution anyone doing this *not* to give the silent downbeats in such rapid progression, or so subtly, that any musician cannot comfortably and securely follow.

Far too many inexperienced conductors feel the need to be musical, subtle, or even apologetic about making some kind of move that might attract attention away from the music. Certainly, one doesn't want to be distracting, but the conductor also should not want to be so subtle as to lose what s/he is trying to communicate.

Giving such silent, "marked" downbeats also occurs regularly even in symphonic repertoire. There will be instances of grand pauses ("G.P."), fermatas, extra measures, and composed silences, all of which require the conductor to mark the downbeat. It is of utmost importance to remember that the ensemble is depending on the conductor to relay to them how time is passing—vis-à-vis their own individual part. The conductor must always be thinking of *everyone* in the ensemble, and never assume that just because you're paying attention to one section in the ensemble, everyone else knows where you are.

Slightly differently, you will have occasion to conduct narration, too. With narration scores, however, there will be sections in which the speaker goes on while the accompanying ensemble underscores a lengthy passage, yet you must synchronize the succeeding statement. Probably the two most common examples of such repertoire are Prokofiev's *Peter and the Wolf* and Copland's *Lincoln Portrait.* Both these compositions will have moments, too, where a particular chord in the accompaniment must be timed exactly with a specific word in the text. These can be quite tricky, but again, it makes sense to practice them—speaking the text and conducting—by yourself at your own study desk.

Grand pause bars are another example of time pausing. If there is an open measure for the entire ensemble marked "G.P.," you can get to that measure and stop conducting, as everyone will automatically know they've arrived at the "G.P." It is not necessary to make a point of giving the downbeat of that silent measure, because there's no question as to where one is in the music. It is most important, however, that your baton also pauses by not indicating any motion or beats after the initial downbeat of arrival. However, if there is an open measure with *no* "G.P." indication (e.g., Schumann's Second Symphony, last movement) and you stop conducting without giving that silent downbeat, you run the distinct possibility of members not counting on your having arrived at that measure. Why? Remember, all musicians are looking only at their part, and are counting the downbeats they see from you against the measures they have in the part. Therefore, if you don't give the downbeat, they are going to wait to see your next downbeat before they count that measure.

SECTION B. Technique Musically Manifested

In this section, we will explore how the basics should next be developed for greater efficiency, effectiveness, and musicianship. To begin with, it will be important to understand that as conductors we are *preparing* our musicians for what is to come. Without that understanding, we would only be followers, not leaders. The music will not happen unless we do something *first*—a gesture, that is, designed to lead the players to begin making the music. Of course, there will be exceptions, when the ensemble is moving along at its already-established pace, during which moments the conductor is essentially joining in with the action moment-to-moment. But there will almost always be certain other factors that come into play—a ritard, a fermata, a cutoff, a change of tempo that will require the conductor to *take charge*, to *lead*, to *prepare* the upcoming moments and transitions in such a way as to keep the ensemble together.

The successful conductor will recognize those moments and be prepared in advance for them. So, all emerging conductors must clearly understand that, unlike all the experience you gathered conducting recordings at home, now one can't just follow along. Rather, *you* must be the leader, and *you* must lead first, before the sound even begins.

The remaining lessons in this section deal with the related aspects of how your conducting techniques should adapt to the musical character and requirements of what you're conducting. Not every beat is the same, even though you might be tempted to think that by reading only the basics in section A. In fact, you will find yourself over time even developing an ability to *not* conduct some beats, allowing your ensemble to progress as a living organism on its own. Further, I speak of your own "style," not so much as some model you've abstractly devised or modeled after someone more famous, but rather as the natural growth of your own musical and physical attributes. This section then concludes with a summation of principles and reminders of what to do (or not!) when on the podium.

13

Every Beat Is a Preparation for the Next Beat!

Every move you make is but a preparation for the *next* musical moment (which hasn't arrived yet!). Therefore, when leading a specific musical event, your gestures will occur *before* the sound by one beat. This is important, for example, with synchronization of tutti entrances (your *upbeat* is where you indicate the character of the downbeat entrance) and for after-beat entrances or accents (the gesture of syncopation you give after which the entrance occurs).

It's the quality and timing of the upbeat (preparation) that makes the downbeat inevitable and automatic. The ictus (wrist-flick) you give at the downbeat then is the precise confirmation of the event that you've just prepared. No sooner is the ictus given than the beat automatically converts into the next preparation for the next beat, and so on and so forth. The quality of the preparatory beat then is *predictive* to the sound that ultimately comes from the ensemble at the moment of ictus in the next beat. Remember, this is a *predictive, anticipatory* gesture; your gesture in the previous beat is not the sound itself, but is generating the sound of the next beat.

I know the concept can be confusing, but if you can, grasp it as a continuous series of "and...now/and...now" where the "and" is the preparation, and the "now" is both the arrival as well as the beginning of the next "and."

Once the music gets started, it's likely you'll have a chance to relax and go with the flow of the music, allowing the ensemble to proceed as if on automatic pilot. Imagine holding the reins on a team of horses. The team is moving along nicely with your guidance and direction, needing help only when changing speed or direction or intensity. The same is true with an ensemble of professional musicians.

Conductors who don't realize the importance of beat-to-beat preparation usually find themselves not being able to successfully manage the flow of the ensemble because they ultimately end up following the ensemble, which itself is following the conductor. It's a slippery slope!

So, every beat is but a preparation for the next. It sounds so simple, and is easy to comprehend intellectually, but employing this into real-time conducting gestures is far more difficult. Why? Let me back up a step or two first. Remember that a conductor is always operating at several different levels of musical consciousness simultaneously:

- *Evaluating* what just happened in that last moment of music.
- *Asking*, was the ensemble in synch with itself, and rhythmically with the music? Was it in tune? Was the character of the ensemble's music-making what you wanted? If "no" to any of the above, determining when to stop (in rehearsal) to fix issues—now? or at the end of the phrase or section, movement, piece?
- *Conducting* meter and dynamics in real time. You're making all the right motions: rhythm, dynamics, pulse, ictus, style, are all correct; you're giving all the right cues; you're leading with all appropriate expression and inspiration.
- *Preparing* the next moment of music before it happens!

While you're doing all of the above, you're also thinking ahead, preparing the next moment as well as the direction of the phrase you're currently in, and how it fits within the general flow of the work. Remember that the "next moment" includes myriad situations, such as:

- cueing a person or section after they've had to count a particularly long rest, and cueing musically;
- paying attention to clarity of beat for an upcoming change of tempo, ritard, accelerando, etc.;
- shaping the music as it happens. You alone have the awesome responsibility of knowing what comes next, of what the piece is supposed to sound like. You alone—because you're on the podium—have been given the charge of creating something artistic out of a bunch of notes. But it's the ensemble actually making the sound! Conduct as a collaborator, then, leading, guiding, shepherding your team so that they will respond in sync, together, and inspiringly!

So, by saying that every beat is but a preparation for the next, the conductor is evaluating the current moment, which may require adapting his/her technique to modify the ensemble sound. The quality of your beat will determine whether the ensemble responds in kind. Some examples include:

- Does a musician/section need to see a strong gesture of syncopation before their entrance?
- Does a musician/section need to be reminded of the legato you talked about in rehearsal?
- Does a musician/section need your guidance in order to make an attack in the proper dynamic, or perhaps some togetherness with others?
- Does a musician/section need a last-instant reminder regarding their passage, according to what you rehearsed?
- Is there a musician/section accidentally pulling at your tempo, requiring a corrective gesture on your part?

These are only a few of the more obvious examples, intending only to give a glimpse into the wide variety of preparation beats you need to give. The experienced conductor likely would agree that all of this really goes without saying, that what we are doing is employing Rule no. 4, "Showing the Music," guiding the musicians, maintaining the flow of the composition. Observing many of the world's most famous conductors, you won't notice a lot of "correction" going on. But those orchestras don't need a lot of *correction*. What they do need and want is *guidance, leadership, expression,* and your *showing the music*!

ANECDOTE

I once had occasion to coach a non-musician friend who, by virtue of his financial contribution, had won the opportunity to conduct his local professional orchestra. He didn't read music but was fairly serious about doing well and not wanting to embarrass himself in front of his friends. I agreed to help him with some private lessons, and after several sessions of learning how to conduct, he stood on the podium for rehearsal, lifted his arms, acknowledged that the orchestra was ready to play, then said to them, "Okay, go!" without making even the slightest move. Even after having lessons, he still didn't get it that *he* had to make the first move in order for the piece to begin! *Every* beat, especially the first one, is a preparation for the sound to happen!

14

The Three Stages of Conducting Maturity

In my decades of teaching conducting, I have come to understand that there are three basic levels of progression from beginning student to professional in terms of conducting technique.

The first level constitutes learning the basic patterns, what direction to move on what beat in what meter. The second level is learning how to adapt the basic patterns, considering different tempos, styles (e.g., legato, staccato), dynamics, musical inflection, cueing, and related techniques such as cutoffs, fermatas, tempo changes, etc. The third and most professional level is understanding that not every beat needs to be conducted, and that while a pulse is always a requirement, the most important thing a conductor can do is indicate the quality of the music at any given time.

The trouble is, it isn't possible to just begin conducting at the third level. Beginning conductors who decide to imitate the idiosyncratic techniques of famous conductors they've seen on stage or online ultimately will fail, as they don't have the disciplined technique of their idols who, by the way, themselves first learned the basics before adapting into their own style. It's a little like a beginning violinist taking the violin and going through all the same mannerisms they've observed in, say, Joshua Bell's playing. In that case, the notes, the phrasing, the technique still have to be there *before* the posturing can take place. And in the conductor's case, the technique still has to be there to create the right notes from all the right players in the ensemble! The discipline of paying attention to levels 1 and 2, then, are simply essential for getting to level 3. It's rather like the old adage about learning the rules before you can break them.

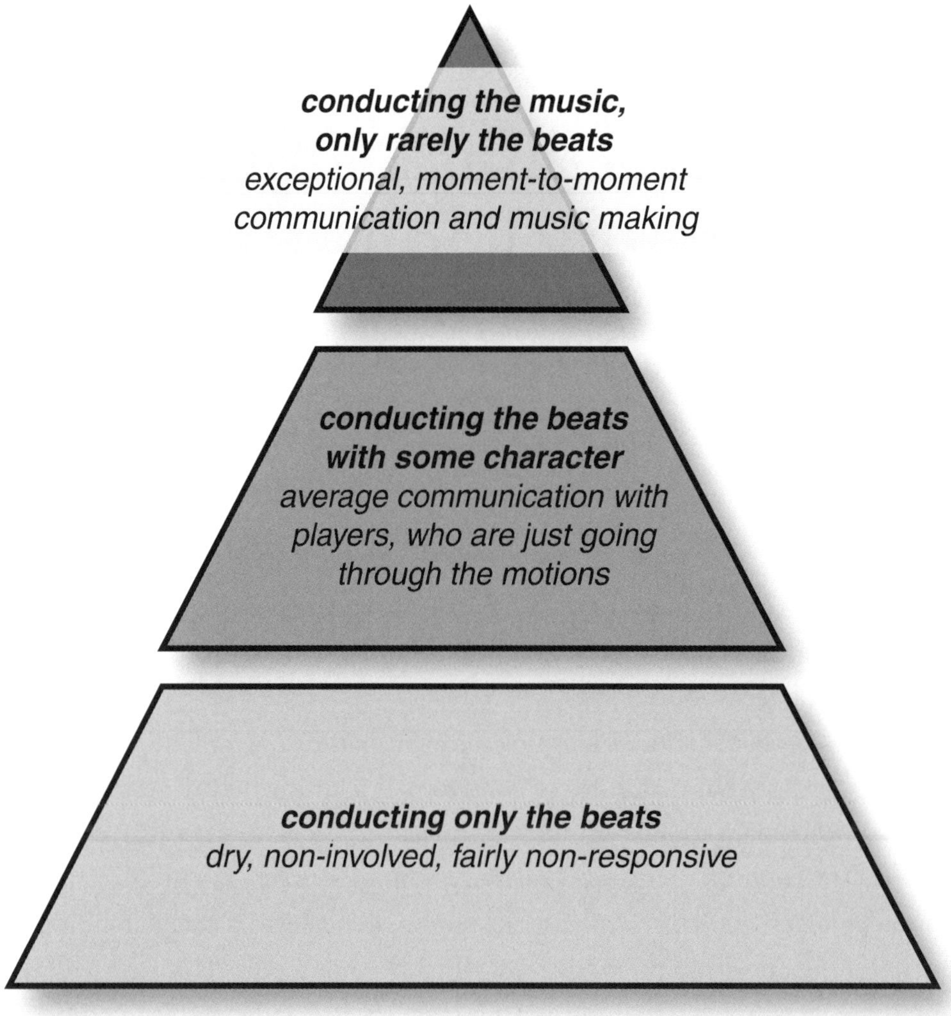

FIG. 14.1. Three Stages of Conducting Maturity

ANECDOTE

I can remember the exact moment when it occurred to me that I hadn't yet attained that highest stage of conducting maturity. I had been rehearsing an orchestra very intently, working out all kinds of details, and after rehearsal was conversing with one of my colleagues in the orchestra when she said, quite simply and straightforwardly, "You know, you don't have to give *every* beat." That one, short piece of advice changed my conducting forever, freeing up the orchestra from the too-tight reins I had been holding, and allowed my conducting technique to become so much more musical in terms of shape and flow. It was a transformative moment in my career, and is advice I now use repeatedly with my own conducting students.

Ultimately, when you reach that top, highest level of conducting maturity, you'll realize that everything we talk about in this book comes together into a magical whirligig of concentration, intention, and attention as you make gestures demonstrating your interpretation of a composition. You'll be planning, preventing, managing, evaluating, responding, yet leading, all simultaneously in a fantastic swirl of energy and music making. You'll find it's not just about you, but rather how you are leading your ensemble, moment by moment, to the composition's uplifting, obvious conclusion. It's hard to describe the precise feeling of wonder, of flow, of soaring that one experiences on the podium, but it is there, and you will find it.

15

Less Is More

Professional musicians want to see a clear beat and to receive your musical guidance. That's all there is to it; *they* will make the music. You are the guide, the shaper, the sculptor. Ultimately, you are only there to help them do their best and to guide them. You are not to put on a choreographed show! To do so would be non-authentic and disingenuous, which ultimately results in disrespect from the musicians.

Reading the conductor interviews later in this book, you will see many describing their conducting style as becoming increasingly economical over the years, using my favorite phrase, "Less is more!" Take their advice to heart. Be economical—and meaningful—with your gestures, though no less musical or involved. Back off technically; let your ensemble go of its own accord. Breathe, and give them the freedom as living, thinking musicians. Conduct only with your right hand. Reduce the flapping of both arms moving in mirror image to each other. The more you "mirror-conduct," the less effective you will be with any gesture; the ensemble will tire of watching you, and will do so only peripherally.

The baton can be exceptionally musical, if used as an instrument and not as just something to hold onto. Of course, all conductors use the baton in different ways, but by letting your wrist manipulate the stick expressively, you can communicate so much more with a simple stick motion than by constantly waving both arms. Besides, the waving of arms actually accomplishes the *opposite* effect: musicians will gradually ignore you.

ANECDOTE

My own teacher, Walter Hendl, had a conducting approach learned from his teacher, Fritz Reiner, who in turn was influenced by Richard Strauss. With all three, minimalism of baton technique was the norm. Nevertheless, Walter's orchestra members focused entirely on the tip of his baton precisely because he wasn't constantly waving the stick in the orchestra's face. His gestures were with the baton, and were so musically and subtly expressive that when he truly wanted to make that rare, large statement with the whole baton he was especially effective.

16

Conducting "Style"

There are as many styles of conducting as there are conductors. Every conductor's own unique physique ultimately determines their own style, so long as their motions are natural, genuine, and authentic. Be effective by being yourself! With no preconceived motions your conducting style should be whatever's appropriate for the moment. Your conducting should be a direct result of your moment-by-moment evaluation of your ensemble's sound. Rarely will you actually conduct the same passage with the same gesture from rehearsal to rehearsal. Conducting is really a cause-and-effect process. It is *not* pre-determined. It's a non-verbal facilitation of musical ideas, based on your evaluation of the sound currently being produced. Your next gesture will demonstrate your confirmation/agreement with the sound, or, you will adapt your next gesture to bring your ensemble what you prefer.

ANECDOTE

While I was a conducting fellow at Tanglewood many years ago, Eugene Ormandy was guest conducting the Boston Symphony but had agreed to attend a rehearsal of the student orchestra—his first-ever opportunity to do so. I was chosen to conduct the student orchestra in rehearsal for his appearance. My teacher at Tanglewood was Seiji Ozawa, who for weeks had been mentoring me with his mantra of the time: "Show the Music." By this, of course, he meant for me to be as physically expressive as he was when conducting. So, for Eugene Ormandy's visit, I was going to "show the music" like nobody else, and I utilized every Ozawa gesture I knew. After rehearsal, Ormandy came on stage to greet the orchestra, my conducting colleagues, and me, and when asked a question about conducting, he said, "the first thing I learned about conducting was to plant my feet firmly on the podium, and if I was to move my body at all it was to be from the waist up." My heart sank, as this was the polar opposite of Ozawa's approach to conducting. Lesson learned: Don't be someone else; only be yourself. Your style is yours alone.

17

Podium Presence

On the podium, you are in charge. Accept the awesome responsibility with grace and humility, while understanding that you alone are accountable for the end result. Your presence on the podium should show a combination of (1) willingness in accepting this responsibility; (2) self-confidence in hearing, evaluating, and demonstrating the music; (3) comprehension of the musical issues involved in the music, and (4) self-confidence in making decisions, offering constructive criticism, and personally connecting with your ensemble musicians positively and musically.

Professional musicians and many audiences will see right through you if you attempt an imitation of Boulez, Nelsons, Gergiev, or any other idiosyncratic conductor. Over time, you will develop your own unique technique likely somewhere between those extreme examples. Whatever you look like, make it 100 percent *you*! Be *authentic*! Be *genuine*! Be *yourself*! Let your physical motions reflect the music and portray your leadership.

A final thought: Be *involved*, making the music happen through your gestures, in service to the composer. Emerging conductors often think that once they're beating all the beats within the correct diagram, their job is done. Not true! Beating time is only the beginning! Resist being a time-beater, and allow yourself to engage with your ensemble in a style that's uniquely yours.

ANECDOTE

Podium presence can of course be defined in many ways. I believe Leonard Bernstein best personified what presence means. Maybe he overdid it on occasion, and maybe his gestures sometimes were designed more for the audience than his performers. But he was so comfortable on the podium that he is an excellent model as to how to relate to standing on a box and waving arms in front an ensemble. I had the privilege of being in his conducting class at Tanglewood, and just observing his natural conducting style was true inspiration for me. The lesson? Be free and spontaneous with your gestures, as they should reflect your feelings about the music. Yet remain conscious of your leadership responsibilities to your ensemble. Do not plan ahead, or choreograph in advance what you do on the podium!

18

Physical Dos and Don'ts: A Summary

Conducting is more art than science. The reason one sees so many different styles of conducting in those with successful careers is that, beyond the very few generally understood rules, it is totally up to you to make gestures that effectively communicate to your ensemble and create the results you want. If the sound you get is *not* what you want, the thinking conductor will try something different until the results *are* what you intend! Loops and circles with the arms, hands, wrist, fingers; jabs, dabs, pokes, and sweeps with your baton; smiles, frowns, eye-cues, and head nods—all of the above and so much more are a part of the conductor's gesticular vocabulary.

BATON

The baton is your instrument. Facilitate the tip of the baton with your wrist to indicate your every musical thought. While my emphasis always is on the wrist, all baton motion begins with the shoulder, causing the entire arm to move organically, operating as one entity.

Psychologically, your primary focal point is in the expressiveness of the *tip* of the baton. Some conductors hold the baton just because they're supposed to, making it anything but the expressive instrument it can be. These conductors think it's their hand that musicians are watching. If that's true, it's because the conductors are not doing anything with the baton. Dynamics, rhythmic meters, phrasing, and timing can all be done with a flexible wrist managing the baton's movement.

HANDS AND ARMS

Your hands can be amazingly expressive if you put your intention on wanting them to be so. A good look at some of the best choral conductors will find some very expressive motions, utilizing flexible wrists and fingers. The extent is almost limitless to which hands can express music's character. A point, a grasp, a swirl, a punch, a wavy flow, are all common motions used by the most flexible of conductors.

A gesture is not made for the sake of the gesture itself. Instead, it communicates an idea or generates a response from the musicians. It cannot be a planned move but must be a spontaneous result of what the conductor wants to hear, either in preparation for an event or as a corrective measure.

The arms are there to provide support for the hands. Motion of the arms, beginning with the shoulder, should translate to an ever more effective gesture in the hands. Your arm movement must be *organic*, flowing comfortably from shoulder to baton *tip*, manifested ultimately by the wrist. With this approach, one can express so many different shades of dynamics and styles and even cues to avoid having to stop in rehearsal to verbally express something.

A reminder must be given here about mirror conducting. Many successful conductors do a lot of mirrored arm flapping. I'm not saying one should never mirror-conduct, because, of course, all of us do. Somehow, it's natural to raise both arms when conducting. I will acknowledge that, yes, every conductor conducts with arms mirroring each other. But, the *effective* conductor is able to keep mirroring to a minimum, maintaining a greater independence of motion in the hands and arms, allowing for more different gestures to more musicians, even simultaneously. Maybe tradition holds that the baton gives the beat and the left hand adds finesse and expression, but who would not want the ability to conduct single-handedly, comfortably, and effectively? It's a skill all conductors should develop, for both effectiveness and versatility.

It takes practice, concentration, and a bit of courage to develop a sense of complete arm and hand independence. It's so much easier with both arms moving in mirror image, and it's so much harder conducting with only the right hand/baton. I personally admit to occasional mirror-conducting, but I'm also very proud of, and comfortable with, conducting a full symphony orchestra with my left hand/arm totally disengaged and simply hanging at my side. Unfortunately, that is not the typical image of a conductor from either the musicians' or audience's point of view. But if you have effectively rehearsed your ensemble in such a way as to render your histrionics superfluous, then any histrionics you engage in are automatically superfluous and non-authentic! A look at great conductors from not too many years ago shows an admirable tradition of conducting by gently leading with the baton, not by choreographing with both hands.

My arms and hands often are completely independent of each other, freeing me up to concentrate on a wider, more inclusive focus on my ensemble. I can give time and overall character, phrasing, and balance adjustments freely with whatever hand I choose.

I sometimes will require my own conducting students to conduct an entire semester doing absolutely nothing with the left hand. It's an excellent first step toward developing real independence of hands. The exercise begins with getting the beat pattern to be second nature, without any thought to the baton's direction. The next step is adding dynamics and some musical style to the pattern, always *leading* the ensemble by preparing what's coming next in the music.

The final, baton-only exercise is to add cueing. This requires adjusting the baton's beat pattern to more variable fields of motion, dependent on the section being cued. The pattern itself remains essentially the same, but the direction the baton goes to make the cue causes the field of motion to move accordingly.

Whatever gestures you use, they must be totally *yours* and *spontaneous*, not planned for audience effect or your own ego's pleasure. All musicians, both professional and amateur, can clearly and instantaneously detect the inauthentic conductor who's on the podium only for his/her own satisfaction, from the one who genuinely is there to reflect a thoughtful, knowledgeable interpretation of the music and who is present to collaborate with the musicians.

EYES AND EARS

Your ears dictate your music making moment to moment; your eyes determine the character of your communication. Really, whatever you may choose to do with your arms (beat patterns, left/right-hand expression, etc.) makes absolutely no sense and has no meaning unless it's a result of what you are hearing and how you connect visually with your performers.

Your hearing simultaneously evaluates the sounds your ensemble is making against your musical vision. Your ongoing gestures reflect your study of the score, the ensemble responds, and your ears determine if that sound is what you intended. In turn, your mind interprets what you just heard and makes an instantaneous judgment as to how to conduct the next beat or moment. Sometimes, this happens extraordinarily rapidly: places like crucial dynamic, tempo, phrasing, or balance changes, especially in fast music. How you manage such places—within the overall context of the composition as an entirety—will determine your success with that particular ensemble.

Your eyes are much more important than you think. When conducting *any* ensemble, lead the musicians with your baton, but *connect* to your musicians with your eyes. Sometimes the most effective gesture you can make to a musician or section is a wink, a raised eyebrow, a smiling glance, or a nod of the head. Conducting is, after all, communication, and human beings communicate best through facial acknowledgment and expression. Connect with your individuals or sections when they have an important entrance at all times. Also, before giving physical cues with your hands, check to *see* if that musician or section is ready to enter. You may not even need to give a "normal" cue with your hands when a simple, smiling confirmation of the entrance might suffice!

When speaking to a large ensemble, develop the habit of addressing them with a roving but connecting eye. No single person being addressed should ever feel like they are being singled out with your comments, but direct your comments to all like any good public speaker, where everyone in the room feels like you are speaking directly to them.

HEAD

Get your head out of the score! Memorize as much of the music as you are able, and force yourself to establish direct eye contact with as many of your players as possible, as often as possible. Actually communicate with them visually by extending your baton to them so that it, too, communicates everything you would with your head and eyes. Your head, the tip of your baton, and the musicians' eyes should be a direct line of communication always.

Many younger, emerging conductors have a habit of immediately dropping one's head into the score upon an initial downbeat. So many conductors do well at getting the ensemble prepared to begin ("ready"); they will maintain excellent eye contact with the ensemble on the upbeat ("set"); but on the moment of the actual downbeat ("go"), the head drops into the score. This does absolutely nothing to encourage confidence in the ensemble's ongoing communication with you, the conductor. If nothing else, at least memorize the first few measures, or phrase, to instill confidence in your music-making to follow.

VOICE

When speaking to your ensemble, wait to begin speaking until you see that everyone is ready to listen, and be sure your voice is heard by all. Many emerging conductors begin speaking immediately after stopping, without realizing that musicians need a moment or two to (1) realize you've stopped, (2) physically stop their own playing, (3) switch from playing position, (4) find the place in the music you're directing them to, and only then (5) listen to what you have to say. It makes no sense to address anyone or any section in the orchestra if even one of them doesn't hear what you have to say.

Given the time pressures of most rehearsals, it can require a bit more patience to wait long enough to get the attention of all your musicians. They will appreciate your patience, however. Ultimately, this is a great investment of time, in establishing the ensemble's collective attention when you stop to give comments.

Section C. Real World Principles

If only a conductor's life on the podium could be as simple and easy as giving a downbeat, gently rehearsing with colleagues, and two-and-a-half hours later saying "thank you." But alas, conducting is not so easy. At the very least you'll face time management pressures and dealing with other musicians and non-musicians, many of whom are much more experienced than you. And you thought—ha!—it was all about you.

This section of the book offers you but a sampling of the kinds of issues and people you'll face, not to give specific guidance on how to deal with them but rather as food for thought. Every person and every circumstance you come across will be unique, so specific guidance is impossible except to say that all issues are about human relationships with human consequences. A collaborative attitude, on your part as conductor, will go an exceptionally long way to building positive relations with your team, your ensemble, and your co-collaborators.

Finally, I include two concepts in which I believe strongly, that I share with all my own conducting students. First, managing your conducting issues as a series of either big (important) or little (not-so-important) rocks, all of which you're trying to fit into the same small container. Whenever you're on the podium you need to determine what your big- or little-rocks issues are, i.e., what's really important to accomplish at every moment.

Finally, an analogy I use with my conducting students—especially those with particularly large, hyperactive, artless techniques—is one where I ask them to imagine themselves as wagon drivers pulled by a team of horses. The horses are the ensemble; you are holding the reins, sometimes with tight control, sometimes loosely. You read the horses' energies and abilities, you steer them in the right direction, but *they* are doing the work, not you. Success comes directly from your ability to manage and lead your team, in the right direction, down the right path, and at the right speed, always in support of the team.

19

Time

> *Conductors are time-shapers. It's what's most basic.*

As conductor, you are the only person responsible for showing the time. Your musicians follow your lead, and to them it makes little difference how you look. That's why there are so many idiosyncratic approaches to the art of gesturing, because there is no one way to look. Just a quick glance at conductors' online videos shows incredibly different looks. Try viewing videos of Bernstein, Järvi, Orozco-Estrada, Kleiber, Mälkki, DePriest, Dudamel, Alsop, and Ozawa for some telling examples of valid conducting looks.

Time is what you give from the podium—accurate, cleanly delineated, and musically shaped time. Your effectiveness will come directly from the gestures you make to produce musical success. Learn the basics indicated in this book, and apply them to your task. No player in an ensemble wants to see you uncomfortably gesturing, or worse yet, simply following along to what the ensemble is doing, without ever taking charge!

TIME MANAGEMENT

Conductors should be aware of, and counted on, for their ability to watch the clock and use their allotted time effectively. On the podium, you are charged with getting done what most needs to be done given the time available.

There are countless stories of conductors who intend to run a piece at the end of the rehearsal but who discover too late there's not even time to finish the run, or who can't finish their own outline of what they want to accomplish. This is just one reason why knowing what your big rocks or little rocks are is so important.

ANECDOTE

Time is precious but always limited. I often recall my very first audition for my first full-time conducting position. I had the second half of a rehearsal for a concert that same day, and somehow found myself four score pages short of concluding my last piece when the personnel manager called "Time!" To this day I am extremely grateful to the orchestra's music director who shouted to the personnel manager, "Oh, just let him go on!" I finished the overture, and got the job. Since then, I have been exceptionally focused on getting the job done in the time allotted.

20

Always, Sometimes, Never

Textbooks are great as a beginning guide or occasional reference, as one begins a conducting career. Once an opportunity arises, however, to actually conduct a rehearsal, concert, or recording session, a conductor is constantly and continuously making choices of *how* to use (or not) the rules set out in any methodology. In fact, as conductor you are always evaluating whether the ensemble actually is responding to your guidance, and simultaneously determining what to do next.

So, despite all you may read in this or any other conducting text, there nevertheless are universally-accepted guidelines that you should always, or sometimes, or never do:

ALWAYS:

- Be prepared. Whatever it takes—however much sleep you must lose—know the score intimately!
- Make a downbeat in a downward motion.
- Serve the music.
- Be sure everyone is ready to begin before you start conducting.
- Be kind, courteous, non-judgmental, and, yes, even (genuinely) smiling.
- Constantly evaluate your own actions and words.
- Strive for clarity of gesture rather than choreography of effect.
- Be loyal to the composer and yet musically creative yourself.
- Be supportive of your musicians.

SOMETIMES:

- Every beat is preparatory, sometimes not.
- In serving the music, you follow a composer's instruction, sometimes not.
- You may give every cue, sometimes not.
- You may lead each musical moment, sometimes not.
- Taking the reins, you may lead the ensemble in another direction, sometimes not.
- You may force (inspire, encourage, insist, etc.) your ensemble to go beyond what's comfortable for them, sometimes it's all about their comfort.

- You may back off and let your ensemble go on their own, sometimes you take control.
- You may mirror-conduct, despite my exhortations against doing so, though hopefully not habitually.
- A cutoff may not be managed by clearly making a preparatory circle, sometimes you may purposely be somewhat less than clear.
- A preparation beat in beginning a new phrase may not be in tempo.
- The size of your beat may not directly correlate to the volume of the ensemble.
- You may not subdivide the beat, when your ensemble is doing just fine without you getting in the way.
- You may not conduct the most obvious musical voice. Sometimes, you may conduct the accompaniment.
- You may not be true to the beat pattern as diagrammed in any textbook if you can get better musical results.

but NEVER…

- Give a downbeat with an obviously upward motion.
- Frown, scowl, or scold any of your ensembles or players—ever!
- Be unprepared; musicians cannot be fooled and will lose respect for anyone unprepared.
- Waste time.
- Appear to know more about your musicians' instruments, even if you think you do.
- "Pull focus," psychologically from the musical moment (or people).
- Begin conducting if any musician isn't ready yet.
- Begin speaking in rehearsal before all musicians are ready to listen.

Many emerging conducting students don't understand the principle in rehearsal that it makes little sense to say anything to the ensemble if they're not paying attention to you. In the race against the clock, conductors often quickly blurt out directions to musicians when the musicians are already talking amongst themselves. Wanting to avoid wasting time, they nevertheless are counterproductive by not going with the flow of the moment. Some points to remember:

1. When stopping in rehearsal, be sure everyone stops playing before you say anything.
2. Once they've stopped playing, establish eye contact with the musicians you're addressing.
3. Speaking directly, first tell them the specific passage you're commenting upon.

4. Maintaining direct eye contact, make your comment for their adjustment.
5. Watch, as you would any conversation, for their acknowledgment (or not, for you to reiterate or explain).
6. Address the whole ensemble when you're ready to begin, asking them first to find the specific rehearsal letter or number, and only then (not before!) counting any additional measures that need counting, slowly enough for them to stick with you.
7. Raise your baton, make sure everyone's ready, and go. It may seem cumbersome, but it is the most valuable, generally accepted way to keep all musicians on the same wavelength, in the same measure, and attentive to your comments and suggestions for improvement.

ANECDOTE

A conductor I observed was young but more experienced on the podium than others her age. She was exceptionally musical and was very comfortable with making whatever gestures she needed to at any musical moment. She was also quite passionate with her music-making, which under normal circumstances would have been a good thing. But her passion on the podium caused her to be impatient, to appear condescending to her players, and to wildly gesticulate or speak to her ensemble in an almost cartoon-like, hyper-intense manner that only created quiet ridicule on the part of her ensemble.

Here's a rundown of her rehearsal [mis]behavior: she began speaking to the ensemble before everyone was finished tuning; she gave her very first downbeat when there were still musicians not yet ready to play; before even finishing the first phrase, she dropped her hands (expecting the ensemble to immediately stop, which, of course, they didn't) and began lecturing them about the intensity of the composition, speaking totally fabricated storyline analogies and singing with such an exaggerated approach as to be comical. She then began the piece again, and again didn't give enough time for everyone in the ensemble to get into playing position. The rehearsal went on like this for a couple hours, when everything appeared to be mismanaged, with no good musical or psychological results.

At least the orchestra was polite about their reaction to her mannerisms, and no one chose to resist or respond negatively. But there was a lot of eye-rolling and smirking within the ensemble, where the musicians clearly wanted out of there. Everyone was uncomfortable, and no one was happy or even willing to give any more than the bare minimum in return to the conductor. To this observer, she clearly needed some instruction on how to relate to a group of fellow humans collaboratively and artistically, and how to manage all the things we're supposed to manage besides waving a stick. The rehearsal I observed not only was quite uncomfortable, but also seemed endless, like we'd never get out of there!

21

Leadership

Conducting is so much more than simply standing in front of an ensemble, waving your arms, and expecting your musicians to follow you unquestioningly. Perhaps symphony conductors of half-a-century ago could get away with that kind of attitude, but it is totally unacceptable and unreasonable today to be anything but a collaborator. Yes, first among equals, but the emphasis is *equals*, not *first*. After all, there's only one person—the conductor—charged with the responsibility of providing context, guidance, and determining quality of detail. Musicians in professional ensembles understand that. They will love, respect, dislike, or question the artistic decisions you make, largely dependent on how you embody your understanding of leadership.

That's why leadership is so important. Conductors are defined in today's terms, not some old-fashioned notion of tyranny. Of course, you would be seen as egregiously self-centered and egotistic to behave as if you were the only person who had all the musical answers. Reject the old-fashioned notion that the musicians better follow you no matter what, or else! Reject the old-fashioned paradigm of the conductor being separate from the ensemble, of not collaborating with fellow musicians.

For many years now, I have been a believer of servant leadership. No longer aloof, today's conductor works together with all members of his ensemble to create a musical event greater than the sum of its parts. The conductor must be as much a servant—recognizing, acknowledging, and addressing the needs of his or her ensemble— as a leader. In short, today's successful conductors truly are collaborators.

For those seriously interested in leadership issues, there are of course many publications available, though you'll find them mostly in the business section of any bookstore. I highly recommend author James Scoullar's *The Three Levels of Leadership*. Eminently readable and easily applied to the world of the arts, this would be an excellent, comprehensive beginning text for conductors. According to Mr. Scoullar, there are four dimensions to this thing called leadership. In applying his principles to conducting, we can say that conductors must be concerned simultaneously with these four dimensions of activity:

1. Showing an overall concept of the composition mentally and physically that inspires musicians to willingly listen, contribute, and work together;
2. Leading the continuous improvement moment-by-moment of all details as they relate to the composition;

3. Serving each musician's effectiveness contributing to the whole; and
4. Managing ensemble unity of musical thought and presentation.

It could look like this, graphically, where the hot spot in the middle where all four dimensions intersect represents "Collaborative Music-Making."

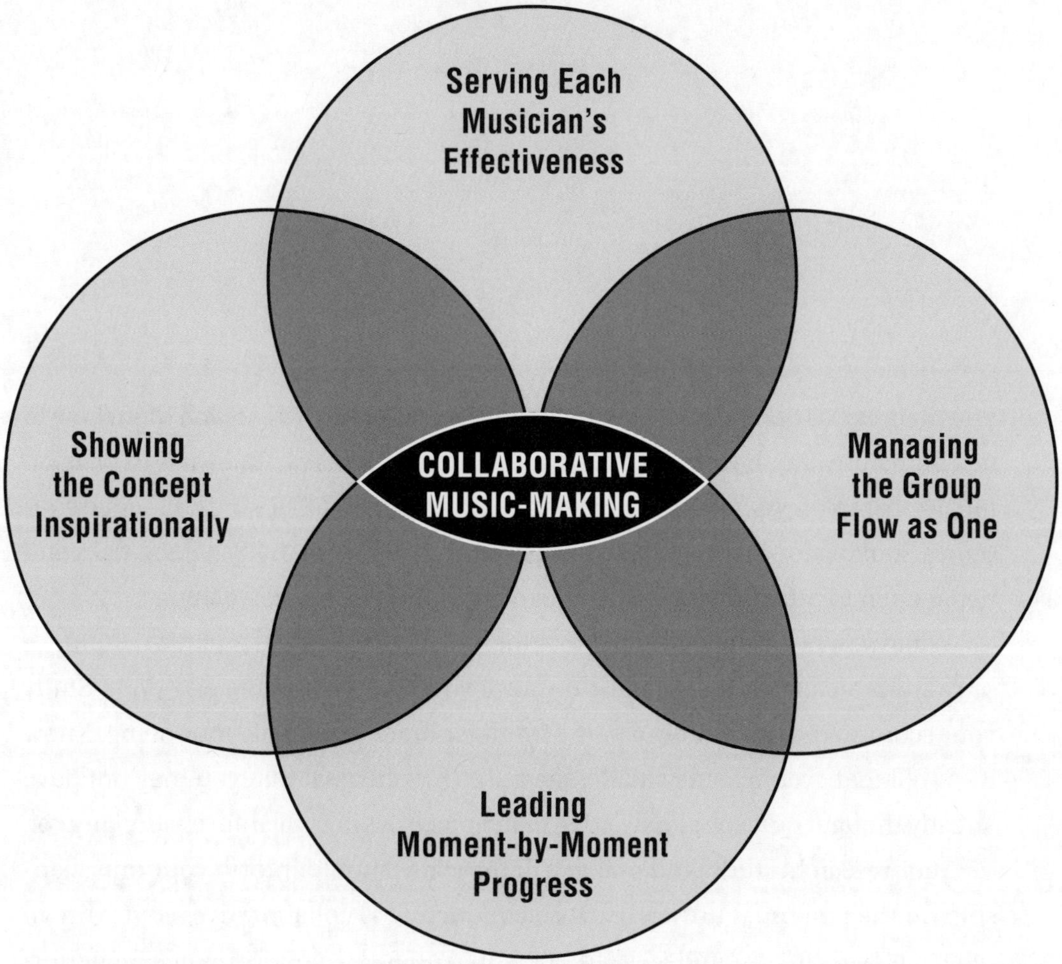

FIG. 21.1. Collaborative Music Making

Be gracious and humble. Remember that you primarily are serving the music, and you have been given the awesome responsibility of conducting. Don't even enter the stage, studio, or rehearsal room if you're not prepared. But assuming you are, enter the stage with an authentically pleasant, collegial attitude of genuinely wanting to develop a relationship with the musicians.

ANECDOTE

Some time ago, I had occasion to observe a guest conductor with a regional orchestra who since has become a good friend. It was his first rehearsal with this orchestra, and the first time I had ever observed him. His repertoire was serious, a classic. And while he was serious, too, in his demeanor, he also was exceptionally pleasant throughout. After rehearsal, a musician said of him, "He certainly enjoys himself while conducting," which I realized made all the difference to her. Sometimes that's all it takes. Smile, genuinely. Otherwise, it's counter-productive. A real leader enjoys working with his/her people!

22

On Being Musical

Fritz Reiner was quoted as saying to his students that he could teach them how to be conductors, not how to be musicians. Whatever it takes, find ways to develop musicianship on your own! Listen to other performers of all kinds. Practice your scores, looking for intent and meaning. Conduct with creativity, taking risks and being open to other ideas. Only you can develop your musicianship.

When you're on the podium, be authentic. Don't conduct a tempo or phrase or ritard or change a balance just because you heard someone else do it. Study your score so that it's wholly a part of you, embrace it with all your being. Know it so well that even if some small issue arises in rehearsal that you may not have already thought out, your knowledge of the piece overall will inform your answer.

Your research, study, and practice of the score should inform your musicianship on the podium. Further, because conducting is collaborative, your work in rehearsal with an ensemble will add personal nuance in performance. In performance, you will be the obvious center of attention for the audience, but refuse to let their eyes affect your gestures or interpretation. You are there to make music with your colleagues, not to put on a show for the non-musicians in the room. Remain authentic and truly reflective of the musical leadership you are providing, and if you become aware of the audience, be mindful to not make moves that will detract from their appreciation of the music.

In rehearsal, allow and encourage your own personality to create a relationship with your ensemble. It makes no difference if you've never seen the musicians before, or if they have no idea who you are. Create a relationship with them as a collaborator (literally, "laboring together"), a musical colleague, a first-among-equals leader, and inspirer/teacher to those you're leading. If you are generally a serious person, it's okay to be serious, so long as you are also pleasant in your relationship with your fellow musicians. If you have a natural sense of humor, use it! In other words, be yourself! Just don't be mechanical. Conducting is not just about metronome markings, or making commands "from above." It *is* about personality, expression, and communication.

As stated earlier, we first learn the beat patterns. Next, we learn how to adapt the beat patterns according to the most basic elements (dynamics, style, tempos). The ultimate, most difficult step is in showing the music, learning which beats not to conduct, and how to make music according to your understanding of the music. This is so much more difficult for a conductor, as opposed to an instrumentalist who has the tangible and tactile ability to actually touch his/her instrument. Conductors make music by pointing a stick, gesticulating, and employing psychological strategies to get other people to come along on a collaborative path. Singlehandedly, you're literally "working the room" to make music happen!

There are examples of professional musicians and teachers saying that the music lies not with the notes, but in the space between the notes. The same is true with conducting. It's not so much the beats you give but the flow between the beats that gives us musical expression. With that connection or flow, we would simply be time machines, mechanical, expressionless automatons needing only a metronome, not a leader. That is not making music. It is the connective tissue, then, that binds the beats, creates the expression and, in fact, makes the music.

When conducting, you should be so comfortable with the basics of your motions as if they are second-nature, with all gestures naturally flowing out of your conception for the music according to each and every moment's requirements. You will then be free enough to concentrate on the natural flow of the music, your personal expression, your communication with your musicians, and how you want to shape the musical idea. Every gesture, every look, every twist and turn you make should be to facilitate a musical effect, and should always be for your musicians, not your own pleasure nor the audience's visual entertainment.

23

Working with Others

GUEST ARTISTS ON STAGE

There are as many different guest artist types as there are people. If you're lucky you'll conduct internationally renowned performers of all types. You will be conducting artist friends of yours, youngsters giving their debuts, and those not accustomed to adapting to a conductor. Some artists will be recommended by your marketing department because of their apparent appeal; others you will have by reputation; still others may be completely unknown to you but you like their repertoire. In some cases, both you and the artist are new to the ensemble. In all situations, you are there to support the soloist. It is their rendition the audience has come to hear, so you should not impose your own ideas. Your job as the servant-leader is to do everything possible to make your guest artist comfortable. Certainly, in some cases, you can suggest alternate ideas in private conversation with the soloist. All artists want their performance to go well and many love to collaborate spontaneously with conductors, so feel free to suggest a change knowing that, ultimately, it's a decision that's best made when the two of you are in total agreement.

Get in their groove! Whether it's a pop artist who remains in a constant tempo throughout their four-minute song(s), or the cellist in the Dvořák concerto, the servant-leader will surrender to the soloist by getting deeply into their rhythmic flow. Think of a piano accompanist playing for a solo recital. In some moments, there is parallel thinking, playing, and motion; in other moments, there will be surrendering to the phrasing of the soloist. But accompanying pianists can respond instantaneously, while the conductor uses a stick to generate a response to the subtle, sometimes unpredictable musical thinking of the soloist. This is yet another reason why baton technique and clarity of gesture is so important—especially for large, classical ensembles.

COMPOSERS AND ARRANGERS

Composers and arrangers are always grateful for having their works performed. In rehearsal and performance/recording, they will listen to your session and will expect to offer comments, suggestions, and other edits when asked. As conductor, you can decide when that is—either during a working rehearsal or, one-on-one, afterward. Depending on the piece, the composer, and the venue, they will either sit in the auditorium or sound booth or on stage close to you. The complexity of the piece itself and the personal relationship you have with the composer will determine your choice, knowing also that it will never always be the same, but that you should always ask the composer their preference.

Arrangers in general are more accustomed than composers to suggestions from the conductor regarding edits the conductor may want to suggest. After all, it's not their original concept, and if the arranger is present it's likely because you requested or commissioned their arrangement. I have found all arrangers to be really understanding, and willing to adapt their arrangement to the ensemble's (and your) needs and ultimate expressive goals. After all, they're probably hoping you'll call on them again!

An exception to the above would be when you're conducting, say, a guest pops act that has an entire show of arrangements and their arranger has come along. In that case, you must respect the show as they've created it, and refrain from any tendency to fix what you perceive as inadequacies. This is their product, not yours, so go with the flow as amiably as if it's exactly what you created yourself.

Finally, be sure to acknowledge and introduce any composers and arrangers present to your ensemble, *and* to the audience if they're present at the performance. It's a small but meaningful way to include your musicians in the bigger picture, and to acknowledge the creative achievement of the composer/arranger.

STAGE DIRECTORS AND CHOREOGRAPHERS

Working with stage directors and choreographers is a true test of your collaborative abilities. Having one or the other inevitably means that you're involved in a staged production (opera, music theater, ballet, dance, etc.) in which as conductor you play the role of "accompanying" the players, dancers, or singers on stage. I put accompanying in quotation marks because too often that's what others think the ensemble you're conducting is doing. Never let that be the case, however. No one else in the entire production company (including the composer, if they're present) is given the responsibility of ultimately determining the music's shape in performance. The stage directors in musical productions or choreographers in dance are the ones responsible for the performance concept, or the "show," if you will. Some will know the score intimately, others will not. Some will be sensitive to your concerns, others will not. In the beginning stages of production, as conductor you should seize the opportunity to be involved in the earliest, blocking-type rehearsals as often as possible, giving you more opportunities to discuss (collaborate!) musical issues with the director or choreographer and to express your musical intentions. Again, this always will be a test of your leadership and communication skills in terms of finding alternate solutions to which all parties can agree, even if it's not what you originally had in mind when studying the score before rehearsals began.

In opera at least, each early blocking rehearsal begins with a music-only work-through (with you conducting) of the scenes to be blocked. It's a terrific grounding process for keeping the singing cast in line with the overall conception, but also occasionally serves to point out inconsistencies in interpretation between you and the stage director. This is yet another circumstance requiring collaboration and, sometimes, compromise.

Most importantly, be faithful to the overall musical expression and your composer's intent, whether or not they're present. Flexibility and understanding where the director is coming from are key, given what you understand the composer's intent to be. The more a conductor can acknowledge and understand the various possibilities different from your own that a given musical moment may represent to the directors is incredibly important. This is the give-and-take, collaborative paradigm with which you simply must be comfortable. Be sure to read the interview with Madeline Smith in which she talks about the creative team of artistic leaders, all of whom must work together. Ego displays and inflexible attitudes are the death of many careers!

PERSONNEL MANAGER(S)

The personnel manager has the most direct contact outside of rehearsal and performance with the musicians in your ensemble. S/he manages the audition process; hires the musicians and their substitutes when absent; supervises and acts accordingly in all matters of musicians' attendance, absence, and compensation; devises seating and rotation; oversees communications regarding all manner of rehearsal and recording schedules; watches the clock to make sure you're not going overtime; listens and responds to all the complaints musicians may have regarding working conditions; and manages the dismissal process. The conductor must have an absolutely trusting relationship with this person. *Every* ensemble has a personnel manager and issues of personnel management. It is not important that you be best friends with this person, but you must have a positive working relationship in which there is mutual trust and respect for each other's responsibilities and duties.

In terms of human resources, your personnel manager places the product you require on the stage so you can do your job. S/he must have open communications with you so that everyone is working with the same understanding of the desired result. This person often needs to work further in advance than you might be ready to even think about for any particular session, just because the process of contracting all desired and appropriate personnel is often so complicated. This is one reason why you'll be asked, for instance, to supply specific rehearsal schedules much earlier than you'll be ready to devise them.

LIBRARIAN(S)

The librarian also will be thinking about and acting upon your musical needs far in advance. Librarians are responsible for securing, disbursing, managing, and often editing all the musical materials your musicians are reading. This means dealing with publishers, composers, and arrangers who require advance deadlines for supplying materials, and assuring that the materials when received are in fact accurate, communicating with string principals who determine bowing, adding in editing marks you as conductor may require, and getting the parts, hopefully in advance, to all players who require time for practice before your session. This may be somewhat different in a studio recording session (see my interview with Peter Boyer) where the music is placed on the musicians' stands the morning of! Your librarian must have a clear idea from you as to what edition you require when multiples exist, and you need to be sensitive to the early timelines librarians require for making all the necessary preparations to the music. In session, the librarian should be close by (often they're one of your musicians on stage) and available to address and fix any musical material emergencies that arise. Even under the best of circumstances, there will be situations in which ensemble members need their parts corrected or adjusted or photocopied to facilitate page turns. Your librarian must be effective, efficient, organized, with excellent time management skills, and able to turn on a dime as it were, in responding to the latest crisis of the moment. Librarians should also be pleasant and flexible, willing and able to respond quickly to address musicians' issues.

I have seen incomplete sets of parts: sets in which the winds and the strings are different editions with different rehearsal lettering/numbering; sets which have been used so often by so many other—often student—orchestras that parts are almost unreadable due to all their markings. This can happen despite the librarian's conscientious efforts to secure the most accurate sets possible.

After all sessions and performances are complete, librarians usually have strict guidelines for cleaning the parts back to their original condition when they were received and deadlines for returning.

Be sure to read *A Manual for the Performance Library* by Russ Girsberger for an in-depth understanding of the librarian's job.

OFF-STAGE MANAGERS AND CREW

If you're conducting a large ensemble in concert, you will have a stage manager working the production. This person is in charge of "calling the show," which means calling all performers on stage, communicating with front-of-house management for shepherding the audience and closing the doors, signaling the lighting manager to go to concert mode and for the ensemble's tuning process to begin, and retrieving and sending guest performers on stage. In opera rehearsal, this person is also the chief steward of the daily rehearsal process, taking direction from the stage director to communicate with all characters and crew.

If you're conducting a large ensemble in concert but of a pops variety, you'll also have a team of lighting and sound (amplification) managers and technicians, all of whom will be making the performance happen according to your preferences in suiting the music, including the placement of microphones in the ensemble. There will also be even more stage crew on hand to facilitate the often-complicated task of moving the grand piano, setting up the drum set and/or the entire band, and otherwise smoothly and quickly adjusting the stage set-up to pre-determined settings.

If you're conducting an opera or other large-scale staged production, you'll have a production stage manager (PSM) whose oversight will include the above but also all the lighting, sound, set, props, costuming, and make-up personnel. In rehearsal, they manage the daily rehearsal schedule at the stage director's direction—coordinating all required personnel and related requisite materials. During the show, the PSM calls all the staging and lighting cues, in addition to calling all the appropriate dancers, singers, and actors to the stage (and conductor to the pit) when needed. This is an incredibly complex but exhilarating responsibility, though they get no public recognition in the performance!

If you're conducting a recording session, in the booth you'll have sound engineers, "second" engineers, producers, and often composers and arrangers who are following every musical step you take with your ensemble, and whose advice and suggestions you will need for re-takes and other edits.

In short, these few paragraphs barely scratch the surface of the people and teams with whom you'll be working, and there will be as many variations as there are musical genres and productions. In the most professional situations, there are experts whose knowledge is valuable to you. In smaller operations, there likely will be fewer individuals covering more responsibilities—possibly including yourself. In any circumstance, however, you're only one of many "experts" who know how to do their job. Teamwork is, of course, the key word.

24

Different Disciplines

SYMPHONY

Symphonic music is so complex, and rehearsal time is usually limited enough that conducting it requires a more advanced, detailed, and expressive baton technique. When conducting symphonic music, stopping to verbally explain what you want as conductor should be treated as only the very last resort, or as a specific teaching moment. Ninety-eight percent of the time, however, the conductor should be able to express his/her musical wants and desires simply by using a well-developed baton technique.

This takes practice, because it's not just about clear and accurate beat patterns. Rather, it's all about knowing when to give beat patterns and—more importantly—when *not* to (i.e., letting your ensemble move along on its own). It's also about how to manipulate each beat pattern to get the musical effect across to the ensemble, because you're showing the *music*, its flow, direction, and intensity, not just the beats.

SYMPHONIC POPS

Time is most important when conducting symphonic pops. As I stated earlier, conductors can be defined basically as time-shapers. The accuracy, consistency, and constancy of the music's time, as well as a clean and easy-to-understand conducting technique are most important. Pops arrangements, especially the ever-popular "selections from…" musical theater and film score standards are filled with tempo changes, many of which aren't predictable and often are sudden and unnatural. Like anything you conduct, you must know how the tune goes. It must be clearly in your mind even before you finish the previous tune, and your technique must be there for each and every musician according to what his/her needs are at that one transitional moment.

The overwhelming majority of pops music that you conduct will be tonal and—except for some extraordinarily symphonic film scores of late—will not be composed with a great variety of orchestration. In other words, most pops music will be simpler in concept and structure, much shorter in time, and more direct in expression than, say, a full symphony. Scores are generally not available until the last minute, are often written in the arranger's shorthand if not published, and you will have little time to prepare on your own.

Unlike standard, orchestral, published repertoire, pops scores are often abbreviated (some pages may not even have notes, but rather just a shorthand indication of the material), many times exist in only photocopied, barely-legible manuscript. Some standard pops scores are written only in "short score" (reducing the orchestration to two or three staves). These are "Piano/Conductor" scores, and often are all you can get.

When studying/preparing a score for this kind of experience, the "road map" becomes your primary focus, meaning preparatory beats, metronome indications, tempo changes, fermatas, ritards and accelerandos, essential cutoffs, meters, and mixed meters. With extremely limited rehearsal time, your total focus will be on giving the beats clearly for the ensemble's benefit. The last thing you want to do is screw up their performance by giving a wrong beat pattern or making some other mistake for which only you are responsible. Spirit and character should be your next most important focus.

When dealing with a guest artist who also is the composer, you are there to serve the artist. What they want is what you should give them. If you're too fast or too slow, they will tell you, and unquestioningly, you will need to change. Always be there for your soloist, whoever it is. Breathe with them, glance at them when possible, and look for their body language, which will tell you how and when to enter or cut off a passage or a chord. You will be so much more successful if you can put your musical self into their shoes and get in their same groove. You may be the conductor, but when working with a soloist it cannot be about you! Rather, it is about how you can successfully manage your ensemble to be in total synchronization with your pops soloist/group.

Simply put, your beat must be clear and accurate. What more could an ensemble member under your baton want for them to feel comfortable? Inspiration? Well, not necessarily, in this repertoire. Given the usually limited time for preparation, the best the conductor can do is provide a comfortable, clean setting to allow the musicians to make their music together, as an ensemble.

IN THE PIT

Conducting singers, actors, and dancers on stage with instrumental musicians in the pit is an extraordinary experience, with extraordinary responsibilities. While the conductor's basic task of ensemble togetherness and time-shaping remains the same as always, some of the obvious, basic differences as compared to conducting an ensemble in the studio or on stage are:

1. You must be seen by all performers. I have been in situations where not all musicians in the pit could see me, and others where the performers on stage had no visual connection to me in the pit. Both instances are extremely risky and should be avoided if at all possible. In the pit, move the personnel into different configurations if need be; it is not necessary to hold on to traditional protocol in terms of who sits where. For performers on stage, it is your responsibility to assure that all performers can see you, whether live in the pit or via closed circuit televisions off-stage. Not having the correct setup can result in musical mistakes leading to disaster.
2. Since pits rarely can fit a standard symphony orchestra, string sections are inevitably reduced. That demands creative seating arrangements allowing for physical comfort of your ensemble. A traditional pit arrangement has all strings to one side, all winds to the other side, with brass and percussion in the rear perimeter of the space. Your repertoire and the actual space you have will determine the best possible solution. Keep in mind, this should be your call. On the other hand, if you are a guest conductor, you will want to be more accommodating to the ensemble's past practice.
3. Your overall approach is definitely collaboration. In the pit, your primary task is to keep the pit ensemble together with the performers on stage, all of whom have been trained to *not* look directly at you. That's not the point! They're acting out, singing, or dancing a musical play that does not include watching the conductor. Your rehearsal preparation should have been secure enough to prevent any surprises between the stage and you. Individual singers, ensembles, and on-stage choruses may briefly glance in your direction for an entrance cue, but otherwise they're concentrating on their role only.
4. Your conducting technique itself will be different from "normal" on-stage concertizing: your field of motion will be much more variable, depending on who in the pit or on stage needs to see the baton at various moments. In soloistic opera aria moments, you likely will want to have constant eye contact with the vocalist, anticipating and matching any subtleties of tempo and phrasing, while your baton will remain lower for ease of the pit ensemble's going with you. In large tutti passages with an inexorable flow to the music, your baton likely will raise higher to be seen more clearly by the on-stage performers so as to avoid any accidental deviations of tempo.
5. Your rehearsal technique also changes in a pit ensemble situation. In many productions, you will be involved in all early piano rehearsals, including the painfully slow-moving technical rehearsals where the stage director is determining and constantly revising the stage blocking and other production cues.
6. After some weeks of putting the production together with piano, you will have several rehearsals with orchestra alone. Time will always feel short, especially remembering that while you and the cast are relatively prepared, the orchestra is now beginning at square one!
7. Following the orchestra-alone rehearsals (exception: it is permissible and often desirable, to bring in leading roles and/or ensembles to rehearse with the orchestra musically) there will be the "sitzprobe." This is the first time

> the entire cast and orchestra play through the entire production together, and can be either a nightmare or refreshingly positive. Orchestra in the pit (for the first time), all cast seated (that's where the "sitz" comes from) on stage, often with their scores, with the primary purpose of doing a first-time run-through from beginning to end of the entire production. Sometimes, I've also had the opportunity to do a "wandelprobe" in addition to, or instead of a sitzprobe, in which the cast may move about the stage to their blocking positions while still paying primary attention to the music.

The sitzprobe will be followed by at least one technical rehearsal, with conductor in the pit conducting piano, which is all about the technical (lighting, props, set design) cues required. These rehearsals can be long and tedious, as every time a technical cue needs to be adjusted and/or set, everyone waits for the cue to be entered in their computer programs.

Following the technical rehearsals come the dress rehearsals, at least the first of which is with conducted piano accompaniment. Except for the absence of the orchestra, this is truly a dress rehearsal with all costuming, make-up, lighting, and stage set adjustments happening—you hope—just as in performance. Only major errors will be reason for stopping, which does happen occasionally, but the primary goal is to get from beginning to end. Lastly, there are the dress rehearsals with orchestra present, during which ideally all glitches and wrinkles have been resolved and ironed out. There should be absolutely no stopping in an orchestral dress rehearsal.

CHORAL

In choral repertoire with orchestra, the chorus master must be clearly aware of your musical intentions before s/he even begins the choral preparation. Ideally you and the chorus master have a session alone discussing all large and small musical issues. Based on that discussion, the chorus master will want to edit the choral parts accordingly, making adjustments of voicing, pronunciation, breathing, and phrasing, paying particular attention to placement of consonants and vowel inflections. This should all be done far in advance of putting the chorus together with orchestra.

When rehearsing with chorus and orchestra initially, the conductor already should have rehearsed the orchestra alone so that most of the time can now be spent on transitioning the choral singing to the orchestra's level of understanding and sound overall. Choruses have a natural tendency to sound like they're singing behind the conductor's beat, which is an outcome of their naturally waiting to hear the orchestra to which they are singing along. Definition of attacks on the beat and overall ensemble precision will be significantly lacking under these circumstances, and the conductor must implore the chorus to make their sounds match the ictus of the baton in the same way as the orchestra.

Choruses respond enthusiastically to even more eye contact and conducting gestures from the conductor. Be there for them with your conducting technique, don't mouth the words, and politely insist that they follow you also with eye contact in order to discern every nuance you indicate. Lazy choruses often sing directly into their music, which is held too low because of lack of space with the row in front of them, or just due to laziness and lack of attention.

Finally, make sure your chorus has a warm-up room available before every rehearsal and performance, separate from the rehearsal space. This is the time your chorus master prepares the group in vocalizing and cleaning up any musical details—even spot-rehearsing with piano—before joining the orchestra. I have also found it helpful to drop by the chorus warm-up room just to say hi, to thank them for a fine job, and to see if they have any musical questions. As most choruses are volunteers, the personal connection you establish with them will result in a better musical product and a more committed chorus.

STUDIO RECORDING/CONDUCTING TO VISUALS

Studio recording and conducting to video games and/or film are definitely related in terms of conducting technique and responsibilities. But often, there is a limited emotional or spontaneous element in recording sessions or matching a click track.

Conducting technique in these situations needs to be clear and concise, not confusing and not allowing for variable interpretation by the ensemble's musicians. Focus for the players must be on the baton, and the less distracting the conductor is with gestures of emotion with either hand, the better off everyone will be. Find the courage to conduct only with the baton hand; leave the left hand for turning pages or the occasional confirming cue. Be more businesslike in your approach, less spontaneously "musical." What's important in recording is the accuracy and precision of the ensemble, and what's important in accompanying visuals is the precision of the timing and synchronization with the screen.

ANECDOTE

I heard via others once that a young conductor with a fairly significant conducting career was invited to conduct one of America's larger opera companies, performing Puccini's *La Bohème*. Not being that experienced in opera, this young conductor studied the score, apparently without regard for age-old musical traditions, and without paying attention to the needs of the singing cast. In piano rehearsal, then, this conductor had very specific ideas regarding tempo and phrasing that often went against tradition, and definitely against the singers' preparation. Because he remained egotistically insistent on his own views, the rehearsal/performance run was a constant struggle. Ultimately, it wasn't successful, nor was the conductor ever asked to return. When dealing with experts in different disciplines with which you may not be all that familiar, make the effort to learn as much about that discipline in advance no matter how good you think you are. It's okay to buck with tradition, but you'll be more successful doing so if you're actually aware of the traditions you're bucking!

25

Rehearsal Practices

REHEARSAL SCHEDULES

One of the most important tasks given conductors is devising rehearsal schedules. They must be carefully considered, with great thought put into the process because rarely will you want, or have, the ability to change the schedule once it's established. So many variables must be taken in consideration: difficulty and/or familiarity of the repertoire, spacing of rehearsals (daily? weekly? doubles?), availability of soloists, and relative ability and attention span of the ensemble are just a few of the most obvious ones. You must be completely aware of your ensemble's capabilities as well as the relative difficulty of passages they will need the most, or least, help given the time available.

Here are some basic considerations in drafting a rehearsal to keep in mind:

1. **The Ensemble**

What is their musical and technical level?

On the higher end of the scale, much more can be left up to the individual musicians. Little errors or lack of synchronization will automatically take care of themselves. Rehearsing can be faster-paced as the individual ability to grasp their part technically and your musical instruction is quicker. Rarely will there be a need to drill notes within a section, though occasionally giving them "another shot" at a passage is warranted. Much rehearsing can be done with an emphasis on style and quality of playing, less on technique per se, and can be done in smaller, more isolated moments.

But on the lower end, there will be a greater need for repetition, drilling, and more playing-through larger sections. More time for explanation and under-tempo repetition should be planned, even for sharing relevant contextual issues pertaining to the music. Lesser ensembles appreciate more contextual information from the conductor than higher ensembles, but even the most professional ensembles in new or unfamiliar repertoire benefit from increased context.

How close is your relationship with them?

You will rehearse an ensemble familiar to you somewhat differently from an ensemble unknown to you. On the familiar side, you'll already have a relationship that can serve as an excellent basis for rehearsing, allowing you to predetermine when and with whom you need to go easy, or how far you can push in asking for what you want and still remain effective. You also likely will have the freedom with your friends and colleagues to do significantly more detailed stopping and starting, especially if you've established a sense of respect in which the musicians trust you to eventually put all the details back together for overall understanding.

With ensembles unfamiliar to you, your rehearsal plan should be a little more generic, allowing time for unexpected issues to arise. At the very least, give an unfamiliar ensemble the opportunity to get to know you by spending some early time in rehearsal reading the repertoire at least in large sections if not in their entirety. You are sizing them up, figuring out areas requiring your attention, but they are sizing you up as well, learning how to respond to you. Not so much can be planned in advance on your part in such situations, as you don't really know how they're going to respond to you or to the repertoire. Spend as much time early on in rehearsal assessing the ensemble's collective personality. Read them as people, and be alert to how they're responding (or not) to your technical and/or verbal direction. Do you see glances (eyebrows raised, rolled eyes) between musicians when you speak to them? Do you make any gestures that are not generating a musical response from the ensemble? These would be cause for alarm on your part, to which you should change your manner to prevent such reactions. Be personable, as you are building a relationship with colleagues.

There is yet a third category, which is an ensemble preceded by reputation. Any studio orchestra in Los Angeles, for instance, is accustomed to sight-reading, to deciphering and playing (perfectly!) their own parts, and to not needing anything but an exceptionally clear beat. Your rehearsal schedule for this kind of orchestra—or, in fact, any fully-professional orchestra—must be made with the assumption that the musicians already know what they're doing. You must immediately have the big picture of your conception in mind.

Are they full-time, or paid by the service, or volunteer?

In short, full-time orchestras are totally accustomed to playing together, which they usually do with great style unique to them. Per-service orchestras can be also really terrific musicians, but the fact that they are per-service means there's a higher risk of less consistent personnel. Volunteer orchestras usually are comprised of avocational, less experienced musicians with less time to prepare their own parts in advance, but requiring more time in rehearsal to "wood shed" or drill difficult passages as well as training principles of ensemble playing. They likely also are participating more for their own pleasure, so a conductor's personality becomes even more important for them to remain enthusiastic.

What is your assessment of their abilities relative to the repertoire?

If the ensemble is unknown to you, this can be difficult to exactly determine, but you should have at least some kind of idea in advance of who you're to be conducting. Ask yourself if you can assume they're completely prepared individually. Know in advance the areas of the music that will require special focus and rehearsal time in terms of phrasing, dynamic contrast, intonation, ensemble, or rhythmic command.

2. The Repertoire

How difficult is the repertoire?

Frequent mixed meters, abnormal key signatures, and extensive arrays of unusual numbers of notes in a given beat (5:3 or 11:8 or 13:16, for instance) or simply a lot of technical passages is obviously going to be more difficult. How you rehearse, then, will be just as different as the music itself. Early on, you will want to get the ensemble to the point where technically they can handle the demands, even if you're nowhere near the ultimate tempo. If you have a together ensemble, then much of the remainder of your rehearsing can be spent uplifting the entire ensemble to your final tempo and a finished product overall.

How familiar is the ensemble with the repertoire?

Are you conducting a world premiere or anything else unfamiliar to the ensemble? If so, a greater percentage of your rehearsal time will be spent with that piece. Are you conducting something the ensemble's done a million times? If so, you can

1. Play through the piece as a reminder for the musicians.
2. Stop here and there for attention to detail.
3. Rehearse only the "corners" (changes of tempo, phrasing, etc.).
4. Don't rehearse at all (just say, "Ladies and Gentlemen, you already know this piece. I trust you. See you at the performance.").

Whatever choice you make, it should be based solely on what you understand the ensemble's level of comfort to be with the piece and with you as their leader.

Are there considerations with instrumentation?

Several considerations come to mind. If you are in a multiple rehearsal situation with multiple compositions requiring varied instrumentations, it's often a good idea to give the musicians with less to do a rehearsal off. If you are doing a piece requiring fewer players than on the otherwise large ensemble program, and if the piece is significant in duration, devote one rehearsal on just that smaller piece. Do you have a soloist who is contracted for just the final rehearsal? If so, and if it's a difficult piece for your ensemble, spend a larger portion of that time with the soloist in that rehearsal. Remember that almost all orchestras have 2½-hour rehearsals, but when conducting a per-service orchestra there will be [justified] pressure brought to you by administrators to try to save money by not having absolutely everyone at absolutely every rehearsal. In your rehearsal schedule, think creatively how you can still make artistic progress but also make the administrators happy with saving money and musicians happy by not wasting their time. Certainly, avoid making such accommodations if you feel there is strong artistic merit in not saving money just for the sake of doing so.

In one-rehearsal situations, I've found it generally to be more helpful to go in program order, as that often helps the ensemble become familiar with the overall flow and their own pacing. Also, if a piece involving extra musicians is a work that's totally unfamiliar, or particularly difficult, or involves a soloist, or the composer/arranger is going to be in attendance, the more important issue is that of being in service to the music. Then individual musicians will be more than responsible at giving their time to the rehearsal effort.

What is the repertoire's relative difficulty vis-à-vis rehearsal time?

Given what you've decided about the difficulty of the score(s) you're conducting, having assessed the ensemble's ability, and now looking at the total rehearsal time available, your decisions about rehearsal schedule now will be made with the goal in mind of leading, guiding, and indeed, raising your ensemble to the best possible standard of performance incrementally step by step, rehearsal by rehearsal, and day by day.

If you have the time, it's usually best to have a run-through at the beginning of the rehearsal process, at least in large sections if not the entire work. In some classical repertoire, it's possible to play through up to the recapitulation, especially if you've decided there are stylistic and interpretive issues you want to fix in the primary material. The run-through serves the purpose of establishing basic musical parameters of tempo, style, and character without having to stop and explain, and gives the musicians the opportunity to acquaint themselves with their own parts and you as conductor. The run-through can be quite helpful in that regard, and can save you significant time in rehearsal, if you conduct expressively. If you mechanically beat time, you will waste time because you'll be forced into stopping and verbally explaining what you otherwise could have shown with the baton.

If your rehearsal time is too limited to allow a first-time run-through, some detail work, and a final dress run-through, your next step will be to determine which of those three elements take priority over the others. Is your ensemble of the quality that can handle all the detail work, and leave the dress run-through up to the performance itself? This could also be your choice if the music is familiar; you can safely assume the ensemble knows how the piece is supposed to go, so work on the details and your interpretation, and let the final run-through be the performance itself. If the repertoire is perhaps not so familiar, but you and the ensemble know each other well, then another choice might be to skip the early run-through in order to dig in to detailed rehearsing from the get-go. Good, solid, beneficial detail work is often appreciated by ensemble members; after all, they all come from similar musical training which is to rehearse enough, and in enough detail, to get the work right!

If your rehearsal time is extremely limited, have in mind the "road map" of the score, and at least point out, if not rehearse, the really important transitions (tempo changes, cutoffs, fermatas, dead beats, etc.). Then, if you have time, play through large sections of the work with the goal of putting those transitions into context. That will be your priority, and can be the most help to any level ensemble, because it is done with them in mind, for their relative comfort and the assumed confidence you place in them to play the non-rehearsed passages well enough.

Sometimes, if I am conducting a program of, say, more than the normal two to four compositions, if the works are a combination of familiar and unfamiliar to the orchestra, and if the rehearsal schedule is spread out over more days than I would prefer, then when devising the rehearsal schedule, I will actually calculate the amount of time I devote to each composition over the entire rehearsal series to see if that time is roughly equivalent to the percentage of time it takes to perform the piece. *Roughly* is most definitely the key word here, as there can be so many variable factors, all mentioned above. But I do find it to be a handy reference nevertheless, as it helps me keep on track, sticking to what I've posted to the musicians within any given rehearsal.

3. **The Schedule**

How many rehearsals?

A studio recording session will read/rehearse/record each passage in the same—one—rehearsal. A youth or family concert with a symphony orchestra will have one 2½-hour rehearsal at most. A pops concert with a symphony orchestra generally has one rehearsal, but sometimes two, especially if it's a special program (e.g., holiday, film accompanying) requiring lighting, sound, and other extra production values. A subscription classical concert usually will have four rehearsals (sometimes only three, if the program is traditional and standard enough).

How compact? (Weekly? Daily? Twice daily?)

Assuming there are multiple rehearsals at all, a volunteer ensemble often rehearses once weekly for maybe six or more rehearsals, requiring much more in the way of rehearsing with a focus on reminding and reinforcing what happened in the previous week's rehearsal. Progress within a given rehearsal will likely be not as rapid or significant as more time will be spent paying attention to the bigger picture—reinforcing last week's progress, plus new detail work, plus introducing challenges to be worked on in the next rehearsal. Musical progress in this case will also be directly related to how much fun the volunteer members are having in the process in addition to better playing and ensemble.

Some freelance professional orchestras rehearse on three or four consecutive evenings. If so, rehearsals can be more tightly planned, as there will be greater retaining of musical information from rehearsal to the next rehearsal the following day. You will be able to plan on a much better flow of improvement and continuity. You also will be able to factor into your schedule many more of the variable considerations mentioned above. Keep in mind, however, that in this situation, your musicians are coming to rehearsal at the end of their day, which presumably has been filled with other activities, day jobs, and responsibilities. It may take a few minutes each rehearsal to get back into the groove you left the night before, as well as an extra ounce of patience on your part as you work with musicians who likely are tired from a long day. If so, give them a few minutes to play before honing in on your rehearsal details, and during the course of the rehearsal be mindful of the need to back off from time to time and let them play—again—some of the passages you've just been working on.

Full-time professional orchestras have the best of all worlds, in a way. They rehearse in the daytime when minds are freshest. They can easily schedule double-service rehearsals for maximum efficiency, and as all musicians are contracted for the same number of services, there is greater versatility and flexibility in asking for certain players to be at any number of rehearsals, as opposed to the freelance orchestra in which, if the player isn't requested at a service, s/he is not paid, either. On the other hand, with full-time orchestras, conductors must be even more diligent in not wasting anyone's time (the worst possible evil besides not making good music collaboratively). These orchestras are often overworked with having to rehearse and perform any number of masterworks programs, youth concerts, and pops concerts, often week-to-week. That's why they appreciate being let out of rehearsal early if you've accomplished what you intended; on the other hand, if they perceive you're letting them out early just to get on their good side, they will hold that against you if they feel there's still work to be done.

Are the rehearsals in the same location as the performance?

A relatively minor concern, but there are still some ensembles that rehearse in a room physically and acoustically different from the performance room, which definitely will affect your scheduling of the one or more rehearsals you actually have in the performance space. This means you need to anticipate both the musical moments and the musicians involved that will require your attention in the actual performance venue. Oftentimes, the acoustics are so drastically different in the two different spaces that making the adjustments to the final location can take more time than you might plan otherwise.

Which musicians need additional, non-musical consideration?

Perhaps you have soloists with specific availability needs. Or, an important orchestra musician has been excused from a rehearsal preventing you from doing their big solo passage. These, and so many other not necessarily predictable situations can (and will) occur when you least want them to, and usually when it's most inconvenient for the musical progress you're planning, but they will occur!

SOME RECOMMENDATIONS FOR VARIOUS SCENARIOS

One Rehearsal

Go in program order, for all performers to get a sense of the flow, and a must if you have technicians doing lighting or sound cues. An exception might be a soloist who needs to rehearse at a certain time for logistical or other, non-musical reasons (example: this is your only rehearsal with a pops group who will perform the second half of your concert, but due to time required to set up all necessary electronica, drum set, sound shields, etc., it will be best to begin the rehearsal with the pops group) to avoid taking time out of rehearsal for non-artistic reasons.

Two Rehearsals

Treat your final (second) rehearsal as you would just one rehearsal above. Paying attention to your soloist(s), giving the ensemble the opportunity to run through at least large sections if not the entire work(s), adjusting final touches and nuances, making sure your ensemble is comfortable with all the transitions, and getting them inspired to the message of the music are all most important at this time.

The first rehearsal, then, becomes a real working rehearsal. Given all the considerations mentioned above, this is the rehearsal when the musicians are freshest and most ready to absorb your musical direction. Use it to best effect by rehearsing smartly—which means to build your musical blocks from the biggest issues up. Or, using another analogy, this will be your first chipping away at your sculpture block, establishing the overall shape which will get nuanced in the next, final rehearsal. In some cases, choral (with orchestra) concerts are prepared in two rehearsals, where the first rehearsal is without chorus, paying attention only to orchestral issues. The same will be true with a pops concert rehearsal, where the first rehearsal is orchestra only, dealing with the orchestra-only repertoire and perhaps a look at the pops material so as not to require time in the dress rehearsal. Another option could be to include soloists as a portion of the rehearsal, if there are significant solo passages that would benefit from a pre-dress rehearsal such as this.

Three Rehearsals

Again, the final dress will be the same as above, and the first of three rehearsals again will be more introductory in nature, but since you have the second rehearsal in between, the first rehearsal can be a bit more relaxed, still giving from your point of view the overall shapes and concept, but also allowing the ensemble to become more familiar with the music.

The second rehearsal in this instance can be so detail-oriented that you don't spend any time at all on running through the works. Have in mind very specific musical moments to be rehearsed; plan this out as an outline which has enough flexibility built in that you're able to get through the list entirely, watching the clock the whole time, and without getting swamped. This second rehearsal should have a feeling within the ensemble of fixing all important details, establishing all appropriate balances and musical understandings, with enough repetition built in to the rehearsal so that the next, final dress can be exciting and inspiring.

Four Rehearsals

Now you have some real flexibility, but always keep your goal in mind, which is to have the ensemble ultimately feel that they are fully prepared for performance. Assuming that your first and last (fourth) rehearsals are the same approach as all the above first and last rehearsals, now you can really accomplish much more detail work in the intervening two rehearsals. Depending on the repertoire, of course, here are some options to consider:

1. If the program includes an entire symphony, devote one rehearsal entirely to that piece, doing the movements in order of declining instrumentation so those who have less involvement can leave early. This will give you a full service to help you firmly establish the approach to the piece.
2. But do not have musicians leave early from the first rehearsal of a double-service day, if you want them to return in the second service. Giving musicians a longer lunch break does no good for them, as it gives more down time most can't use wisely while away from home. Not often, but I've been known on a double-rehearsal day, to begin the first rehearsal with the smaller instrumentation, eventually bringing in all others with later call times by the end. Then I've started the second rehearsal with everyone but let the "extras" go as the movements or pieces decline in instrumentation.
3. All the above notwithstanding, it's more common on a double rehearsal day to have full orchestra in the first, and reduced orchestra (whether pieces or individual movements) in the second.
4. Another example, in the case of an oratorio, would be to have one rehearsal focusing only on orchestra, but the other rehearsal—whether same day or not—focus only on solo arias and ensembles.
5. Having four rehearsals also gives you the opportunity to *not* rehearse a piece in a given rehearsal, allowing for more concentrated time on another work that might require more time. In a normal symphony concert of, say, four compositions, I might choose to concentrate on two different pieces each of the first two rehearsals, do spots in perhaps all four pieces in the third rehearsal, then run-through in the dress.

These are only a few obvious options out of the myriad choices you will have. Every concert program and every ensemble (and conductor) is different, so your choices for each program also will be different. Be creative, and keep in mind your ultimate goal, which is to prepare your ensemble to the point where they feel prepared and will give their all in performance.

AND IN CONCLUSION...

Be ready to make decisions on the spot when necessary.

The conductor's base knowledge of the score must be sufficient enough to address the most *un*expected question, and to either answer quickly and effectively and efficiently... OR ... at least to know when it is better to simply suggest to the musician, "Let's take a look at that during the break..."

Suggesting to sideline the issue (go "offline," as they say) will be welcomed by all other musicians who don't want to be sitting waiting for you to resolve someone else's issue.

> *At times, when a section or the entire orchestra is struggling with a passage, just say, "Let's try it again."*

There are countless musicians who would agree with me that sometimes all it takes to make a passage work satisfactorily is to simply have another go at it. Emerging conductors tend to want to fix every little thing, however, not really allowing for their ensemble musicians' own ability to improve on their own. But musicians appreciate the trust and, yes, even empowerment that a situation in which they can solve their own issues creates.

> *Never stop in rehearsal to address or fix anything that could be changed on its own or by a gesture from you.*

So, what do you do instead? Use the left hand! Or, change your baton technique to address the issue. Be creative, and experiment with any gesture that will produce your desired result. Whatever the gesture, it must come authentically from you, not a textbook. And be friendly, collaborative, and guiding. Anything but will create additional psychological issues with your musicians that you really want to avoid!

> *Watch the clock, but do not rehearse the full two-and-a-half hours if you've done all the work.*

Always watch the clock! Always know how much time you have left to rehearse, and always calculate minute-by-minute what your big rocks issues are to accomplish in the time you have left, no matter what you listed in your advance agenda/outline! And just because your ensemble has been hired for a full two-and-a-half hour session doesn't mean you have to keep them there right up until the last second. Most importantly, leave your ensemble at the end of a rehearsal with a sense of satisfaction, at having achieved some real progress in putting together the music. A friend once advised, being only partly facetious, "The best way to get invited back is to let the orchestra out early!"

> *Do not lose momentum. Always keep the attention of the orchestra at a high level.*

For both psychological and union reasons, you never want to waste your ensemble's time in rehearsal. You play a role as much psychologist as conductor, so be sure to learn basic principles of human behavior and group dynamics. How you *pace* a rehearsal is as important as the actual music rehearsal itself, which in turn is variable depending on the repertoire, the venue, and the purpose of the event. First, be sure to have a specific goal of what you want to accomplish in any given rehearsal, for instance:

1. Letting the ensemble play through the music. This should be your goal in a final, dress rehearsal, but can be crucial in the first of a series of rehearsals, especially if you and the ensemble are new to each other, or if the repertoire is unfamiliar. This also works well for studio recording of new pieces in which the repertoire can and will fall together on its own by virtue of your own professional musicians.

2. Intense stopping/starting, working on many details, usually reserved for after the ensemble is already familiar with the overall piece. While maintaining a positive rehearsal flow, and with attention to the group psychology, the conductor can be quick and efficient with suggestions and guidance, giving feedback in almost rapid-fire timing. Follow up by allowing the musicians to play some major portions of the piece essentially on their own, putting all the pieces back together. Remember, your job is to make sure they get the big picture!
3. A combination of serious, detailed work balanced with playing through larger sections. This should be your default mode, and works well when faced with minimum or insufficient rehearsal time. You become servant-leader, helping in any way you can to make the product finished.

26

Relating to Your Musicians

Believe that your ensemble members are your colleagues.

All musicians in ensembles are there because they want to do a good job, even if it's just for the money in a freelance situation. I learned a long time ago that no musician comes to rehearsal or performance *wanting* to do poorly. Whether they are fond of your conducting or the repertoire you're conducting, all musicians still have confidence, dignity, and pride in being able to accomplish what you ask of them. So, treat them with respect, praise them when they do well, feed their spirit, sense of camaraderie, and satisfaction of achievement non-gratuitously when you are satisfied. The more you trust and appreciate them, the more they will trust and respect you.

In rehearsal, remember that individual musicians are often registering issues important only to them or their section while they're playing. As soon as you stop, then, the musician will feel they can speak with their stand partner or section leader to discuss the issue. Do not take offence at this, but pleasantly acknowledge that the musicians are dealing with issues that are crucial to them. If you want to make a comment that includes their attention, wait until they're ready to listen. It is also possible to pleasantly interrupt any conversation the musicians may be having in order to efficiently and effectively address your own issues.

Musicians like to know when they are doing well. Acknowledge when they do!

A simple nod, smile, or sometimes even wink or an actual thumbs-up (in rehearsal) can do wonders to any musician's sense of belonging and self-satisfaction. Remembering that all musicians really do want to perform well—it gives them great pride individually—conductors must therefore also remember how important it is to the musician to have his/her work acknowledged, recognized, and appreciated, even if for a fleetingly brief moment while the music is still going on. Many emerging conductors fail to take the time to be positive and appreciate the musicians' work, even if it's something simple like saying "excellent!" after running or rehearsing in detail a significant portion.

At the end of a rehearsal, the musicians like to feel that they have accomplished something.

Orchestral musicians may grumble at times about having to rehearse, but they really do want to work, and they do expect the conductor to work them. Kindly, yes, but insistently so, too. Therefore, a rehearsal must have a satisfying flow for the musicians, and by rehearsal's end, they should feel like they actually accomplished a lot! Even with the hard, detailed, slower-moving rehearsals, there should be a sense of accomplishment at the end.

When rehearsing a large symphonic work with a huge, climactic ending, remember that endings like those are taxing both technically and psychologically. To reach that point significantly before your rehearsal time is over puts you at a disadvantage: you don't want to spoil the climactic moment you just had, but you don't want to let the orchestra go too early. Find a way, therefore, to not get to the climax too soon, pacing it so that when you reach that moment the musicians can just play out on their own. That is when their feeling of accomplishment sets in. Then let them go and say "thank you," and "see you next time." Apply this principle to all kinds of situations, inside a rehearsal as well as at the end. Work vs. Play, Intensity vs. Relaxation, Seriousness vs. Humor, Accomplishment vs. Release—all should be a constant and continuous flow.

Be a humble leader, a "primus inter pares."

Gone are the days of tyrannical behavior from the podium and utter servitude or fear from the musicians. Ensemble musicians everywhere want a musical leader/conductor who will work with them, who acknowledges all that they have to offer on their own, and who is able to carve some really interesting and effective musical sculpture out of the music at hand. The only way in which a conductor is "primus" is that s/he, unlike everyone else in the room, is charged with the responsibility of putting the musical product together. For that reason and that reason alone, musicians will accept (though, sometimes only begrudgingly) the directions, corrections, and musical adjustments made from the podium.

LEADING AND TEACHING

You can feel the music all you want to, but unless you have developed the ability to *lead* and *teach* your ensemble, elevating them to a higher level of understanding, you have failed. Open your ears to the sound being presented to you, and determine the steps and methods you are going to initiate to make your ensemble better than they are. Begin your rehearsals at the level of their current understanding and ability, and recognize your responsibility to show them the way to their finished product. You must infuse every minute, every hour, every rehearsal with an obvious sense of progress.

Conduct the front stands, but look at the back of the sections.

When dealing with a large ensemble consisting of sections of many individuals playing the same part (e.g., a string section in an orchestra), be sure to address the entire section by connecting visually and verbally to the back stands. The most difficult places to sit for string players in large orchestra sections are at the back. They have a hard time hearing the conductor, seeing their Principal chair leader, and understanding any detailed discussion that might be going on between the conductor and the Principal chair. Too many emerging conductors conduct and speak with only the first stand of each string section, causing all others in the section to feel ignored, to not pay attention, and to disregard anything they may have missed. By speaking to and visually connecting with the last stand, you automatically bring the entire section into hearing distance and into your field of attention. You must be very conscientious of this until it becomes habitual.

Eye contact with your musicians is a most basic goal. Many conducting teachers, my own and myself included, often use the phrase "the score in the head, *not* the head in the score." It's such a simple concept, but with so many emerging conductors, I see the head drop down to latch onto the score even at the very first downbeat of a work! Or at crucial moments like fermatas, ritards, and cutoffs. If any, *these* are the moments when you should be establishing visual communication with your musicians! Be constantly self-critical.

No matter how much experience you have or don't have, believe in yourself and your ability to improve—continuously!—provided you remain present in the moment, continuously listening, scrutinizing and analyzing what's being given to you and evaluating how to support, change, or fix what you're doing. Never get so involved in the act of conducting that you stop listening to what you're there for, which is: to lead, to guide, to adjust, and to inspire in each and every moment of activity. And I'm talking about your entire relationship you are constantly building with your musicians.

When changing tempo, use a clearer but smaller beat to get your message across.

Generally speaking, when wanting to go slower, expand your field of motion. And when wanting to go faster, contract the field of motion. Yes, it's counterintuitive to do so, but so much more effective. In the most critical tempo changes, give the ensemble the clearest beat possible so they can easily and comfortably determine both the ictus AND the flow from one changing beat to the next.

> *Give the ensemble something to watch.*

I've heard conductors complain that their ensembles don't follow them. "Why won't they watch me?" they ask. And I reply, "Give them something to watch." It's really quite basic: if your ensemble is not following you in your crucial moments, your gesture is not effective at leading them, because:

- You did nothing different to catch their attention in time.
- You didn't lead, probably opting instead to follow them.
- Your timing with your gestures was off.
- You've developed a culture of their not watching, because you're not connecting with them.
- You're not sure yourself what you're doing.
- They've learned over time that they cannot depend on you.

> *A conductor's ideal dream should be to rehearse their ensemble so well as to render him/herself superfluous.*

It goes without saying that a conductor's work is mostly done in rehearsal. Clearly, there is repertoire in which a conductor is essential. But shouldn't it nevertheless be our goal as conductors to lead and train our ensembles to the point where they can play their repertoire without the "intrusion" of a conductor's ego? What if conductors were more like servant-leaders, serving their musicians through leadership rather than autocratic means? What if fewer conductors made the music-making with an ensemble much less about them and their ideas, but much more about what s/he can generate in terms of collaborative music-making with all the musicians?

It's likely you can still find online the infamous video of Leonard Bernstein conducting the Vienna Philharmonic in Haydn's *Symphony no. 88* (fourth movement) in which, after getting the orchestra started, he simply stops conducting, at least with his arms! His trust of that orchestra goes so far that he frees up the atmosphere by allowing the orchestra to play on its own, with only a wink, a glance, a nod, a twitch here and there to guide his fellow musicians.

27

Big Rocks/Little Rocks

One of my favorite metaphors was taught me by my friends at the Stephen Covey Leadership Center (Principle-Centered Leadership). The folks there demonstrated the very simple principle that if you fill up a period of time dealing first with the little, urgent, non-important minutiae, drudgery, and menial tasks, you will not have any time to spend on the really important, *non*-urgent big issues with which you must deal as a leader. At the Covey Center, they demonstrate this by taking a large bowl and filling it up first with little pebble rocks, dramatically demonstrating that there is no room for inserting the big, important rocks. On the other hand, if the same bowl is filled with the big rocks first, there will still be room to insert as many little rocks as space allows.

Transferring this to the task of a conductor, the "Big Rocks" are those issues that are the most basic and fundamental to your ensemble's development at any one time *as an ensemble* (correct notes, togetherness, rhythm, dynamics, entrances, basic style, balances, basic structural understanding, tempo changes). The "Little Rocks"—while still important! (an individual's intonation, subtle dynamic shadings, and phraseology)—will only create frustration if your most basic, Big Rocks, haven't been addressed, solved, and reconciled first with your musicians.

Ideally, your big rocks in a given rehearsal will be addressed so that in the next rehearsal there's a different set of big rocks. Over time, the big rocks (musical issues) of course become smaller as the issues are addressed and fixed. Consequently, each successive rehearsal will have a different set of big rocks/little rocks. This is a terrific shorthand speak for conversations between me and my conducting students as they're planning any given rehearsal: what are your big rocks today?

28

Are You the Horse?

Speaking of my conducting students, I have a favorite analogy that I use with them: You are not the horse; you are but holding the reins and managing the horse. In other words, that team of horses (ensemble) that you're leading knows full well how to run, how to step over potholes, and run around rocks and trees. They can, and are, doing *their* job. But they have no sense of direction; a team of horses needs guidance. That's your job—from your place on the carriage (podium), holding the reins (baton), and by using a variety of motions, you are managing (conducting), moment-to-moment how the team (ensemble) starts, stops, goes left or right, speeds up and slows down, maneuvers around major turns, and otherwise successfully reaches the end of the [musical] journey. This includes, by the way, knowing when to not interfere and let the team pace itself!

Reading a textbook on how to hold the reins and facilitate a team of horses without crashing and burning certainly will be helpful, but only once you get on that carriage and give trial-and-error some experience, will you be achieving any real success at leadership. Moment-to-moment, you are managing your ensemble, knowing when to lead, when to take the reins and impose your leadership, when to back off and simply maintain the pulse. In the process of doing so, you'll inevitably find that any textbook is only the beginning of your developing a gesticular vocabulary, because you are managing your ensemble artistically, musically, and not only as a textbook exercise.

In rehearsal, keeping the horse analogy for now, you wouldn't stop the team of horses mid-trail to explain what it is you want differently from them. Rather, your commands will be issued by how you maneuver the reins. Imagine then, your baton as the reins for the orchestra, refraining from stopping and talking to the ensemble and concentrating only on how you can better express your musical commands by making the baton itself more useful.

Too often, emerging conductors seem to have the attitude on the podium that they have to make the music happen all by themselves! They employ lots of perspiration and wild gesticulations trying to make the music happen! But for the most part, it's just wasted energy, is not effective, and runs counter to any notion of collaborative empowerment of the ensemble. Conductors, through their leadership skills only *allow* the music to happen, through oversight of details and leadership of the big picture. In terms of conducting, you should relax, and "ride" the orchestra as if it were a horse. Feel what this "animal" is capable of, manage and guide its progress, and give it room to express itself in its own, unique way.

PART II

Technical Suggestions in Standard Repertoire

Here follows what I hope will be a very helpful section as your conducting technique develops. The musical excerpts listed here are from the standard orchestral repertoire. These are the kinds of excerpts found in conducting auditions—precisely because they contain many of the technical problems encountered by conductors for centuries! With orchestral music, you will find a greater preponderance and complexity of tempo changes, fermatas, cutoffs, cueing challenges, and essential score-reading problems than any other discipline except opera.

Pop music may have the occasional fermata or tempo change from introduction into song, but generally speaking, there is little real *technical* concern. Conducting to a screen, such as in film and videogame accompaniment, also generally consists of multiple segments of straight-out tempo, any exceptions to which are dictated by a click-track or other device. But any conductor will benefit from practicing these excerpts, quite simply because the specific issues all remain the same, no matter the genre.

A fermata remains a fermata, and there are a limited number of ways to get out of a fermata, all of which are discussed in this section. Similarly, tempo changes, cues, cutoffs, and all other manner of standard conducting gestures remain the same in principle whether it's a Beethoven symphony, a John Williams film score, a Richard Rodgers medley, or an Aaron Copland ballet.

Using these detailed, measure-by-measure descriptions in print along with the videos for these excerpts, I hope to provide you with a real basis for both understanding and successfully conducting not just these examples, but all others in which the issues and applicable principles remain the same.

The scores for these excerpts and video demonstrations/explanations of me conducting them are all available on the Hal Leonard website library, and the titles of each video and notation excerpt PDF are at the beginning of its respective lesson. See the first page of this book for the URL and your unique access code.

29

Beethoven, *Egmont* Overture, Measures 1–16

The first thirty measures of *Egmont* require a very clear beat, both in the 3/2 (especially if you're subdividing) as well as in the 3/4 (especially if you're conducting in "1") to delineate the new tempo. Maintain the 3/2 pattern musically, meaning it must show the dynamic variations and cues, but especially the gesture of syncopation eighth-note pickups that happen so frequently. Remember, this opening introduction is setting the dramatic mood for what is to follow (not just in the overture but in the play, too!), and your musical approach must be aware of, and sympathetic to, the dramatic needs of the story that follows.

Measure 1

Egmont.pdf

Give a strong downbeat for the *tutti forte* entrance.

Have in mind the degree to which you want the diminuendo to occur. Make the diminuendo with your left hand only; save the baton for giving the next downbeat.

How long you hold the fermata will depend on your overall tempo for the beginning. *Sostenuto ma non troppo* can easily be interpreted as "in three" (not necessarily "in six"). If that's the case, this measure's fermata should last the length of approximately two measures in tempo. Any longer than that and your winds and brass will run out of air and your strings out of bow. (They should not have to change bows here.)

The fermata may be a left-hand cutoff if you want the next downbeat delayed, or the baton can cut off as it prepares for the next downbeat, in tempo.

Measures 2–4

I believe that measure 2 does not have to immediately follow measure 1. But how much space to allow before beginning measure 2? As long as your cutoff of measure 1 is with your left hand, you can wait to prepare measure 2 with your right hand for as long as you want (being stylistically appropriate, of course).

Are you conducting this in six? If so, *beware*. Every conductor I've seen conduct these measures in six creates a discrepancy from what Beethoven wrote. What sounds instead is this rhythm:

FIG. 29.1. *Egmont* Overture as Normally Conducted. Equal length notes and rests.

…which is *not* what Beethoven composed. Rather, by writing staccato half-notes, Beethoven wants separated half notes, not equal quarters and quarter rests. Just comparing this version with Beethoven's, there is no way this comes close to the power as expressed in Beethoven's staccato half notes. But if conducted in six beats to the bar, usually this is the end result, because your players interpret your beats 2, 4, and 6 as releases from beats 1, 3, and 5.

Having said all that, assuming you're beating in 3, you should conduct beat 3 as a release, then a gesture of syncopation quarter-note preparation beat for the eighth-note pickup.

Measures 4–5

Be sure beat 3, divided, is piano! The downbeat of measure 5 *is* a quarter-note this time! Begin *gently* conducting in six, here. While the four woodwinds may not really need it, it helps with the violin 1 entrance in measure 7.

Measure 8

This one measure is more difficult than you might expect, thanks in large part to Beethoven's wanting to emphasize his simultaneous 9-8 and 4-3 suspension-resolution in such a short amount of time. Get out of tempo slightly to bring out the suspensions—and also to allow both the resolution and diminuendo to happen on the final quarter without jumping immediately into the next downbeat!

Hold the final quarter-note C-major resolution just slightly longer, as if it were a mini fermata, which then gives you time to make a bold preparation for the upcoming ***ff***.

Measure 9

This measure is different from measure 1 in three very important ways:

1. It is not just ***f***, but ***ff***.
2. It is not a fermata but is in tempo.
3. There is no diminuendo this time!

Do not beat out all the quarter or half beats in this measure, but *do* mark the passage of time for all players to pace their breath and bowing.

Because there is no diminuendo, string players can play the whole note in two bows (down/up), putting them in proper position to play the next measure forcefully without having to retake their bows. Winds and brass likely will take a catch, out-of-tempo breath for themselves, but you must be listening for consistency in those sections, assuming you want everyone to treat the transition from measure 9 to measure 10 the same. (Please note: it should be possible for winds and brass to play measure 9 into measure 10 *without* breathing in between, but they will then have time for a catch breath between the two half-notes in measure 10.)

Measures 10–11

See measures 2–4. There is no need to beat out the third half-note rest, but the baton must still mark the next, silent, downbeat.

Measure 12

Be sure to give a definitive, piano, "dead" beat here so that everyone understands the first sound in the clarinet is in fact on the "and" of the beat.

Measures 14–15

This is a very important V7 to I progression mid-point in the introduction. Be sure to conduct the shape accordingly, perhaps allowing for a fraction more time to establish the D-flat major harmony, but also to set up an appropriate *subito* ***pp*** in measure 15.

Setting the tempo in measure 15 is extremely crucial for violin 2 and violas, especially if you're taking a little time on the V7 chord before their sixteenth notes begin. Conduct violin 2 and viola with a very clear preparation in advance of the downbeat. Then pay attention to violin I if you wish.

15. Beethoven, *Egmont* Overture

30

Beethoven, Symphony no. 1, Fourth Movement: Measures 1–14 and Measures 225–248

With no storyline to follow, it's the conductor's responsibility to determine the *musical drama* inherent in Beethoven's early symphony. As always, a firm understanding and strict observance of the ***ff*** fermata and the ***p*** and ***pp*** dynamics that follow will create a successful interpretation.

EXCERPT A. MEASURES 1–14

Measure 1

PDF Adobe Beethoven-1-Excerpt-A.pdf

In four, ♪ = 63. Hold the beginning fermata with a stylistically appropriate length. Maintain the ***ff***, not allowing any diminuendo. Cut off the fermata with a strong gesture, going to the right, creating a dead third beat, which then in turn becomes the preparation beat for the violin 1 pickups.

Measures 2–5

Unlike the pickups, the downbeat eighth note has no staccato dot, meaning it should be at least approximate full value. Your second beat will show the violins when to release. This is true for the entire series of four downbeat eighths. Musically speaking, it makes sense to make a point of having long downbeats in these measures, as Beethoven continues the idea in the *Allegro molto* with the downbeats of measures 8, 10, and 14, though in a faster context.

Measure 5

Probably the most difficult measure of the entire introduction, because you have to show not only the subito ***p*** downbeat, but also the preceding crescendo above ***p***, the second beat cutoff, and the following ***pp*** in tempo. Practice this on your own at first!

Violin 1 sections not accustomed to playing this piece are often struck with fear at playing together the ***pp*** thirty-second notes, for a number of reasons:

1. Many think it's a faster passage than it is.
2. It's not clear that the thirty-seconds begin on the "and" of beat 3.
3. Many conductors give the section The Hand, indicating the softer dynamic, rather than encouraging a together entrance.

Measure 6

Hold the downbeat appropriately, but allow the baton to float higher, to be ready for the dead beat you're about to give. (Caution: Do not float in such a way that you encourage a response from the orchestra!) The dead beat becomes both the cutoff of the fermata as well as the first of two beats of the *Allegro molto* section. The dead beat is given only with the wrist-baton, not the arm, because its intention is to release the sound in the fermata, not to make anything happen. Therefore, measure 6 has a total of three beats given by the baton. Younger orchestras often need the explanation that measure 6 actually has two downbeats. This is good to do, as there is the risk that someone (or more!) in the second violins, violas, or celli/bassi will enter a measure early, ignoring the single measure rest that follows.

16. Beethoven, Symphony no. 1: Fourth Movement, A

EXCERPT B. MEASURES 225–248

Measures 236, 238

Beethoven-1-Excerpt-B.pdf

At first glance, the chord in each of these measures is simply a tutti tie from beat 2 into the next measure. But closer study shows some important sixteenth notes the timpani must play on the second beat before the fermata. Of course, the lone timpanist will play that part anyway, but to not lead the player in that moment is irresponsible in a crucial timing moment such as this. The conductor should be in charge here, as it is your responsibility in terms of pacing the tension/release that Beethoven has composed.

Measure 239

Conducting this measure clearly requires almost the same technique as I describe in measure 6 of the same movement (see above). Give the downbeat, allow the fermata to establish itself, but then get your baton in the proper position (letting it float upwards) so your next, downward move will be both the cutoff of the ***ff*** fermata and the first, dead beat of two beats preparation cueing in the second violins. Like measure 6, this measure again will have a total of three beat gestures, which is best explained verbally to the orchestra. The most effective way to tell the orchestra is that you give the downbeat twice: once as the release of the fermata, and once as the downbeat proper.

17. Beethoven, Symphony no. 1: Fourth Movement, B

31

Beethoven, Symphony no. 5, First Movement: Measures 1–7

For emerging conductors, this is probably the most difficult passage to conduct. The two greatest mistakes made by young conductors are:

1. to show the downbeat in measure 1 as an upbeat, because that's the music's effect, rather than giving a downbeat because that's the music's print, and
2. after each fermata, to dive right into the following measure (measure 3, measure 6) without enough time for the strings to retake their bows for proper positioning.

Consider this pairing of fermatas seriously! What was Beethoven's intent? Should there be a longer silence than what is implied by the single eighth-note rest in measure 3 and measure 6? How many times, and in how many variations does Beethoven employ this holding musical gesture? Should the single-measure or double-measure fermatas always be the same throughout the movement? When is it appropriate to make a ritard into any of the fermatas?

It is not for me to provide answers, only to ask the questions. This is not an issue that can be taken lightly, and whatever your research teaches you about the pacing and structure must be extraordinarily clear in your baton technique. All orchestras aspire to doing this piece, and those who have performed it often most likely also have done it many times with different interpretations. Given the overwhelming familiarity at all orchestra levels, though no orchestra knows what to expect from conductor to conductor, your interpretation must be musically convincing.

Measure 1

PDF Adobe
Beethoven-5.pdf

The first measure has three upbeat notes. But in the manuscript, they are in response to a silent *downbeat* eighth rest given by the conductor. Do not give an upbeat! The trained orchestra knows an upward motion from a downward one, and if they see you give an upbeat, even an encouraging one, most orchestra members will wait for the downward gesture before they make a sound.

Your preparation for that downbeat is best if it is the equivalent of an entire 2/4 measure in your tempo. This tempo is too fast to indicate a quarter-note preparation. Even if you think your baton technique is amazing, a quarter note in a "normal" tempo for this movement will move so quickly as to render it impossible for an entire string section (and two clarinets!) to easily comprehend as the clear tempo indication of the symphony.

Measure 2

The biggest question regarding this measure is that of how to release the held note, making the preparation for the next measure. There are three basic choices:

1. Make the release of the fermata and the downbeat of measure 3 one and the same gesture. The difficulty here is in raising the baton during the fermata as preparation for the next downbeat without creating a diminuendo or other unintended effect in the strings ***ff***. It is possible to do it effectively, however, if you allow the baton to rebound from your original downbeat (measure 2) in a non-rhythmic way so as not to create a false response from the orchestra.
2. Once you've given the downbeat for measure 2, hold the baton there (down) for the length of your fermata. Then lift the baton just as you did at the very beginning of the piece, in an encouraging way, causing the orchestra to release the fermata on your upswing and preparing them for the next downbeat in measure 3. Doing so, however, automatically creates a longer silence—equivalent to a full 2/4 measure plus an eighth-note rest—because your preparation for measure 3 will be the equivalent of a full half-note pulse as with the beginning of the piece.
3. If you accept the premise that any fermata *and* the space created by its cutoff is inherently a suspension of time, you have the freedom to time the next entrance of music in any way you like, given stylistic norms. So, cut off the fermata with the *left* hand only, without moving the baton until you're ready for your next preparation beat. Therefore, your pacing of any fermata-plus-release-plus-downbeat combination can be achieved with an infinite number of timing relationships. This left-hand/right-hand combination can be effective musically. Simply give the verbal direction that you intend to cut off each and every fermata with the left hand, but they should wait for the baton to indicate the next downbeat—however long it may take to show it! It is most important to remember, however, that this method will work only if your baton does not move in sympathy with the left-hand cutoff!

Measure 5

In my teaching studio, I expect students to show this fermata measure with another downbeat, even though there's nothing new in the music. Why? It's an excellent discipline to get into the habit of conducting *all* downbeats in the music, especially when any one or more musicians is counting rests. While the woodwinds and brass in this piece wouldn't necessarily miscount their measures' rest at this place, there are numerous examples in other repertoire where the conductor must be sensitive to those musicians not doing anything but counting measures of rest by showing them all downbeats.

So, your downbeat in measure 5 is, in effect, a silent beat, even though you will want to use the baton to maintain the ***ff*** dynamic. Be clear, but not forceful in how you show this downbeat; you want everyone to understand where they are in the music, but it makes no sense to give a huge ***ff*** downbeat as if something new were happening musically. The downbeat also does not need to be exactly in time. This is only a utilitarian move on your part as the orchestra's shepherd to make sure all your sheep are in the same, right place as you.

Measure 6

Obviously, the transition from measure 5 into measure 6 can be treated the same as in measures 2–3, with the only difference being that in measure 6 you're only cueing the second violins' entrance as opposed to the whole string section, and at ***p***, not ***ff***. This will only affect the quality of your beat, not the beat itself. It will be possible to conduct this transition with any one of the three options listed above.

18. Beethoven, Symphony no. 5, First Movement

32

Brahms, Symphony no. 1: Fourth Movement, Measures 269–289 and 375–391

At some point in our musical training, we learn that in the music of Johannes Brahms there is a surprising rhythmic complexity that waits to be discovered. Similarly, while the music itself speaks directly to an audience, there are times with Brahms that require a more advanced approach to conducting technique, especially due to the complexity of the inner voices in particular and how they relate to the leading line.

Here are but two classic examples from Brahms' first symphony that at first appear simple but which I've seen student conductors totally fail to achieve. In the first example, the conductor is required to conduct forceful beats in silence to which the orchestra responds in unison. To the conducting student who is more accustomed to conducting along with the music, this is a serious, unsettling feeling of having to lead in silence and yet trust the orchestra to respond with its after-beats. The second example is a relatively easy exercise in creating an orchestral accelerando, during which the conductor will make a transition from one beat pattern to another, keeping the orchestra together while increasing tempo with everyone in sync.

EXCERPT A. MEASURES 269–289

Measures 279–284

Brahms-1-Fourth-Excerpt-A.pdf

The conductor should give gestures of syncopation on beats 1 and 3 of each of all six measures. It may seem odd to the emerging conductor, as no one plays actually *on* your beat. In terms of conducting technique, nothing else really matters other than creating the powerful after-beat effect this music has. This is like a series of "shout out" responses every two beats of music, and to enhance the effect, there is a tradition with some conductors to lead these six measures somewhat slower than tempo, increasing the dramatic intent of the theme in measure 285. Your gestures of syncopation must be as clear and forceful as the music demands for the orchestra to respond in kind.

Measures 285–289

Numerous conductors get carried away in the sonoric majesty of the climax here, totally ignoring the need for all the second violins and violas to play—together!—a rhythm of six repeated notes per beat. That rhythmic inclusion in the fabric of the orchestration, as well as the straight sixteenth notes that follow, and the timpani eighth-note triplets two measures after that show me that Brahms' music here continues to be driven by a classical rhythmic pulse. I am not suggesting rigidity—nothing of the kind. Brahms' music definitely has underpinnings of classicism, but its language remains of his own "romantic" time. The challenge to the conductor is to balance between the two aspects.

19. Brahms, Symphony no. 1: Fourth Movement, A

EXCERPT B. MEASURES 375–391

PDF Adobe Brahms-1-Fourth-Excerpt-B.pdf

This passage has an important orchestral accelerando that the conductor must facilitate successfully. Two other classic examples include the finale to Beethoven's Fifth Symphony and the "Infernal Dance" in Stravinsky's *Firebird.* I have found that when making an accelerando requiring a transition from one beat pattern to another (in this case, four beats into two), it is clearest to make the switch *sooner, not later.* To continue the original pattern's accelerando too late, the uncomfortably fast beat becomes incomprehensible. To switch to the new pattern sooner allows the orchestra to listen to itself without interference from the conductor, and yet gives the conductor greater control from the podium in the more crucial, later stages of the tempo change.

Measures 375–391

Please note that Brahms does not indicate any accelerando until *after* the initial eight bars of the phrase. The conductor then is faced with the decision in the next eight bars when to transition into "in two" from the already-established "in four." This can be a remarkable, and remarkably exciting, musical event if facilitated successfully. Begin measure 383 by directing the cellos, basses, and contrabassoon as the leading voices, meanwhile paying attention to the after-beats in the second violins and violas to assure the rhythmic solidity of the ensemble. With the ensemble being comfortably together, go "in two," ultimately driving the tempo to the *Più Allegro.* Remember, change your beat pattern sooner, not later. If you wait until measure 389 to go "in two," you would be changing both your beat pattern *and* the composite rhythmic gestures at the same time. While not impossible, it's often risky, and doesn't help the orchestra's comfort level.

20. Brahms, Symphony no. 1: Fourth Movement, B

33

Dvořák, Symphony no. 9, Second Movement: Measures 105–110

PDF Adobe
Dvořák.pdf

Too many budding conductors mess up this simple passage by trying to insert too many motions, non-essential cutoffs, and otherwise awkward preparations coming out of the fermatas. This passage is simple enough to conduct *only* with the baton, with no extraneous motion from the left hand. Simply beat time up to the silent beat, arriving at a rest for all musicians, stop ("freezing" your beat pattern right where you are), then restart with the preparation for the following music entrance.

Measure 107

Here's a classic case of not needing to make an actual cutoff movement or gesture....at all! Simply conduct a full three quarters, go to beat 4, and STOP! Adding an actual cutoff at this point, with either hand, only confuses the issue for the musicians and tends to add an extra, superfluous, non-essential beat. When you've held the fermata your desired length, proceed as you would from any other fermata, making a preparation beat for the next downbeat.

Measure 108

A big mistake on the part of some emerging conductors is to stop beating somewhere in beat 2. The music continues, however, through beat 2 and stops on beat 3. Encourage first violins, violas, cellos, and basses to play a full half-note all the way to the third beat, so they don't leave the second violins to play their last D♭ eighth note all by themselves without the supporting chord of the others. After you've stopped on the beat 3 position for the desired length of time, come out of it by making a preparation for beat 4.

Measure 109

21. Dvořák, Symphony no. 9: Second Movement

Same as the previous measure, but with the issues displaced by another beat. Conduct a full three beats in this measure, without allowing anyone to finish playing until you've reached beat 4. Stop the baton on beat 4. Then continue from this point to make the preparation for the next downbeat.

34

Mozart, Symphony no. 39, First Movement: Measures 1–10

The entire *Adagio* introduction is a wonderful exercise in subdividing with creativity, dynamic contrast, and musical phrasing. Some beats will be forceful and forte, others lyrical and piano. Still others variously maintain momentum, help the ensemble, and indicate lengths of notes. All details can be shown at this tempo!

Measures 1, 3, 5

Mozart.pdf

The downbeat must be together, and this is an example where the initial preparation doesn't really have to be in precise tempo. Your most important goal is an absolutely simultaneous entrance, but it's actually the next few beats that really determine the tempo.

After the downbeat, only mark the next two eighth-notes of the measure. The next important beat is the fourth eighth-note, a gesture of syncopation for the timpani. Conduct the fifth eighth-note, but only mark the sixth. Be clear with the seventh eighth-note, again for the timpani. Conduct the eighth eighth-note as a gesture of syncopation for the entire ensemble to play the final sixteenth note together.

Measures 2, 4, 6

Use the second eighth-note as a preparation for the *subito* ***p*** in the winds. The fourth eighth-note is a gesture of syncopation preparing for the sixteenth note. Give the fifth eighth-note as preparation for the violins on the sixth eighth-note. Mark the seventh and eighth eighth-notes, but come out of the eighth as a preparation for the ***f*** downbeat in measure 3.

Measure 7

Gently indicate the ***p*** downbeat for woodwinds and low strings, but use the baton to emphasize the after-beats in the first violins.

Measure 8

The underlying voices in this measure are essentially double-time the previous measure. Lead it clearly so, at the same time indicating a phrasing in the first violins to the high C and returning through the lower E♭.

Measure 9–10

At this point, your basic objective is to maintain the even flow of the tempo while letting the music express itself within a slow two (half-note), but remaining conducting divided beats. At the same time, pay attention to the first violins' entrance in m. 10 for accuracy of rhythm, not rushing, not slowing down, etc.

22. Mozart, Symphony no. 39, First Movement

35

Rimsky-Korsakov, *Capriccio Espagnol*, Fourth Movement: Measures 1–27

A performance of this movement can easily fail if the conductor isn't prepared. The various cadenzas are a conversation, where individual voices are given a statement, with the conductor determining context. Plan all timing issues in advance.

Measure 1

Rimsky-Korsakov.pdf

Cue the snare drum with a baton downbeat. Then give two beats preparation (one "dead," one "live") to the brass with the left hand (no baton, as the orchestra is not counting rests). Some conductors choose to make a ritard going into the final ***f*** downbeat fermata; others proceed exactly in tempo. It's a personal choice, though you should be sensitive to your principal trumpet's abilities on the high C's.

During the brass fanfare, the overall diminuendo/crescendo inverse swell is not in the snare drum part, which plays only a continuous ***f*** roll. At the end of measure 1, the brass make a diminuendo *before* the snare drum does. The score shows the brass disappearing into the snare drum ***f*** sound, followed by the snare drum's own diminuendo. At the end of measure 1, without moving the baton, the left hand shows (1) the brass diminuendo, then (2) the brass cutoff, then (3) the snare drum diminuendo, in that order, with the actual timing of those events up to the conductor.

Measure 2

Give the downbeat with the baton, signifying the snare drum's arrival at ***ppp***. Do not cue the concertmaster's solo entrance, and do not conduct the concertmaster. They will do much better without your interference.

At the end of this violin cadenza ("*Cadenza II*"), the fermata is the high A note, not the following rest. So, the concertmaster's release of the final note is your cue for the *a tempo* at [L].

Measure 3 (at [L])

This is the same tempo as the *Allegretto* beginning of the movement (♩. = 69).

Measure 12

Some conductors include a ritard here, for which I find no musical basis. It is more impactful to create surprise by proceeding in tempo to *Cadenza III.*

Measure 13

Give the downbeat for the violins' pizzicato chord and timpani entrance with the baton, but the left hand should control the diminuendo in the flute and clarinet, and their cutoff.

Maintain the timpani ***pp*** roll audibly, both for support of the flute but also so there's room to manage the smorzando, which you should do with your left hand once the flute arrives on the high A. Like before, the flute's *release* is your indication to have the timpani conclude its smorzando within the one beat that Rimsky-Korsakov prescribes.

Measure 14

Give the downbeat with the baton for the beginning of *Cadenza IV,* signifying the end of the timpani roll and the entrance of the cymbal. Cue the clarinet with the left hand but don't conduct, rather listening for the important peak notes in the arpeggios (C arpeggios with rising G, C, G, C) on top. With the baton, catch the clarinet's last note, the low A as beat 2, which you continue conducting in two. You must conduct measure 15, even though no one but clarinet is playing, because that's a measure rest printed in everyone's parts, which they are all counting.

Measure 20

Your baton downbeat signifies the triangle entrance. With the left hand, guide the woodwinds on their diminuendo and cutoff. Referring to the printed score, the harp enters immediately after a single eighth-note rest—even before the woodwinds cut off—eliminating the need for a harp entrance cue. Pay attention instead to the woodwinds; they are playing the same notes as the harp, and lengthening their note slightly could serve as a filler carrying the harp sonority longer.

The harp finishes its first musical phrase on the high A, but the triangle continues until the harp plays the low A as the glissandi begin. Catch the harp's final glissando note, which for all intents and purposes is the second beat of the bar, following which you begin conducting in two, even though you're giving two beats in total silence before the brass entrance.

Measures 22–27

23. Rimsky-Korsakov, *Capriccio Espagnol*, Fourth Movement

Rimsky-Korsakov writes a wonderfully stereophonic alternating violin passage—only if they were seated apart—so don't hesitate to opt for Rimsky-Korsakov's *feroce* by having all violins play all four measures.

36

Tchaikovsky, *Capriccio Italien*: Measures 1–27; Measures 275–297

The first musical example is a clear and extended passage for the "Italian six" beat pattern, with various dynamics, rubatos, cueing, gestures of syncopation, and cutoffs. Why the "Italian" pattern? Because some measures will be in six, some in two, and more so than the "German six" pattern, the "Italian" lends itself to ease of transitioning between the two patterns.

The second example is a fantastic example of an accelerando, but one that begins very slowly and ends quite fast, going from a slow "in two" to "in one" at the culmination of the accelerando. This is a terrific exercise for the emerging conductor to set up a "groove" and manipulate it to a much higher level (speed) without leaving anyone in the dust.

EXCERPT A. MEASURES 1–27

Measures 1–7

Tchaikovsky-Excerpt-A.pdf

Easily can be conducted "in two," without any need for subdividing. Long, slow beats but with extremely clear, definitive ictuses will help the brass immensely.

Measures 7–15

The conducting problem in these measures is how to comfortably yet clearly indicate the sixteenth-note pickup in all occurrences. Based on your tempo in the first 7 measures, the woodwinds and horns will already have a basic idea of your overall tempo. Conducting only two slow beats in measure 7 will not be very helpful to the winds and horns, who are panicking over playing the sixteenth-note pickup together. What works is to give the impression with your baton that you are dictating the sixteenth-note pickup by actually "shaking the stick" at the players on each one, and allowing the "in two" pattern to still take effect in the intervening beats.

Measure 16

The silent downbeat of measure 16 (and also measures 18, 20, 22, etc.) must be marked, but clear enough so the orchestra knows the actual rhythmic placement of the rest. The second eighth-beat is also silent, but for the conductor is the preparation for the third eighth-beat, which in turn is the gesture of syncopation for continuing.

Measure 17

Do not conduct every eighth-note in this measure. Rather, conduct beat one, then don't make a conducting gesture until the next downbeat (make it look like a downbeat!). If your stick moves in the right direction, the players will be with you all the way. Even when no one's playing, continue marking the passage of time by allowing your baton to actually go through the motions of the large "in two" feeling.

Measures 19–27

The successful performance of this section will depend on the musicality of your rubatos. Think very clearly how you want this tune to sound, knowing exactly where you want to take time for relaxation, or push the tempo for intensity, or simply remain straightforward. Be free! Sing it to yourself! Be musical! But keep the stick moving in such a way that you're keeping everyone together and in sync.

24. Tchaikovsky, *Capriccio Italien*, A

EXCERPT B. MEASURES 275–297

Measures 281–291

Tchaikovsky-Excerpt-B.pdf

This is a terrific example of an exciting accelerando starting from virtually nothing and ending up at the Presto "in one." You will have been conducting "in six" up until this point, but at measure 281 you can begin conducting "in two," without changing the tempo—yet. Optionally, in order to prevent any misunderstandings with any of your players, you can maintain "in six" in measure 281, but go "in two" immediately afterward, in measure 282. Whichever method you choose, do not change the tempo until after you have changed your beat pattern. Here now are ten measures in which you are managing your violins and violas, progressing from ♪ = ca. 132 to 𝅗𝅥. = ca. 96. That's a huge, over 400 percent, increase in tempo, but so much fun when it comes off perfectly! Begin "in two" either in measure 281 or measure 282, manage the accelerando but, still "in two" for perhaps four measures, transition to "in one" before you need to, and push the accelerando to its culmination. Don't forget the crescendo/diminuendo while doing so; it can actually be quite thrilling to all if your pacing is immaculate!

25. Tchaikovsky, *Capriccio Italien*, B

37

Mendelssohn, *A Midsummer Night's Dream*, Overture: Measures 370–404

This passage looks simple, but it is deceptively difficult and tends to cause the emerging conductor to lapse into lethargic music-making by falling into the soft-means-slower pitfall without being true to the real needs of the ensemble. Over a total of twenty-eight measures, the melody is broken down into motifs, separated by fermatas, and slows down over at least half the passage until the return of the overture's opening chords, which in turn are transformed into additional chords done at tempo! The conductor must study style for a section like this, so that his/her conducting of it doesn't over-indulge musically, or drown in confusing gestures for the orchestra members.

Measures 370–375

Mendelssohn.pdf

This six-measure transition must be treated delicately, as it represents a cornerstone between the previous 350+ measures of *Allegro di molto* and the coming breaking-down of the tune before the recapitulation in measure 394. Maintain the allegro tempo for four measures, and at least the *feeling* of allegro in measures 374–375. You must pay attention to, and lead the shaping of the cellos, in their last two measures of eighth notes. Some conductors make an actual ritard to set up the next phrase; others will make a gentle and minor ritard as a musical and psychological preparation for the even more gentle next nineteen measures. A few conductors will interpret Mendelssohn's marking strictly and not make any ritard until its indication a full eleven measures later.

Measure 378

The second beat of the bar is more important to the conductor than even the first, as it signals the end of the note for all the first and second violins and cellos. There is no need for an actual cutoff, as the music stops on the second beat. So, give that beat clearly and meaningfully, without encouraging any kind of accented release. Keep in mind that just because there's a beat's worth of rest after the violins' first four half-notes, the same phrase actually continues for the next sixteen measures. The conductor's job here is to make the phrase, with all of its interceding rests, actually hang together without sounding like a new beginning each time.

Measure 379

After gently releasing the strings in the previous measure, the conductor must be ready to show a gesture of syncopation on the downbeat of this measure. It's an issue of shepherding your entire first violin section (how many in your section—eight? twelve? sixteen?) to enter on time (after only a half-beat's rest) *and* to continue in a tempo without slowing down on their own.

Measure 380

The same principle applies as in measure 378, but what's different this time is that the second beat signifies both the cutoff for second violins and cellos, *and* the new note, a B♯ quarter-note in the first violins. Again, there is no need for a cutoff for the first violins; they will not play longer simply because it's only a quarter note. The quality and clarity of your second beat, however, will indicate to them both the timing of beginning the B♯ but also a musical ending.

Measure 386

I've seen many beginning conductors be fooled by the fermata in this measure. For the conductor, the fermata is on the second beat of the bar, not the first. You still need to conduct a full first beat to finish out the half-note in the violins and cellos. The move you make (or choose not to) in the fermata second beat will depend on how long you've decided the fermata should last. Most conductors imagine the fermata as simply being an extended rest, prolonging the continuing ritard. If that is the case, conduct up to the second beat, then non-encouragingly and out of tempo, lift the baton in preparation for the next measure's downbeat. That preparation does not need to be in tempo, as it's only a gesture of syncopation, having the first violins enter after the beat, just as they did eight measures earlier.

Measure 388

Same as measure 380 and measure 386 combined.

Measure 394

This is another easy-to-miss example in terms of knowing just how many beats need to be given. Many conductors are fooled by the fermata that occurs for the whole notes in the flutes, forgetting to indicate the *second* beat, when the strings release their half note. And it would be incorrect to tell the strings to play the same length as the previous four half-notes, since those all have staccato, or more like *separation* dots. Measure 394 is a full, resolute, final half-note, completing the ritard, without regard for the *Tempo I* indication that Mendelssohn places there.

Measures 397–404

Beware the deceptive whole notes! After the final fermata in measure 397, the next six measures are whole notes in the *Allegro di molto* tempo! These must be conducted in exactly the same tempo as you will from measure 404. Please note also that of the six whole-note measures, there is a change every two measures: first, the first and second violins enter; second, the winds and horns rearticulate their chord and simultaneously reduce their volume to ***pp***; third, the second violins change the chord to minor. These are small but extremely important changes that psychologically set up the return to the eighth-note tempo in measure 404.

26. Mendelssohn, *A Midsummer Night's Dream*: Overture

38

Debussy, *Prelude to the Afternoon of a Faun*: Measure 86–End

Never conduct this piece as if it's a conducting etude! One wonder of Debussy's music is that while you and your players are counting ferociously to achieve maximum synchronicity within the ensemble, the music itself cannot *sound* like anything but being free, floating, picturesque, and constantly evolving on its own. When conducting this piece, never give the impression that you're beating time or doing anything but allowing the music to blossom with finesse, ease, and an essential inner rhythmic underpinning. It requires great subtlety on the part of the baton technique: being there with every necessary move for the players, within a context of organic growth and structure, it is as if nature itself has come alive musically.

Measures 86–89

Debussy.pdf

The *1er mouv't* to which this refers is, of course, measure 1 of the entire composition. But there is a meter discrepancy between these two versions of the theme. The first time Debussy presents this tune, it is in 9/8 meter:

FIG. 38.1. First Statement of the Theme: Flute in 9/8

But here at measure 86, the same tune is in 4/4:

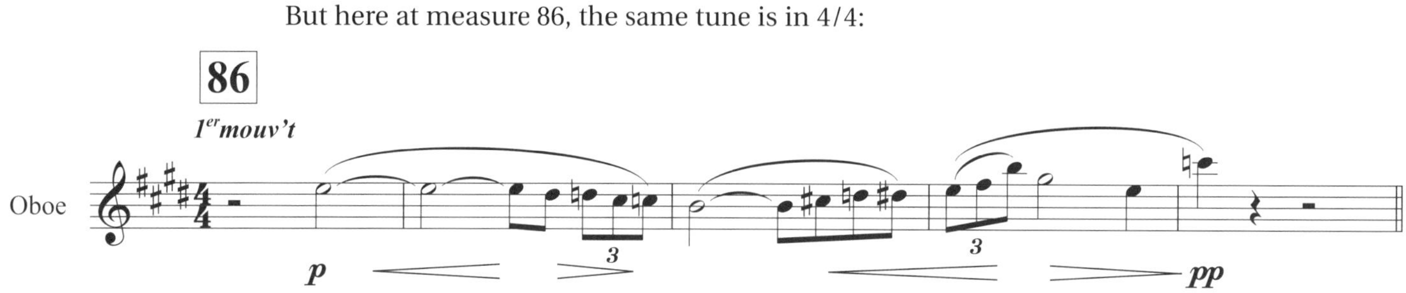

FIG. 38.2. Theme at Measure 86: Oboe in 4/4

Consequently, despite the note values being halved from the eighth note in the first (flute) statement to quarter notes in the oboe at measure 86, as conductor you must see that the pulse both times is essentially the same. In other words, if your metronome in the beginning of the piece is at ♪ = 88, then the quarter note at measure 86 should also be at ♩ = 88. I believe the evidence that Debussy wants the same tempo is found in the fact that, with each statement of the theme, Debussy holds the first note for the same relative length, i.e., 4½ beats in each tempo.

Measure 90

Let the solo English horn follow you while you lead the three French horns, who have a distinctly more difficult time playing the sextuplets in a sudden new tempo. By the way, I encourage the horns to mentally divide their sextuplets into two triplets of three notes, dividing the beat in half as the pulse. There's another reason for that, if you read on to the following paragraph dealing with the clarinets playing sextuplets in measure 93.

Measure 93

Continuing the methodology for the horns in the paragraph above, then it will be assumed that the clarinets will also be phrasing their sixteenth-note sextuplets similarly. The problem comes, then, in managing the retenu, synching it with the first horn in the last beat whose triplet switches to being in three parts. My solution for this has always worked: beats 1 and 2 are conducted in quarter-notes, as nothing changes to the tempo yet. I divide beat 3 in half, which allows me to begin the ritard and is easy for the clarinets to follow the beginning of my retenu. I divide beat 4 into three subdivisions, basically dictating each of the triplet's three parts, while also giving me ample room to effectively manage a gradual retenu. The only caveat to conducting this measure in this way is that one needs to announce and explain it to the orchestra.

Measure 94

Beats 1 and 2 require no subdivision, but beats 3 and 4 should each be subdivided into triplets.

Measure 95

This entire measure is divided into duple rhythms ("in eight"). There is not a single triplet to be found. Conduct this measure in eight beats—i.e., a subdivided four—but increasingly slower: *avec plus de langueur* (with more languor). Be mindful also that your subdivisions in this measure are themselves actually slower than the triplets in the previous measure.

Measure 96

It will feel incredibly slow to you, but conduct this measure in four quarter-notes! The musical pulse is definitely four languid beats per bar, so there really is no reason to subdivide anything for this or the next three measures. Keep the beat exceptionally clear.

Measures 100–101

It is possible to conduct these measures the same way I suggested conducting measure 94, but only if circumstances allow you to trust the harpist to get the right tempo without having to make a major adjustment in the third beat when you do begin subdividing. I prefer to conduct these measures in twelve beats (subdivided four into triplets). It's just much easier to control the overall flow, without leaving anything up to chance.

Measure 102

Assuming you're conducting the previous two measures in twelve as I suggest, then it's an easy transition to simply conduct measure 102 in nine (subdivided three into triplets). And since this first measure is another retenu, even though it involves only two woodwind players sitting just a seat apart from each other, it makes more sense to me to conduct the measure in nine, albeit gently.

Measures 103–104

It helps to return to conducting these measures in three. First of all, Debussy wants us to observe *a tempo*, and second, the only person who would benefit from subdividing would be the oboe, who probably would be much happier not having each eighth note dictated to them.

Measure 105

The only way to accomplish a true *Très retenu* is to subdivide the beats. But two players (flute and oboe) are subdivided into triplets, and more players (all first violins, solo cello) are subdivided into duplets. Which to conduct? It's easier to play two notes against three beats rather than vice versa. Since I want it to be easier for the larger number of players, I conduct this measure in nine (subdivided three in triplets), with the second beat not subdivided.

The question inevitably arises, then, if I'm conducting the section beginning at measure 102 in nine, and measure 105 also in nine, why not just conduct all four measures in nine? Of course, you can conduct all four measures in nine, though I still strongly encourage you not to beat the eighth-notes in measures 103 and 104, as it will restrict the musicality of the solo oboe. You should be there to support the oboist, not dictate the minute flow or getting into the face of a valuable principal player.

Measure 106

If there were only one harp, one might comfortably conduct this measure in a slow four (Debussy: "*Très lent et très retenu jusqu' à la fin*"). But there are two harpists playing, so I would make it comfortable for all by conducting this one measure in eight—again, gently and musically, without appearing pedantic.

Measure 107

Of the four large beats, only beats 2 and 4 need to be divided. Beats 1 and 3 are fine standing alone, the baton simply indicating (in tempo!) the passage of time. This is an elusive measure for several reasons:(a) there is no discernable underlying pulse; (b) the first violins are playing without their first stand; (c) both horns are muted, even though they have the leading voices; (d) violins are not accustomed to playing the lowest voice in second inversion triads. As conductor, your baton must be the glue that binds them together! Once they get it, it will be fine, but the first few times you conduct this in rehearsal, you'll quickly discover it's not as easy as it appears.

Measures 108–110

Relax! These last three measures are [almost] exclusively in four simple beats per bar, though continuously slowing down ("*très retenu jusqu' à la fin*"). That will require a very clear ictus for all beats that have more than one person entering or changing notes. The only exception here is the next-to-last measure of the piece where, in beat 2, the flute has a final, anticipatory third (G♯) of the final E major chord. It is nice to give the flute a little time to expressively play that one single eighth-note, quite simply from the point of view of not wanting to rush over or through it. It is so delicious a move that I would subdivide that one beat for the flute, allowing for a proper placement of the final chord on beat 3.

27. Debussy, *Prelude to the Afternoon of a Faun*

PART III
Interviews

To this day I cannot remember having even one private conducting lesson, even though I graduated with a bachelor's degree in conducting from the Eastman School of Music. The curriculum there at the time was in its infancy, so while I needed to continue private lessons on both cello and piano all four years, specific conducting training was limited to conducting a piano in class situations along with my three fellow majors, plus whatever real hands-on experience I could muster on my own. Feeling the need for more, I decided to observe as many rehearsals and conductors of the Rochester Philharmonic as I could. Often without score, sometimes without patience (Why is he saying that? How could he conduct that music like that?), I spent loads of hours observing conductors' techniques, not just of conducting itself, but how they used their techniques in relation to the professional musicians in the orchestra. Oftentimes I learned more about what *not* to do or say, but there were also revealing, informative, and educational moments as well.

This final section of the book is my attempt to have you "observe" a dozen different conductors whom I admire for their abilities and accomplishments. In some cases, you may not be familiar with their names, but I am familiar with them, their backgrounds, their professional successes, and especially with their ability to thoughtfully share their thoughts about conducting technique and decorum. I believe there is much to learn from all these friends, and hope that you, too, might benefit much more from them than I was able to put forth in the earlier chapters. Read, ponder, and enjoy!

39

Peter Boyer

Los Angeles-based Peter Boyer is an immensely successful composer, conductor, and orchestrator on both the concert stage and in the recording studio. He has conducted the London Symphony, London Philharmonic, and Philharmonia orchestras in recordings of his own music. His concert music has been performed by more than a hundred orchestras, especially the noteworthy *Ellis Island: The Dream of America*, for which he received a Grammy nomination. As an orchestrator, he is frequently found in all the major movie studios, and his work can be found in several dozen feature film scores.

You mention Bernstein as a great inspiration for conducting. What impressed you most?

He and his legacy have become very important to me in terms of being a composer/conductor, and a thinker about music. With Bernstein as a conductor, there's so much one can say; he was obviously a very theatrical person, and also a charismatic and magnetic personality. If one watches Bernstein, the approach from a physical and technical standpoint is unorthodox, in certain respects, but also as it changed over the years and from piece to piece, he seems to have had such a psychological connection to so much music that I don't think he needed to think consciously about what his gestures were going to be. It simply emanated from him, and if that meant extravagant, theatrical, dramatic gestures, then that was what he did. But I don't think he necessarily plotted and planned it out ahead of time. There was a certain flow, spontaneity, and connection to those composers. So, all of that is what I think makes him a unique figure. The really close connection to the music, the combination of intellectual, emotional, and a sense of wanting to communicate so dramatically—all of those things are so important in understanding Bernstein.

I've observed in your own conducting you have a very clean technique. When and where did you learn that?

In graduate school, I studied conducting with Harold Farberman [longtime conducting faculty, Bard College]. His was a very specific approach to baton technique, with clarity being the order of the day.

He talked about avoiding mirroring as a normal course of events. And the contrast between what each hand could do independently. He was very methodical.

How does your conducting technique differ in the recording studio from the concert stage?

I've done recording sessions in Los Angeles and London both with and without click track, a number of which have been my own music, which obviously is somewhat different from conducting someone else's music. But still there are separate roles that have to be clearly defined between being the composer and being the conductor.

A very big consideration is whether or not to use a click track, because it changes your approach. In a way, conducting to a click track is easier because the all-important role of establishing time is taken away from your responsibilities because we're all listening to the same click. That's its whole purpose: to make things easier to do. The click track can occasionally be a hindrance, but much more often than not, it is an extremely helpful thing, especially when time is very short, and when one is marrying it to a visual image when there's so little flexibility. We don't all have that built-in, uncanny sense that John Williams seems to have just with a clock and streamers and punches. In the recording studio, it's always a high-pressured situation in terms of time, and so efficiency is extremely important. Obviously, that's also important in the concert hall, but it's augmented more in the recording studio. I have found that conducting with click track, it's important not to overdo things, to be more minimal in one's approach and gestures, because we all have a click, so we're all going to have the same basis for time-keeping. Also, one cannot talk too much (which is true, of course, in the concert hall as well)! One becomes a kind of traffic cop to facilitate the flow of information, especially if you have someone in the booth listening for you. In the concert hall, it's pretty much all about you, but in the studio, there are multiple levels of things that are happening.

The general approach in the studio is rehearse/record, rehearse/record. It's unusual for the orchestra to have seen the music ahead of time, so you're dealing with sight-reading. Film music is generally going to be divided into cues, which are by nature short. So, with each cue, we'll read it, then record it, then fix whatever needs fixing, then do another take. Having two or three takes then gives you choices for making cuts and edits. When dealing with classical music with a 6- or 10- or 20-minute piece, rehearse/record means having a larger piece of music to deal with. In my recordings in London, we recorded an hour of music in three sessions, i.e., twenty minutes of music in each session, which is quite extraordinary. In that case, I didn't have the luxury of going back to the booth to listen during the session, so I hired a producer who did the listening for me.

How has your own conducting technique changed over the years?

Good question! I haven't looked at my old videos in a long time. I think that even in my early days, I was not getting in my own way and was reasonably efficient, but if anything, I'm probably more economical in the gestures I make. I think the general tendency of emerging conductors is to over-conduct. You know, to a large extent the orchestra can really play together without you, so therefore, don't be so full of yourself that you think you're invaluable. If you're starting from a baseline that they can already play very well, treat that with care, and respect. One should be confident but not arrogant, respectful but not demure. Finding that balance and smiling makes a big difference.

When recording, who else is running the show in the booth, in addition to yourself conducting?

There's a level of technical preparation that has had to occur prior to the session. In most cases, it's going to be Pro Tools, and the click may be generated from Pro Tools. There have to be tempo maps that have been carefully put together between the composer and the composer's team, so that the clicks are sensible and make the right number of warning clicks in to a starting place, that there are clicks preparing into new tempos. Often, things need to be broken into sections, especially if there's an especially long cue, so you make cuts in order to get it done more easily.

There is that communications flow in a recording studio. At the top of the pyramid is the composer, then the orchestrator, conductor, music editor, engineer, second engineers, all of which goes out to the orchestra. When that's all happening at a really high level, it's quite remarkable, and is remarkable to be a part of. In that context, I've been an orchestrator much more than a composer. I've had the opportunity as orchestrator to have these notes that were written by somebody else but then came through me. It's not all that uncommon for an orchestrator to get, say, a 120-bar action cue that's big and dense and loud and full of notes, and to only have a day to get all that on paper. All of that stuff gets printed that morning and goes on to the orchestra's music stands later that day. It really is remarkable, when everybody's job is being done well and everybody's functioning at that level, that you can have something that came literally right off the presses, put down on the stands, the click track goes, the conductor goes, and have it be very close to perfect on a first pass!

Where do you get your greatest satisfaction today?

Being a composer has a built-in level of loneliness attached to the endeavor. Composers spend an inordinate amount of time in the composing studio, alone, trying to work it out. Sometimes, we spend hundreds of hours just to write one good minute of music, so there's a kind of personal cost, as you're not spending that much of your time with people socially. For me, it's unbelievably satisfying, after months of working on something, to be able to get in front of an ensemble of great musicians and to have that sense of energy and community, and then to actually do it. I agree with John Williams who has spoken frequently about that very special trinity of composer-performers-audience that is one of the great gifts that we have as human beings. At the end of the day, it's a communicative art.

What advice do you have for emerging composers who may conduct their own works in the future but haven't yet?

Understand that being the composer and being the conductor are fundamentally different things, and require fundamentally different types of preparation. Don't assume that just because you have composed the music that you necessarily are the expert or best possible person to stand up there and conduct it yourself. Just as one seeks to study composition to get better at that craft, then a composer studying conducting will only help. Be prepared. Don't talk too much. Respect the orchestra. Smile. Listen to what the orchestra has to say, which should be a tremendous learning process. You will be nervous, at first, but listen to the orchestra, because there is that wealth of experience and information that they bring to the table.

From a composer's perspective, what advice do you have for emerging conductors doing your, or someone else's music?

Be as prepared as possible. Know the score as well as possible. Presumably, the conductor has the opportunity to talk to the composer, so that kind of communication is a great advantage. Respect for the musicians is so crucial, and that respect extends in many ways: no condescension, respecting their time, not talking too much… Showing what you want is very helpful, and treating that new music with the same level of respect as you would a traditional composer. Hopefully, the new music, and its preparation, its crafting of the parts, is deserving of that respect, so that when it's put on the stands, there's going to be no barrier because the musicians see something that looks unplayable or is a mess to read.

When I look at the successful, professional conductors who have conducted my music I see that, while they may have distinct personalities, there is definitely a certain commonality of professionalism, preparation, and efficiency in terms of how they deal with their time on the podium. Remember that the flow of communication between composer, conductor, and orchestra is extremely important. One learns to be very efficient in rehearsal with one's comments. Some composers may be less fluent with making comments, so a conductor may need to interpret what's being said by the composer into the language of the orchestra.

What should the emerging conductor be sure to always and never do?

ALWAYS be prepared. Know the score as well as possible. Be respectful to the musicians.

NEVER get on the podium not knowing the music. Never treat the musicians disrespectfully. Never be arrogant.

40

C. Thomas Brooks, Jr.

Choral conductor Tom Brooks is both a good friend and terrific choral conductor. I remain incredibly impressed with his knowledge (as I am with everyone in this interview series) of singing, conducting, and choral repertoire, and the high standards to which he holds himself and others. Most importantly, his desire to teach and to share his passion for music's ability to uplift the human condition is exemplary.

I first met Tom at Indian Hill Music in Massachusetts, where I am the artistic director. We became good friends almost instantly, and since then, he and I have collaborated with our various institutions in all manner of orchestral, opera, choral, and collegiate performances. Now conductor of the Erie Philharmonic Chorus and of the Mercyhurst College Choir (which he actually founded in the 1970s), Tom also remains conductor of the professional Lyricora choral ensemble in Massachusetts as well as executive director of the Salzburg Institute's concert series in Austria.

When and from whom did you learn your first basics of how to conduct?

I actually learned it from Harold McNeil, who was an Eastman grad, and he was at the college we were at. He had a sort of brutal way of teaching. We were all scared to death, but it's a system I've used since, and it works. He would teach us the beat patterns, and then he would have a sequence that ran like a measure of 1, a measure of 2, then 3, 4, 5 (2+3 and 3+2), 6 (both Italian and German), and 8 (subdivided 4). You had to go in that sequence, which he would drill from the top and back down, then back up again. He would put it on a metronome, and place us individually on a very high podium in front of the class. And if we made even one slight mistake, he would say, "Sit down, you get an F." At the end of just three weeks, everybody was flunking, but we were practicing day and night. The result was that we got the patterns into our heads the first three weeks.

Later on, he'd ask for the pattern to be done legato, or espressivo, or staccato, or he'd switch styles in the middle of your sequence. This way, he was teaching you the style and the patterns, but at the same time drilling you. He'd make you switch quickly, making you change immediately. It made you really think.

He would do the same kind of drilling process with preparation beats as well, by calling out the beat on which music begins. If you couldn't immediately position your stick to the right preparation location, he'd say, "Sit down, you get an F." That would be your quiz grade for the day.

For years, I would continue this kind of drill, circling through all the patterns and all the preparations on my own. Then we would conduct to a recording of the Beethoven *First Symphony.*

Any other mentors?

Vytautas Marijosius, a Lithuanian conducting professor at the Hartt School, and former student of Richard Strauss. He had also conducted the Czech National Symphony Orchestra, the Prague Radio Symphony Orchestra, and the Lithuanian State Opera. He mentored me for three years, never charging me a dollar, and became as good a friend as one could ever have. What he taught me was the sense of musicality and paying attention to the parts—paying attention to what's going on, and that conducting precipitated or caused some of the music, that it had to be a certain way. He would demonstrate a plain pattern without expression and say, "This is truth." But anything beyond the pattern, he would say is "expressive." So "Don't be sloppy" conducting the patterns: "What did you mean? Are you saying something with your movement? What are you trying to say?" At first, I didn't have an answer, but had to find one, which started to awaken in me that music is not just a bunch of notes, but there's something happening in the music! Realizing that there's real music-making going on—there's something really happening in the score!

All of that came from him constantly questioning me: Why did you make that movement? What are you trying to say musically? That was the awakening of the *musicality* of what a conductor does.

What, if anything, did you learn the "hard" way?

There were probably two things. Early on, before studying with Marijosius, I chose to conduct the Daniel Pinkham *Christmas Cantata* with brass accompaniment. Because I was new to the field, I had difficulty with this piece's asymmetrical measures and was forced to learn conducting mixed meters.

The second time, I was put on the spot by Marijosius at Hartt. He wanted me to do a reading rehearsal of the Howard Hanson *Second Symphony*, which was fine, as I thought I was prepared. But just before beginning, Marijosius comes up to me and says, "See if you can get through the entire symphony without the orchestra breaking down." This was an extension of his work with me earlier, forcing me to really think about my gestures and what they mean to the players without allowing the ensemble to fail.

But I realized that my commitment came out of fear, and then later, it came to me that if I can turn it on out of fear, I could turn it on any time. I realized that, though we have so little control by just waving a stick, we can exert ourselves over people with this mental energy.

Last, I was doing the von Weber *Mass in G* in Chicago, without enough time to play through the piece. Responding to the fears of one of the orchestra players, I said, "You watch me, and I will get you through this." The concert went well, and that's when I realized that all these things I had been studying in the past could be brought forward into my conducting technique. What I learned from that experience was that if you could call on this ability in a performance, why not do the same in rehearsal? But you have to be the first to exert yourself before it's going to happen from your ensemble.

What would you say is another primary responsibility of being a conductor, and where did you discover that?

One of the first things I realized is that there's more to the whole process of conducting, beyond just drawing beat patterns and preparation beats in different styles. You almost have to be breathing inside yourself as if *you* were going to make that entrance, and then you will have an ensemble respond. The weakness in conducting class is if you're conducting a recording, the music's going to happen anyway, no matter what you do! Then comes the issue of what you want from the music—the revelation that the sound of your ensemble may not be what's in your head, so what are you going to do about it?

When do you use a baton?

I use a baton if I'm doing anything with instruments, not with just a straight choral group.

Why?

I think it's what singers are used to. I think the bigger the group, the more differently you can conduct. You can use flat-hand. Singers like the hands better. A lot of them feel the baton is too impersonal. Right or wrong, that's what they'll complain about.

Can a baton be expressive, or is it simply an extension of the arm?

Absolutely, it can be expressive, and should be expressive without just using the left hand all the time. The baton hand has to be primary. If the musical gesture is everywhere but not in the baton, then I think that's ineffective. And the baton gives you the ability to use the wrist.

Should conductors mouth the text, even silently, to the chorus? Do choruses appreciate that in an orchestral setting?

They need to learn to follow your hands, your beat, especially with the large distance between you and them in an orchestral setting. But like mirror conducting where you're using the left hand all the time, there's no point to mouthing the text.

What are some of the basic differences between conducting for chorus and conducting for orchestra?

I try not to do anything differently, but I think the rehearsal techniques are somewhat different. When you conduct a choir, you're probably going to have less expertise on the part of the singers than you do with an orchestra. When you go into an orchestra, you assume everybody can read music, but when you go into a choir, there are a lot of singers who don't read well at all. They basically learn their scores over the years by tonal memory. You play it, they remember it, they sing it back, so it does change the way you rehearse them. What are you going to do to get them to remember certain things?

So, what are some of the choices you have?

Sometimes it's more note drilling than you would do with an orchestra. You work faster for that reason. Picking up the pace for singers gets them engaged more quickly into the score. Because so many of them learn from an aural tradition, to get them to remember their notes, you have to repeat them as quickly as possible, and several times. The longer they sit there before you repeat a passage, the more they forget all the things they're learning. So, the pace for choral, I think, has to be relatively quick. Then, after working in a quick unit, you can slow down and give them a chance to get their breath back. There are a lot of ways to do that, by changing what it is you're doing. You're coming from notes several times, then you put some technical thing vocally with those notes, and now they start to remember the notes because you've added something here that's a hook to hang your coat on.

You don't do this with an orchestra. Singers' pace? The more they sit around, the less they pay attention, the more de-energized they get, and the less their "instrument" works, because they are the instrument. You have to mentally keep them sharp. Part of keeping a chorus energized is in not drilling one thing too long. Whatever technique you're doing, you're always layering those steps. Next rehearsal, you layer those same steps again, so now you can work faster because of their familiarity with that layer they've already worked on. You keep repeating and building and adding another element.

Overall, I've always felt that you begin with an introductory thing, then you learn notes, then you have a vocal approach, then a musical approach, then an aesthetic approach. You layer them and try to mix them together as you progress in rehearsal.

There are a lot of ways to approach rehearsing. You can approach intellectually, then you have to get to the emotional, because they will respond to the emotional very quickly. Instrumentalists may do that at the end of a rehearsal sequence, when they start to buy into it, but there's a much more methodical approach to getting an orchestra together. And with singers, you can work intensely for a time, then give them a break, but you can't let them out of the chair. If they leave their chairs, it takes so long to get them back in, it's not worth it.

How has your conducting style changed over the years?

I'm much more economical with my gestures now than before. I think I'm just as expressive, but it's smaller, more economical. Part of that comes from thinking what you really want out of the music, and if you show too much all the time, they get numb. I think also, small movements within a phrase can accomplish so much more. When I was beginning, I did a lot of "air-beating," kind of like a rooster that sits on a fence flapping its wings but doesn't go anywhere. Sometimes, conductors just wildly flap away, the only reason being that it makes us feel like we're doing something, when actually we're really not doing anything.

How would you describe the essentials of "podium presence"?

I think there are two things you have to do first:

1. You have to really love music and have a strong aural image in your head of what you want from that music. You cannot get on the podium and be guessing what you might want from the music, or not have decided already. You might change your mind later, but you need to come on with a strong idea of what you want to get out of the score musically.
2. You have to like—almost love—people. You can't do anything without those people. You can get up and wave a baton that makes no music, but you have to have people who are willing to play for you. The old conductors used to do it through fear, but that doesn't work today. Today's musicians cannot make music when they're scared. They have to feel that you care enough about them that they're willing to try to do what you're asking of them.

What are the steps you take in determining what you want in a score?

Conductors need to study style, beginning with the period of music and what the demands are from that era. You have to be serious about discovering the uniqueness of each period and each composer with that period. That will open all the color possibilities in your head. Old Moshe Paranov used to say that with every score he conducted, he would bring the experience of having conducted all the other pieces he ever did before that. A real absorption of historical styles and thoughts means reading the authoritative texts dealing with style and performance practice. You have to take it seriously.

Something else I think conductors don't do is to listen to genres other than those they are currently studying and conducting. The old style of Marijosius' teaching used to be to start with choral music, because singers have to exert themselves to maintain a line. Then, one would go to the opera pit, because there you have to have technique of effective, non-superfluous gesture. You have to be clean and know exactly what you're doing. Only then, maybe, you have the right to conduct a symphonic work. This is a good progression, because it teaches you line, then style, then technique.

Do you have a method you generally follow in studying a new score?

Generally, I'll sit at my desk and try to get all the way through the score once or twice, maybe even three or four times. This gives me the overview, and you begin also to see the sections that make up the overview. The more you do it, the more you automatically break it down into ever-smaller sections. It also gives you a sense of pacing, helping you make decisions musically as to what comes before and after a particular passage. Then, I'll break up into sections, often working only on one section at a time, drilling it in my mind, until I'm confident that I have that firmly in my musical grasp. If I spend significant time on just one section, I'll not leave the score until I've gone back and done yet another complete overview in order not to lose the context of what I've been studying. After doing that for the entire piece, I'll go back and ask myself if my approach has continuity, or have I made decisions in any section that don't fit the context.

Sometimes, I'll think about singers such as Dietrich Fischer-Dieskau, singing a Schubert song so beautifully, and ask myself, what did he do with the phrases? Now if you go to a four-part choral score, all the four parts have phrase, and if you're doing an instrumental piece, is there not an inflection to their lines? I believe that too many orchestras today just play the notes. I work out all that phrasing in my mind: what I want to hear, before we get there together. That's how I study it: each line with all those inflections, all the way through the piece. Who is playing where, and what should they be saying?

Do you use a piano in your score study?

Yes. I do a lot of reading the score myself without a piano. I can hear the music in my brain, without depending on solfege or other tools. But at my desk I have a four-octave keyboard that I'll use if I'm not sure whether I can hear something.

How do you mark your choral scores?

First, I have to do background and textual analysis. I have to understand the text in order to understand why the composer wrote what s/he did. What are they saying? It has to be something—I hope; otherwise, it's not a good piece. Then I'll mark cues, because I want to make sure I'm not missing something important. I'll also mark some dynamic things, and also where I think the stress of the phrase goes. I'll look at a phrase and ask, where is it going? Where is the high point? And I'll make a notation how to come off the high point, not exaggerating a note that's not part of the high point. It's helpful in rehearsal to have made that mark, because you're busy.

I tend not to work too much harmonically, unless there's something that's strange enough for me to stop and analyze what could be a unique color. It'll make me question why the composer is using that particular effect. I'll also keep a page or two in the score that has any research I've done on the text, or something about the composer, or the form of the piece that is unique. I want to make sure that I don't forget that later.

And I will use colors. I've found that red for crescendo and blue for diminuendo is very helpful. Sometimes, I'll use green or orange if it's something that I have to make sure I pay attention to. Sometimes, I'll use two scores, marking up one with all kinds of phrasing and other marks—probably too much in the first round. Then when I've marked it and decided what I want to do with it, I'll go to the clean score and start over again. I never use pen, because I change my mind. I learned something from John Moriarty of the New England Conservatory: that it's okay to change your mind as you continue to grow—both yourself and your musical understanding. This is not something you do from rehearsal to rehearsal, but a year later, you might look at a piece totally differently because you've now matured from where you were the previous year. Actually, if you're not doing that, I would question whether you're actually studying and reading, because that means you're not growing.

How do you plan out a rehearsal, and is it different dependent on the ensemble?

Yes, depending on what the problems are and what needs to be solved. I like to plan out a rehearsal with variety, not being on one thing all the time. I'll work on one specific thing, then relate it to another, and then get to other issues.

My rehearsal planning is generally in terms of the whole scheme. If I have fourteen rehearsals for a concert, then I work backwards. You have to plan it out so it comes out right at the concert. Planning backwards from a dress rehearsal, you're able to think how many times you may have to do a particular movement or piece. I'm actually quite meticulous in planning my rehearsals, and I stick to the plan, which always includes some review in any rehearsal of what we did in the previous rehearsal. In each specific rehearsal, I tend to write down in advance the issues I want to address, because it's too easy to forget. Or, sometimes I make two different plans for a rehearsal, so I can switch if Plan A isn't going to work successfully for various reasons.

What are your basic goals when preparing a chorus in a major work for another conductor?

Bottom line is absolutely that the sound has to be clean and well learned (not heads in score but score in head). Drilled enough that they know what they have to do—accurate notes and rhythm. The choral conductor has to know how much the chorus is going to articulate, based on what you know about how the orchestra is going to sound. If it's low, it has to be cleaner and a little more articulated to be heard. Dynamic markings must absolutely be adhered to, and you've got to come up with a vocal production that sings through the orchestra, that there's enough resonance. If it gets too dark, it doesn't get heard through the orchestra. Once you've prepared the chorus for accuracy and cleanliness, you can hand it over to the orchestral conductor to decide if s/he wants to do some musical things with it. The chorus should be pliable. I often would prepare sections two or three different ways just to get them to be more pliable.

What is your role when you've prepared a chorus, and they're rehearsing with the orchestra and a different conductor?

Sometimes, I'm on the stage, next to the conductor, ready to translate his/her musical request into singers' techniques. Another thing is, if I'm out in the hall, I'll often take notes during rehearsal—not only for issues going by in the moment, but also for sections that I don't think are clean enough in the chorus, which I can then fix later in a chorus rehearsal.

When it comes to balance, there is a difference in the way choral conductors think. Most of them feel that the choir has to be predominant, but especially in nineteenth-century music, that's just not true; they're just another color (choir) of the orchestra, which is perfectly okay. That balance is what the orchestral conductor should be doing; choral conductors should not butt in at that point, unless asked.

Overall, you can't give up. You're always trying to fix something within the choir. You can't relent, right up to the last minute. Always try to fix it, make it better, sharpen it up within the context of the what's going on in the total work. You can't change what the orchestra's conductor has determined, but you can constantly tweak and improve the sound of the choir.

Where do areas of collaboration exist, and with whom?

Early on, I discovered business executives. For me, it was top insurance executives in Hartford who liked to sing but also were interested in what I was doing. Of course, we had music in common, but then I had to find something in common with what they did, to question, to ask, and be interested.

My father-in-law was a farmer, and I learned a lot about music from farming. Farming was a perfect example of preparing ground, planting a seed, cultivation, and getting to harvest, which is exactly what we do in music. I asked him, what qualities does it take to be a farmer? He taught me about paying attention to everything that's going on, to notice if there's disease on the plant, how the weather might affect it, and how to prepare for that. I started thinking, how do I do this with my music? Planning ahead taught me to schedule an extra rehearsal with my choir before the winter set in, because I could count on losing a rehearsal later on due to bad weather.

And from sports I learned—especially from coaches—how to stay with fundamentals. Always maintain the fundamentals because it keeps you disciplined. Without fundamentals, you fail.

What instrumental/vocal training do you think emerging conductors should have?

You need to struggle with strings. To struggle is to begin to learn just what it takes to play. Learn enough about strings to basically know what's going on and to shut your mouth! I learned in a hurry that if you're playing with professionals, ask your professionals. Tell them what you want musically, and let them figure out how to do it. Don't try to tell them something they've spent thirty years doing themselves! Find someone to study a string instrument with, no matter how bad you may be.

Piano is also very important. And I was lucky being a brass player early on that I have a good sense of what is going on for brass players now.

Every conducting student also should take voice lessons, because when you sing, you are the instrument. You are the player *and* the instrument. And if you can sing the phrase, you also feel the phrase. I've worked with people who can't sing at all, and I've noticed that it slows their rehearsal down, because they're always explaining. For good musicians, if you sing it for them, they've got it, which takes so little time to do. Even if it's not beautiful; they don't care, but you've shown them what it is. We're used to listening.

What are the real-world administrative pressures around professional conducting that the newbie should be aware of?

Emerging conductors should learn something about management techniques. How the business and the non-profit worlds work, so they understand how the world around them works.

Today's conductor also has to know something about raising money. It doesn't mean they have to close the deal, but they have to realize they're the front-person when it comes to raising money for their orchestras or ensembles. Donors like to meet the conductor. What does that mean? They need to start to practice early on to be easy with people, to learn to actually like talking to people. Too many musicians today don't want to talk to anybody. Young musicians today need to learn how to dress, how to look good, and be well groomed. You'll be dealing with older people who expect this.

It's all about presentation of self. You have a public life where you're relating to others, and you may have a private life, but that's separate. Nobody should see the private life. In the public life, young students today have pathetic table manners. Learn how to eat well, how to look good, and learn mannerly ways of doing things. Conductors get invited to formal dinners, and if you don't know what fork to use, you're going to make a fool out of yourself.

How to "work a room" and get around that room when you're in a reception, rather than just hanging out in the corner with a drink.

If you're starting to become a conductor, you have to start becoming a different, public person. It takes time, just like it takes to learn conducting. When you're out, be a conversationalist; talk to people; get around; find out about the world; do a little bit of keeping up on things so you can have a conversation with someone you don't know. If you don't know at all what's happening in, say, sports, or politics, or generally in the world these days, that can make a difference to a potential donor or board member or volunteer.

Have I not addressed anything you feel is important, or any last word or advice to the emerging conductor?

Read this book again. One should have a regular reading shelf. Mark your copies, and reread. Rereading, you get so much more from it than before. It's no different from studying a score. Getting the information in your head is the same as getting it in your hands. It takes constant repetition; you have to be relentless. Also, choral conductors should read vocal pedagogy books on voice production. Do not rely on the cute, simple choral conducting techniques you find a lot of places. When you are working on vocal techniques with a group, you have to make sure you are in the *mainstream* of vocal pedagogy. In order to know where that is, you have to read, read, and read some more.

What is your advice to any emerging conductor—what should they ALWAYS do, NEVER do?

ALWAYS treat conducting like it's playing an instrument. Practice and study scores every day. It's no different from being an instrumentalist. Practice! Look at a mirror, even!

NEVER wing it. Never go in not having looked at the music, not having planned a rehearsal.

41

Jack Everly

Jack Everly is a busy conductor of pops concerts these days, and serves as the principal pops conductor for the orchestra of Indianapolis, Baltimore, and Naples, and Ottawa's National Arts Centre. This is an incredible feat, both musically and logistically, so he inevitably has a superb knowledge of pops repertoire and artists, of orchestra behavior and culture, as well as a very special flair for connecting with all his audiences. Having conducted Carol Channing literally hundreds of times in *Hello, Dolly!*, having been conductor of the American Ballet Theatre for more than a dozen years, and conducting his annual Yuletide Celebration for the last quarter-century with the Indianapolis Symphony, shows him to be effectively musical at the very highest standards of music-making. This interview was especially informative and entertaining, even joined at times (in the background) by his dog, Duke.

What was your own introduction to conducting, and who were your earliest mentors?

My high school had a marvelous orchestra, whose conductor, Ralph Burkhart, was patience personified and yet very quietly nurturing and very helpful to me. They needed some bass players the one year, so I taught myself how to play bass. He actually let me conduct the orchestra, too—my first time conducting. Now, also during high school, I had done community theater in my small town, and I had always assembled an orchestra for the pit, so I had both the musical theater and now the high school orchestra experience conducting. Mr. Burkhart taught me the rudiments, but of course, I observed him while playing bass in the orchestra. Mr. Burkhart made the initial, huge difference in the seed of knowledge he was planting for me: how to approach things, the rudiments of conducting, and sometimes more philosophical ideas. He just very gently did all that. It was wonderful.

At Indiana University, what courses did you take besides conducting that you realize now were of most value?

As a philosopher and human being, comparative literature. I loved the whole concept of themes and stories that have been around for hundreds of years and to look at their evolution—Da Ponte, Goethe, Gounod, Shakespeare, or Arthur Lawrence—in the world of theater or novels or films or Broadway musical. It opened up my whole brain to the idea of different treatments of the original material depending on the genre you're involved with.

I also had a marvelous piano professor there, Alberto Reyes. I learned so much from him, not only because of his innate musicality, but also his quiet, patient way of suggesting ways for me to think about my own music-making. It meant the world to me.

What are some other examples of what you did not *learn at conservatory?*

First, understand that my schooling is quite out of the norm, having studied piano, set design, and one undergraduate course in conducting. So, I am not a masters or a doctorate. My experience in my conducting getting better and clearer came through musical theater, New York summer stock. Even in college, I put together my own production of *She Loves Me*. Not only did I put together a thirty-piece orchestra, but I also designed the set!

The school of music where I attended (Indiana University) didn't really know what to do with me. I was accepted into the set design program to study with Mario Cristini from La Scala, who unfortunately died a month before I arrived. But they were very helpful in putting together a combination degree (music and design). But what I didn't learn was: the theatrical pacing of a concert, how to speak to an audience and what do you talk about, where do you find the music, the nuances and details of programming, the arc of a concert from beginning to end, and how all this is very tricky and important, especially in the world of pops. In other words, the basics, or the important things of conducting in the pops realm that simply never get taught.

How important is your conducting technique in a pops situation with limited rehearsal time?

You don't just give a downbeat and follow the drummer! There are times, though, when one's work throughout the evening is a little easier because of a great drummer in an orchestra; it makes the orchestra's lives easier, too. The truth is that a drummer who has orchestral experience and knows how to respond to it and how to nudge these fabulous musicians along gently is worth his/her weight in gold. Where I work, a lot of musicians understand and appreciate that greatly.

Of course, there are situations, particularly in working with a star act, where you of course just follow the star. So, you would be stupid and egocentric if you said, "No, no, this song should go slower." You wouldn't dare tell that to the great Michael Feinstein, for instance.

Do you always use a baton?

Most of the time, yes. If something is particularly choral, then probably not. Also, if it's an extremely pop concert where the drummer is leading us, I think it's too grandiose to use a baton, because it doesn't seem to be that formal.

How has your conducting technique changed over the years?

Like any conductor, we become more finessed. We don't have to be quite so demonstrative as when we started out. One can trust the brilliance of the symphonic musician, a good thing to learn because it's less wear and tear, but it's also about a maturity that's involved with that.

In performance, perhaps I'm a bit more gregarious than in rehearsals because there is an element that is a positive and expected dynamic, on the part of the audience, which is show biz. It's what Lenny [Bernstein] did so well—not that it wasn't organic, but hopefully, you keep it organic so it doesn't get in the way of your incredible musicians. But there's a bit more flair because you are performing, which the audience appreciates and wants.

How did the Symphonic Pops Consortium that you created come about?

There was a need in the industry to assemble a concert in a very theatrical way. So, we would find the sources of music, which is how we always started off, then we would "arc" the evening as far as repertoire, then we'd discover in the program places, say, for the singer to change her gown, then we'd add lighting. It served the industry well, especially as the approach was gratifyingly in demand, and it did so well that now the industry more or less does it on its own.

What are the differences in conducting when in the pit or in the recording studio?

In the pit for musical theater and opera, the nice thing is that the orchestra can hear the singers. In opera, it's a lot easier to do a musical phrase that's ebbing and flowing because one hears where the singer is going. And frankly, that also works on stage for a Broadway night at the pops, where the singers are being heard by the musicians. But in the world of ballet, the orchestra hears nothing but thud, tap tap tap, scrape, and that's it, and we are the only sounds the audience hears. That's a whole different concept of how the musicians are adapting to the phrases, which they're doing strictly by the visual of what you do as a conductor. That took me a while to learn, because I came directly from musical theater; suddenly, in ballet, there isn't a drummer. A Broadway pit is a very small space where you don't have to worry about one hearing what someone else is playing on the other side because it's so small and/or because the drummer is leading.

So, in ballet, my body language needs to show the tempo changes, and one has to be so clear in ballet that if you aren't, you just die (or you'll kill off a few dancers, and then *they* will come for you!). This is body language you would *never* do on the concert stage, because you'd be grossly pulling focus to yourself, and an audience can't even hear the music if you're going to do that. There's too much visual going on, and that's just wrong because the musicians don't require it, the audience doesn't require that extreme of motion. So, there are different things you do depending on whether you're in a pit or whether you're on stage being viewed.

Is conducting Broadway easier, then?

Yes, it is. While it does depend on very specific hand, baton technique, and eye contact with certain players. Example: I was very fortunate to do about two and a half years of *Hello, Dolly!* with Carol Channing. I learned so much about timing and pacing from her, which unfortunately you can't write about because it is so innate and subliminal. If you allow yourself to be in tune with that, it will take you far. This may sound ridiculous, but I don't think I would have been as sensitive to Renée Fleming if hadn't started years ago really listening to someone like Carol Channing. While the voices may be terribly different, what they were doing with the phrase was so intelligent and so musical that you'd be foolish not to listen or absorb it, and understand why they were going where they were going.

In the recording studio, your conducting becomes even more minimal. For one thing, you don't dare want to make a sound or a violent gesture that'll make a squeak or any kind of sound. All must be silent; no audible page turns. There are two ways of doing recording sessions: (1) Singers are in another room with a glass partition; they're somehow hearing the orchestra, they're singing along with you, and you all have visual and audio contact; (2) a whole three-hour session (like in *Hunchback of Notre Dame*) on one song, where the process was: (a) Alan Menken provided a demo of how it was supposed to go, (b) I then view Michael Starobin's full scores, which I'd study and compare to the demo, (c) the demo would change, getting a new one on almost a weekly basis, (d) you show up to the studio, and hopefully you've got it down until they say, for instance, "We'd like these twenty-four bars to be slightly faster, then slow down here" (which might be different from the demo they sent you), (e) you'll do the cut a couple times with your singer, (f) they might then say, do the same cut but with no vocals (you have to precisely remember where the singer was breathing or where the tempo even slightly changed, (g) then later, with the prerecorded orchestra track, they add the singer(s), which could be a month or two later. Then sometime later, they have you return, conducting the singers in a booth with the orchestra track in your ears. The process feels quite convoluted if your training is in live musical theater. But it's the process, so you hopefully adapt to that very quickly.

In a pops program, how often do you get together in advance with guest artists or lighting/staging designers?

What I usually provide in advance is what I call a walk-through of the entire concert, which is a document that explains every moment of the concert. Because, if you don't, it tends to have a very non-theatrical pacing, and I—coming from the theater—prefer a theatrical pacing in my pops concerts, which means that after I've given an introduction, I immediately give the downbeat without taking time to open the score, making sure everyone's ready to play, etc.

I give the walk-through document to the technical people, I talk with them about the particular feeling we might have on the stage in each moment regarding lighting, such as follow-spots. Regarding singers or dancers, if I have worked with them before on the same concert program, I tend not to meet with them in advance. But if there's new music, or it's a new program, then I'll always schedule a rehearsal with me at the piano coaching them. This is very important. Sometimes, you just touch on the very basic things because, for example, if they did the role on Broadway, they already know what they're doing. Frankly, if a performer has done a role on Broadway and wants to advise me on how they want to do it, I'm fine with that. With someone who has not done the role, I try to imbue them with a sense of the role and the pacing, etc.

Also, in places where it matters to them, the orchestras have allotted two rehearsals. On particularly strenuous programs such as *West Side Story*, they allow three or four. Other places don't care as much, so they tend to do it on one rehearsal, and pay more attention to their Shostakovich or Bartók and spend a week on it!

And when will you work with someone in the orchestra in advance of rehearsal?

I will if it's something that is stylistically important, that you don't see on the printed page. For example, there's a quality to what the trumpet solo does in *American in Paris* that you don't do in the tone poem but is done in the film, because that was a famous trumpeter in the MGM Symphony Orchestra who had an enormous sound, a particular vibrato. That's such a particular example in the *approach*, not the *notes*, that you must emulate it the best you can. So, you send that message ahead to the player, even referring them to the original soundtrack, which is often easily available. This is not something they teach at a conservatory.

Any thoughts for conductors on the situation of having only one rehearsal the morning of the concert?

Yes, don't sign the contract! Seriously, "efficiency" is the word of the day, even having in the back of your mind that an unexpected issue might arise (incomplete sets of parts, different editions of the same piece in the parts, etc.). So, you have to allow for the possibility of not rehearsing something, but also being aware that an orchestra may have in their contract they will not play something if it's not been rehearsed. There are all these variables that you must be aware of. A one-rehearsal situation is very tricky.

Also, with one rehearsal, go in concert order. Not just for the orchestra, but for the sound people and others who must have an immediate sense of flow of the concert. Sound people are programming their board as you're rehearsing, so if you do it out of order, they won't have a clue. And, for the orchestra, there's a sense of continuity they get, even if it's subliminal. You would rehearse out of order only if there was something so special that required it. But then, hopefully, you would have enough time to do it again in program order. If not, then skip over it. But if there's something that just has to be rehearsed meticulously, not just a reading, then do it first.

What are the current trends in orchestral pops programming?

The most recent trend is film with orchestra, which I applaud because the scores are symphonic, and it's a marvelous way of bringing in a different demographic to the concert hall who not only have the experience of watching a film they love, but also hearing a live symphony orchestra. My experience with that has been to see people so enthusiastic about hearing the orchestra, even including students who become even more committed to practicing their own instruments because of this inspirational experience.

Another example is Ben Folds, who brings an entirely different demographic to the concert hall. He is a wonderful musician who so appreciates what a symphony orchestra is. And he's constantly telling his fans how important that is, and they're always responding with a big "Yay!" They in turn appreciate the experience because of what he's doing.

Talk about the various collaborators that are important to you.

- Singers. There are a handful of singers whom I adore working with because of their approach to music. That means a sensitivity to the words, the ability to spin a very long line and be musical, the ability to do comedy, or to enrage their emotions. That's what a singer who is also an actor means to me.
- Designers, especially lighting. The industry has come so far that there are many marvelous people who are on staff at various orchestras whom I can trust implicitly.
- Administrators. Generally, these relationships are fascinating and often joyful, because we're all enthusiastic about the various possibilities. But they know what's going on in their community; they know their audiences, and as much as I think I know their audiences, it's great to listen to them and have them advise.

What would you advise emerging conductors should do in advance of rehearsal for a pops program, especially given the extremely limited rehearsal time normally provided?

It depends on what the event is. If it's the current vogue, which is film with live orchestra, you must know the pacing of the film, backwards and forwards. Are you comfortable with the streamers, punches, and/or click-track that you'll be rehearsing with? Which are of course all above and beyond the music.

Obviously, you have to know the music, including knowing where the land-mines might be. Even though it might look straightforward on the page, once you start synchronizing with the film, it becomes a whole different experience.

There is, for example, one sequence in the first *Harry Potter* film, the Quidditch match, which you must rehearse first to give everyone the lay of the land. Players find it's much faster than they thought; it's a very lengthy cue, and the continuity is much more intense than they ever thought. So, in film land, you have to know where the traps are (which we say about any piece of music anyway), but it's especially crucial in film because if you get out of sync, you're dead. Then, you're making the music within the confines of a click.

In advance of a "normal" concert, then, yes, knowing where the difficult places might be as far as coordination. This kind of program tends to be a little more sight-readable, therefore a little less convoluted and/or stress-provoking than, say, a film.

Any basic, bottom-line advice you'd like to share?

In your eagerness to get through all the repertoire you're just dying to do, don't impose things upon your audiences. Never forget your audience. Never forget why you're there. You're there by the grace of the musicians and the management, but long term, you're going to be there because of the acceptance of your audience.

What is your advice to emerging conductors that they should ALWAYS do?

ALWAYS follow your passion. Be courageous enough to do so. Don't do something just because you think you might be successful at it.

...NEVER do?

NEVER preach to the musicians. They know more than you.

42

JoAnn Falletta

Maestra JoAnn Falletta has a remarkable résumé of accomplishments, is seriously committed to women's issues (founder of the Women's Philharmonic) both as performer and composer, and remains a staunch champion especially of American composers. She is music director of the Buffalo Philharmonic and the Virginia Symphony, and also serves as principal guest conductor of the Brevard Music Center. She has won conducting awards and guest conducted orchestras too numerous to mention, and has served at institutions such as the National Council of the Arts.

Your interest in conducting began at a really early age. When and from whom did you learn the very basics of conducting?

I don't remember any one specific person. Most probably, my initial learning came simply from observing conductors, going to concerts, etc. This also gave me an early inspiration for the complete physical thrill of making music, for the force field of energy that conducting represented.

You credit Leonard Bernstein as one of your teachers. What about his conducting and mentoring impressed you the most?

Naturally, he was a huge celebrity, especially in New York City. When he visited with us at Juilliard, he was very kind to us conductors. I'm sure he realized we were terrified to have him observing us. But I learned that conducting is so much more than just the beat patterns. With Bernstein, it was always about the context of the music, not about the technique itself. His approach to conducting was all about the music's emotion and his own commitment to it. In turn, his podium presence was magnetic.

What are your memories from studying with these conductors?

Semyon Bychkov

Such a tremendous conductor! But his technique is uniquely his, and we as students looked quite silly if we tried to imitate him. He is a very physical conductor, and I believe his passion and musical impulses, his strength and naturalness on the podium, cause great success!

Sixten Ehrling

From Ehrling, I learned what it truly meant to study the score. Rather than worrying much about gestural technique, our seminars with him were spent going over a composition, measure-by-measure, and he would explain all his thoughts about what could go either right or wrong at every moment in the score.

Jorge Mester

Mester had a wonderful baton technique, but also a great sense of the psychology of conducting. Our lessons with him had to do with all the hard aspects of technique: tempo changes, using the right hand versus the left hand, managing the various elements of the orchestra and orchestration. He was also terrific at encouraging each one of us to be ourselves. If our nature was to be spiritual, or comedic, or whatever, then that's what we were to be on the podium. Don't pretend to be someone else, or what you're not.

What were some of the most valuable studies for you as an emerging conductor at both Mannes and Juilliard?

I really enjoyed all courses in musical analysis, score reading, music history. Also art history, world history, and literature. As a conductor, you have to be aware of your world.

Was there anything you learned the "hard" way that wasn't explained in your schooling?

In school, we never learned issues of leadership, or the psychology of conducting a large ensemble, or of running a rehearsal. When to push, when to back off, how to tune a chord, how to discipline. So much of this has to come just from observation and experience.

How would you describe your conducting style?

My style has become more and more flexible, and much less controlling. I like to let the orchestra inform the performance, because each orchestra is unique. So, I ask myself, how can I let this piece be this particular orchestra's rendition? I like to create a kind of framework that they move around.

How important is the baton to you? Do you ever abandon it, and if so, why?

Almost always, I'll use the baton with orchestra. Maybe in a choral passage, I'll abandon it, since many choruses are more accustomed to baton-less conducting. But being of somewhat shorter height, I also find the baton very helpful in extending my range of motion and being more present on the podium to the players.

How closely do you follow the textbook axiom that the right hand is for the time, the left hand for expression?

I don't follow this closely at all. Actually, the use of one hand over another often has to do with who's playing rather than anything particularly musical. For example, if the first violins are especially prominent, I might conduct primarily with my left hand just because it's closer to them.

What about your conducting has changed over the years?

I'm not thinking anymore about the beat patterns, but letting the music itself inform what my gestures will be. I'm much freer than I used to be, which allows me to keep my ears open and hearing the music more distinctly. And I now have much more faith in the orchestras I conduct, letting them inform the interpretation, too.

Do you have a method of score study for any new work that you generally follow?

Most importantly, I mark phrase lengths. Conductors have to know the trajectory of the piece and not get caught up only in the details. By marking phrase lengths, you can read and are guided by the big shapes, which is what the orchestra needs to see and feel from you. Each and every orchestra member is concerned with their own details, so it's essential you show them how those details fit into the big picture.

You have had tremendous success. Was there a price paid, or are there any regrets?

I have no regrets. I'm always looking forward, not back. And after time, one realizes that maybe the things that you were so disappointed in not getting or accomplishing years ago actually weren't meant to happen, that life has worked out okay. Sometimes, your advisors (agents) will say don't do such-and-such if you want a career, but I've found that I just want to conduct whenever I have the opportunity. So, whether it's *Scheherazade* with the students at Interlochen or a Bruckner symphony with a professional orchestra, I'm happy making music with them all.

Early on, or even now, *what struggles, if any, did you come across and have to overcome as a woman entering the field?*

I became aware of that issue eventually, but not at first. At first, I think I was just focused so much on my learning how to be a conductor that gender really wasn't a problem. Now, I think orchestras are realizing that times need to change, and that there's really no reason why there should *not* be women conductors.

It is obvious that you are devoted to performing and presenting new, American composers. What advice would you have to emerging conductors embarking on a career as to the merits of that, or any other commitment?

All styles, from a credible baroque style, to a romantic symphony, to contemporary extended techniques, to following a drummer in pop music makes being a conductor today very difficult. Back in the day, one could become a conductor with just the romantic symphony portion. So, finding a particular niche might be helpful. In my case, American composers is a category I truly believe in, and if anyone wishes to commit similarly, my advice is to pick two, three, or four composers to whom you're truly committed. Believe in them, support them, perform them, wherever you go.

What experiences have you had in working around tight budgets or dealing with other constraints?

Most emerging conductors will get started as an assistant conductor, which is a very difficult position. You have all the responsibility but none of the authority or power. You're conducting repertoire that you've never learned, that orchestras generally don't want to be doing because it's so often not focused on them but for entertainment or educational purposes. And doing this repertoire, you usually don't even have sufficient rehearsal time, other than to make sure it ultimately hangs together as an ensemble. Also, very difficult in these situations is knowing how to plan a rehearsal and having time for everything you need to do.

What are your thoughts about the relationship conductors must have with people in these positions?

Concertmaster

This relationship is very important. It must be a partnership, and it must be obvious to all that you and the concertmaster are in synch with each other. The concertmaster must maintain authority, so conductors should not get into micromanaging them, their bowings, or their sound. If there's a particular issue, it's best to speak one-on-one with the concertmaster during the break or outside the rehearsal to achieve agreement.

Executive Director

You must have a good relationship/partnership with your executive director [who is responsible for all non-artistic matters in an orchestra, and with whom conflicts often arise between artistic and financial concerns], who must be interested in, and willing to work with your vision. Not that you should expect to get everything you want immediately. The two of you must work together.

Marketing Department

The marketing department cannot be expected to know as much about the music as you do. It's your responsibility to work with them so that they understand at least the essence of the repertoire you're programming and why it's going to be interesting to ticket-buyers. They also need to understand when there is repertoire that is programmed for artistic growth purposes, not the bottom line.

Guest Conductors

When hiring guest conductors, get the best ones you can afford, and let them do the repertoire *they* are most excited about! It is most helpful to your orchestra to give them as many opportunities as possible to be as good as possible, no matter who's on the podium.

Personnel Manager

Your personnel manager is in a very difficult position, because s/he represents both the players and management (you). One cannot micromanage a personnel manager, so they may have the freedom to work with the various principals in the orchestra in determining substitute and extra musicians, leaves, medical excuses, etc. The musicians in the orchestra need to believe the personnel manager is on their side, but the conductor has the same need. This person must be very diplomatic, must be a people-person, and must have a sense of humor.

What are the differences in conducting a recording session that new-timers should be aware of in advance?

Recording sessions for me are very different, primarily because there's so much concern about the little specifics, the details that will get noticed by critical listeners. Also, there is a tendency to rehearse/record in smaller sections of pieces.

What would you say to the next generation of conductors to ALWAYS and NEVER do?

ALWAYS know the score, and study it even more. There's ALWAYS more to learn!
NEVER gloss over the score!
NEVER get into an us-versus-them podium attitude!
ALWAYS believe in making music together with fellow musicians.

43

Craig Jessop

Some will know Craig from his current work as dean at the Caine College of the Arts at Utah State University. Others will remember him from his years as conductor of the Mormon Tabernacle Choir. Still others will know him from his conducting the U.S. Air Force Singing Sergeants and being commander/ conductor of the U.S. Air Force Band in Europe and later of the Heartland of America Band of the Air Combat Command in America. I know Craig from his incredible background as a singer (member of the famed Robert Shaw Chorale), and from having collaborated with him in Omaha, Nebraska, where he prepared the chorus in my first-ever performance of Mahler's *Eighth Symphony.* Craig is an exceptional musician and amazingly pleasant gentleman, overflowing with integrity. I count our acquaintance and brief working relationship as sent from the angels. Today, you can find him in Utah but also often guest conducting at the Berkshire Choral Festival in Massachusetts.

When and from whom did you learn the basics of conducting, and what were those basics?

There was a woman named Ella Monn, who did a church choir, and whom I could not get enough of. Then, my junior high music teacher, Mr. Arn Olsen, who was an inspiration to me. He was pivotal in encouraging me to do music. Also, the director of choral activities at Utah State University, William Ramsey, heard me sing when I was only fourteen, and he said, "Young man, I think you've got quite a gift. Have you ever thought of private voice lessons?" I said, "I'd love to do that, but my family can't afford it." He said, "Can you mow a lawn?" "Yeah." "If you mow my lawn, I'll give you voice lessons."

He was such a pivotal person in my life. He directed my undergraduate work, he gave me my first conducting lessons, guiding and mentoring in all musical ways. I remained very close to him. He had gone to Columbia University and both sang in and became assistant to the Robert Shaw Collegiate Chorale. Not only that, he was an incredible singer, a superb clarinetist and string bassist, and he played marvelous piano. I still think he was one of the most talented people I've ever known. He had an incredible knowledge of repertoire and literature, and introduced me to the finest choral music on the planet. He opened the world of J.S. Bach to me, which to this day I cannot get enough of. And I say this as someone who grew up in a family of cowboys whose favorite singers were Patsy Kline and Hank Williams!

I had known of Robert Shaw. I had collected all of his recordings, but I had never had the chance to work with him. But when I was forty, I was introduced to him and ultimately became a member of the Robert Shaw Festival Singers and sang with him the last ten years of his life.

What of working with Robert Shaw was the most impactful to you?

The first thing that comes to mind was his holistic approach. Rather than just one thing, it was the synthesis of everything. It wasn't just the music he was doing, but he was able to contextualize the era, the time, the spirit, the philosophy behind the music. He loved texts, and he was able to read into text things that I never had considered, which affected the performance of the music. It wasn't just the dots on the printed page, but he would always use the scripture, "the word made flesh," the word being the spirit. He said our job was to make the flesh the word by taking the dots on the page and turning them into spirit—to go to that moment of creation when it was written down on the page and recreate that inspiration. That was our job, not to just give a bloodless reading of the notes.

Robert Shaw was a true genius in my life. I had never encountered anyone like him. There wasn't any area of human experience he wasn't familiar with. He had one foot in heaven and one in hell. I had never met a kinder or more refined gentleman. And for some reason, he was extremely kind to me. I'm looking at a note he wrote to me when I became conductor of the Tabernacle Choir—after having conducted the Air Force Band and Singing Sergeants—that I had framed, in which he said in 1995, "I always figured our country was a lot safer with you there, leading the band, but I must admit our nation's loss is heaven's gain. Keep them flying—angels, that is!" With him, I was allowed to see what a true master can achieve. We recorded the Frank Martin *Mass* for Telarc at the end of one of our summers in France. I have to tell you, that's when I say I've been to heaven. He opened a world of spirituality that I never experienced before or since.

In your own schooling, what non-conducting courses did you take that you have found to be most valuable later in life?

French, German—language study is really important, whether you're a singer or not. I loved my political science class and my history classes because you cannot isolate music from its time. Music is involved in living, breathing humans, and to have a knowledge of history and an appreciation for the whole human experience is important. I loved my English literature, and art appreciation classes, and I believe that a university experience is absolutely invaluable, which some conservatories lack.

As a trained singer, how did you garner knowledge of orchestral instruments?

In junior high, I played the bassoon, but I learned quickly you had to have a degree in plumbing just to put the instrument together, and I didn't particularly like knives! I barely passed my piano proficiency requirements. But my voice got me places and opened up doors. Bill Ramsey again, who was both a singer and an instrumentalist, did many orchestral and orchestral/choral things, so I grew up singing many of these pieces. That is how I knew this was what I wanted to do.

When I was at Merola in San Francisco with Kurt Herbert Adler, I knew pretty quickly that I did not want to be an opera singer. But Mr. Adler stated that he thought I was going to go in a different direction, which I took as a compliment, not a criticism. So even at that point, I knew that this was not the right place for me. But then, my DMA work at Stanford University was with Bill Ramsey, who himself had a degree in orchestral conducting. Every one of my doctoral projects was with orchestra, and I'm still very close to the Stanford program. Then later, I was conductor of the Air Force Singing Sergeants, which included preparing them for performances with Col. Arnold Gabriel and the Air Force Band. I got to work with many composers and arrangers for all combinations of instruments including string orchestra, which put me in a peer group that I never would have had in academia. Nothing prepared me more for the Tabernacle Choir—both musically and by making contacts in the business—better than the Air Force Band experience.

How expressive can conducting be?

There's no question that the gesture is important. But I also know that you can stand on the podium with your hands behind your back and make music just by your physical presence and your face. Conducting is all about expression, but what separates the greats from the not-so-greats is knowing when to get out of the way. Depending on the level of the ensemble you're facing, you may have to give them everything. But working with the Tabernacle Choir or the Singing Sergeants, I hardly had to do anything because the ensembles were already so tight. In fact, I've learned that orchestrally, less is more! These people know what they're doing; don't get in the way of their artistry. So, knowing when to insert yourself for a transition or for a bit of drama or a bit of mellowness is important, but unless your gesture can bring something in addition to what your artists are bringing, get out of the way! I think new conductors think they're responsible for everything, but the experienced, seasoned conductor views the instrumentalists as collaborators. You're not the boss! You're having a conversation in collaboration. When you can get the trust to the point they will allow that conversation, then the magic happens.

Do you always use a baton?

Generally, yes. That's how I was taught. Sometimes, maybe with an a cappella choral selection that's quite legato and flowing, I won't use a baton. But a baton gives me greater clarity and greater discipline.

Can a baton be expressive?

Because it *is* an extension of the arm, yes, it's expressive.

The elements of rhythm and tempo are so important. In so many pieces of music, there's a very narrow channel where the music works and the magic happens. If you find the groove, the channel, with the right musicians, the music can play itself, which for me then becomes three-dimensional.

Are there any differences between conducting choruses and orchestras?

Number 1 is text, number 2 is balances. Otherwise, notes are notes, and music is music! I think you do the singers a huge disservice if you don't treat them as professionally as you do instrumentalists. Col. Arnold Gabriel always started his Air Force Band rehearsals by singing chorales, which I continued. Their intonation and ensemble improved, and especially their expressiveness improved. You have to agree that the first art is the human voice and that all the great soloists try to create the same kind of expressiveness that a singer would do.

How is your own conducting technique any different when conducting chorus, band, or orchestra?

I don't think there is any difference. Expressivity is expressivity, no matter the ensemble. Strings have bowings, winds have tonguings, and singers have language, but I don't treat them any differently. Because singers generally don't have rhythm, Shaw developed count-singing, which I also used for the Tabernacle Choir. But you have to be willing to take the time to train, to discipline, and just insist on it.

How has your own conducting style changed over the years?

I think I've learned the value of less is more, and again, learning when to get out of the way. Speaking of choruses, if you can build a really strong rhythmic center to that chorus, you can glide instead of having to constantly "whip" them. You can float on top of their energy.

Do you have a specific method for studying a composition for the first time?

I always look to the score and do an architectural draft. I want to see the structure. Is it 8+8, or 32+32, or 7+3? I want to know how it's structured together, and I want to know where the big sections are. If it's a choral piece, I always do a very strong textural analysis, because that's what inspired the composer. How then does the music relate to the text? Then I'll look at the composer's markings—tempo, dynamics, wind articulations, bowings—and text annotations like final consonants. Next I'll look at balances (which I got from Shaw who in turn got it from George Szell), especially between chorus and orchestra, making adjustments wherever necessary.

How do you mark a score?

I'm a fan of Margaret Hillis' color-coding method. I use pencils—green, red, blue, and normal black. Reds and blues primarily have to do with dynamics, red (hot) for crescendo and blue (cold) for diminuendo. Green is primarily for cueing, mostly for solos and singers. And the normal pencil marks tempos, meters, and metronome markings. I also will give bracket marks indicating phrase lengths, conducting meters (2+3, etc.). If I have mixed meters, I'll either literally write 2+3, or a vertical line (2) and a small triangle (3).

Your first job ever was as a high school director. What did you think then were your top priorities as a conductor?

I don't think I've changed at all! My fire for the love of this art form burned bright then and burns bright now. Because of Bill Ramsey, and the incredible training experience I had, I was concerned then about being faithful to the composer, honoring the work of the composer, trying to make sure my ego would never eclipse the composer and the music they had written. To try and create a performance that would reflect as close as possible what had inspired the composer. I felt it then; I feel it now. I think it was because of Bill Ramsey that I had that philosophy. I know he set me on a rock-solid foundation.

Also, I've always loved people, and I never forget that people make it possible for conductors to have a job. Relationships have always meant everything to me, and while that has nothing to do with pitch and rhythm, it has everything to do with performance.

I think my difficulties were insecurities and being intimidated, particularly by instrumentalists. I never felt intimidated by singers because frankly, I was a good singer. But as a musician, I knew I had gaps that I really was self-conscious about. Robert Shaw was good for me because I think he had those same kind of insecurities. He couldn't play the piano very well; he didn't play an instrument, but had an insatiable passion for this art form. He was a workaholic, and just over-compensated by knowing the score better than anybody I've ever known.

In devising any concert program, what are your overarching guidelines?

Col. Gabriel was a master programmer for the Air Force Band. He had a big influence on me, too, because the Air Force Band had to play *for the people.* And generally, these were not the people you'd normally find in symphony orchestra concerts. But Gabriel also wanted integrity. He would open with a march or overture really accessible to everyone. Then he would do the most challenging piece for the band or orchestra right up front, followed by another march, a soloist, and end the first half with another very substantial piece of music. First half was never longer than fifty minutes. Second half, which was show biz (Singing Sergeants, etc.), was always 45 minutes, closing with the obligatory patriotic section and the Air Force song. From his programming, I saw the value of arc-and-flow and of knowing the audience.

At the Tabernacle Choir, we were responsible for 28'30" of music in each of the *Music and the Spoken Word* performances. Generally, the broadcasters would not like anything longer than 4 minutes, so our philosophy there was to do something old, something new, something borrowed, something blue. There always had to be a standard hymn, a folk-song, a choral masterwork, an organ solo, and maybe something lighter like a Broadway tune. Beyond that, I would look for the emotional contour and key relationships. It would be mind-numbing, for instance, to have three pieces in a row all in the same key. You know how you can feel an audience behind you. You don't even have to look at them; you can feel what's going on with them.

Generally, I've tried to manage the emotional flow, to put the most challenging thing up front, and the last thing the audience hears is something absolutely inspirational in some way.

What advice to emerging conductors do you have in terms of their future careers and how they may experience unexpected twists and turns?

It's real life! In my case, the doctoral degree became helpful, and for everyone an advanced degree can help open some doors, especially into teaching. But keep relationships in mind. It's very simple: good relationships are better than bad relationships. Also, never burn any bridges.

To emerging conductors, what would you advise they be sure to ALWAYS and NEVER do?

ALWAYS (1) master the piano, so you can be totally independent in your score study and preparation, soloist coachings; (2) if you want to conduct, go observe and work with the very best in the world.

NEVER think you're better than anyone else or that the music is for your own glory or ego.

44

Jonathan McPhee

Jonathan is actively conducting various organizations in New England. Most significant, however, is his work in the field of ballet. He's recently concluded an almost thirty-year stint as music director of the Boston Ballet, a remarkable feat considering that organization's significant season of productions. He's produced recordings with that orchestra; he has published arrangements for smaller orchestra of standard large-orchestra ballet scores (e.g., Stravinsky's *Rite of Spring*), and he continues guest conducting important ballet companies around the world. Additionally, he has enjoyed great success conducting orchestras on the stage, including all manner of productions of musical theater, operetta, pops, and classical concerts. He continues as music director of the Lexington Symphony in Massachusetts, an organization that he has built significantly both in terms of music-making and audience development. As an oboist and budding conductor, Jonathan had the great privilege of studying both at London's Royal Academy as well as the Juilliard School in New York. He has a remarkable entrepreneurial spirit and serves music and the field of conducting by being extremely active in myriad ways.

Who or what inspired you to begin the study of conducting, and what were the circumstances?

When I was in first grade, I attended a school assembly to watch a visiting orchestra (it was probably a college orchestra) do a Christmas concert. I was completely enthralled by the fact that the person conducting was thinking the music and the musicians were playing what he was thinking. It was the communication aspect that made me decide this is what I wanted to do. I remember coming home and telling my parents about what I had experienced and announcing that I was going to be a conductor. From that day on, I started to examine what skill sets I needed to develop and to prepare.

Do you have an early mentor you'd like to acknowledge, and what about that teacher was important for you?

I had many people who helped me at the right time, as an oboist, then as a conductor, starting with my school music teachers. My move to London, England at the age of twelve, was the most important step. When I graduated high school in London early, I was accepted into the Royal Academy of Music at age sixteen. My guiding force was the oboist Leonard Brain, older brother of the famous horn player, Dennis. Leonard played oboe and English horn in the Royal Philharmonic Orchestra and introduced me to Music Director Rudolf Kempe (who also had been an oboist). Both shaped my style as a conductor and musician and opened a world of learning opportunities for me.

Was there anything about your conducting career you feel you learned the "hard" way, that your schooling didn't provide?

I could spend an hour on this question: "What I never learned at Juilliard." I was very lucky after graduating from Juilliard. I was almost immediately thrust into the ballet world with relationships with Martha Graham, Mr. Balanchine, and Robert Joffrey. I learned how to build and manage music budgets, negotiate performance rights, research music that was nearly impossible to find, work within the confines of a Collective Bargaining Agreement (CBA) with the musicians' union, learn how to work in a theater environment with several different unions (basically what you can touch and what you cannot touch); that's a starter list. Mr. Joffrey taught me how to speak with donors and serve as a representative for the company. To put it another way, school teaches you how to play your instrument and hopefully how to play as a musician with other musicians. Everything else you actually need to build a career and survive, including entrepreneurship, you have to learn the day you walk off the stage after receiving your degree.

What is your general process of score study, when studying a work new to you?

Break it down in phrases, then build it up in sections, then movements. Analyze. Find out as much as you can about the composer, other works by the composer, how the piece relates to its time and place (context), then stand back and try to see the big picture.

What are some of the specific markings you need to make in your ballet scores based on the choreography you're dealing with?

In addition to my normal musical markings that any conductor would have in their orchestral score relating to the music and musical structure, I have production marks (stage cues, cues I give dancers or production staff, cues dancers give me, light and curtain cues, etc.). I also have quite a bit of choreography marked in my score. I try to learn as much of the choreography as I can. What is incredibly important is to understand how the movements relate to the music, style, tempo, character, etc. (This is done by observing ballet masters and/or choreographers working with the dancers in rehearsals.) You will always find "reminder clues" that I write in my scores about all of these things.

What are some of the most basic differences between in-the-pit-ballet and on-stage-orchestral conducting, in terms of specific technical, musical, or leadership approaches?

Pit work—whether it is opera or ballet—requires the highest level of multitasking. The conductor must be aware of not only the musical performance he/she is shaping in real time, but of what is happening in terms of production activity (sets, scenery, exits, and entrances on stage), the needs of the singers on stage or dancers if it is a ballet, and always, the needs of the orchestra in the pit. Often, conditions in the pit are a concern: low light, weird configurations of the orchestra setup, etc. Technical clarity by the conductor in communication with the orchestra is essential to allow them to relax and do their job. The rehearsal schedule is often minimal due to the overall expense of running a large operation like a ballet company or opera. There is also usually a large volume of music that must be covered in that limited rehearsal time, as opposed to a standard orchestra concert program.

What is a normal rehearsal sequence (from piano to orchestra to dress) for a ballet production, and what expectations are there of the conductor?

1. Ensure that the music for a production can be obtained, rights cleared, and annotated piano rehearsal materials obtained.
2. Once the ballet masters have taught the choreography to dancers to allow for large sections to be put together, the conductor attends the piano rehearsals and shapes the music to ensure that the technical constraints required for the choreography and dancers make musical sense. This is truly a collaborative phase that requires insight and patience by all.
3. Orchestra alone rehearsals to prepare the musicians.
4. Technical rehearsals with conductor and piano to work out the production aspects on stage.
5. Dress rehearsal with conductor, orchestra, and full company in costume with scenery and lights.

In ballet, when do you need to have the dancers watch you?

Most dancers learn early that having an eye on the conductor can be a great help. A conductor's upbeat preparation is virtually the same as a dancer's "*and*," which is a verbal preparation before a movement. If in doubt, when they see the conductor's arm go up, they know where the downbeat is going to be. Mr. Balanchine frequently built in cues that the conductor gives to the dancers on stage. Cues go both ways. Conversely, the conductor has to be just as aware of the dancers on stage as any of the musicians playing in the pit.

In ballet, how much say do you really have in terms of tempo? And are there other areas of discussion the conductor might have with the choreographer/ballet master?

This is a very complex issue that I have spent whole interviews trying to crack for people. Conducting for ballet is not just about tempo. Rather than giving this an honest answer, people tend to give a flippant answer, like, "There are only two tempi in ballet: too fast and too slow." That infuriates me, because that is the mark of someone who doesn't understand, and cares even less, about the entire art form. To be a successful conductor for ballet, one needs to have impeccable skills as an orchestral conductor. Beyond that, one needs to have respect for what the choreographer and dancer brings to the music, and then collaborate with all of those artists so that together you can shape a valid musical performance that allows the composer's intent to shine through the art of the choreographer and artistry of the dancer. And you need patience.

How does the role of music director differ in the ballet world from that of a symphony orchestra?

The music director in a ballet company spends much of their time as a member of the senior staff managing the entire music budget, heading off potential problems that involve the music in ballet productions, and serving as an artistic advisor to choreographers, dancers, and artistic directors. In addition, they frequently monitor or negotiate rental and royalty agreements as well as grand rights for music used in stage performances. Sometimes, there are new commissions that involve the music director in the selection of composers and working with the composers. There are all of the other normal responsibilities that go into running an orchestra, such as doing substitute auditions, auditions for permanent positions in the orchestra, advocating for the musicians within the ballet company structure where needed, improvements in working conditions, applying the terms of the collective bargaining agreement to day-to-day operations, dealing with personnel issues, and managing the library staff and rehearsal pianists for the company. The music director guides sound issues in the theater especially if they involve recorded music or if you are in a theater that needs to have sound reinforcement. The music director is the musical voice for the organization, which means working and collaborating with the various departments such as development, marketing, public relations, and the educational wing and volunteer organizations. One of the most important aspects of the job is also working closely with the production department for scheduling and artistic coordination on everything from events to rehearsals and performances in the theater.

Any final word of advice?

Final thoughts: being a conductor is not about power. If you think that it is, you need to change fields now. The orchestra is the most complex and expensive instrument you will ever have the pleasure of playing. It is a living, breathing organism made of individuals. Each of them brings their collective history, strengths, and weaknesses. Together, they create or recreate something that is impossible for anyone to do on their own. Your job is to allow the creative genius of the composer and choreographer to live through the environment you shape for the individuals in the orchestra and dancers, and to touch an audience in ways that will live within them forever.

What would you advise young conductors to ALWAYS do, and NEVER do?

ALWAYS be prepared, be respectful, be honest.

NEVER think it is all about you. It isn't!

45

John Morris Russell

John Morris Russell has the unique privilege and opportunity to follow Erich Kunzel's footsteps in continuing to serve American music in all forms for all audiences as conductor of the Cincinnati Pops. Native Ohioan John rose through the ranks in the Cincinnati Symphony as the best possible person to lead this outstanding performing and recording orchestra, while also maintaining his hand in classical symphonic music as well. I was especially interested in hearing how he and the Windsor Symphony made lemonade out of the 2008 financial collapse of a lemon, as that is an important lesson for us all. John has done amazing work with Cincinnati Pops and often conducts at the Hollywood Bowl, the New York Philharmonic, and other orchestras such as those in Vancouver, Buffalo, and Cleveland. His energy is palpable, and his audiences truly enjoy his music-making and energy.

When and from whom did you first learn the very basics of conducting?

I grew up in suburban Cleveland, in a family where everyone was expected to learn a musical instrument. I don't know where it came from, but in my home there was a little book entitled *The Technique of Conducting*. And as a kid, we'd go to Cleveland Orchestra concerts all the time (my very first concert was attending the Cleveland Orchestra, with George Szell conducting the Dvořák Eighth Symphony). Boy, this is good, I thought! And I remember looking at the book at home, mindful of George Szell, and thinking, this might be fun. But I didn't really think about conducting seriously until college. I was a trumpet player, a total band geek (concert, jazz, pep, garage–you name it!). But I started developing some physical issues with the playing that made me aware that even if I wanted to make a career playing the trumpet, it just wasn't going to happen. That's when I thought maybe I should try this conducting thing.

Even in my brass ensemble days, I was the one who would take the lead at getting the ensemble to begin, going, "1-2-3-breathe! and go." So, I quickly learned what we try to teach emerging conductors today, that it's so easy if you just breathe! It was so natural as a wind player for me not to have those problems of having an ensemble begin a passage. Then, I realized that if I was going to go into conducting, I'd better learn how string instruments work, so I took Suzuki violin lessons. What I found when I first picked up the instrument was not knowing what to do when I got to the end of the bow—I'd be gasping for breath. And the teacher said, no, just move your arm back the other way and you don't have to breathe or anything. But I was breathing with each bow!

On the podium today, is there anything you do that specifically reminds you of your past mentors?

Charles Bruck, successor to the Pierre Monteux School for conductors, would have some principles that would get drilled into us students. The first example is: ONE is DOWN! Also: CLARITY is EVERYTHING! And: BREATHE! That was the Bible for us! The whole Charles Bruck approach was that you physically sing the music inside of you, and your body takes over for you. Therefore, you don't need to manipulate or maneuver by consciously moving one way or another.

I used to attend conducting workshops sponsored by the American Symphony Orchestra League (now League of American Orchestras), and I would be so overwhelmed. Soon, I realized that a large percentage of what was "taught" in any given workshop was just hubris, but that there was always going to be at least 15 percent of stuff you could rely on. So, for me, weeding out the crap from the really important lessons was relevant to what I needed to know. Every conductor is so individual, you have to become a really good filter to know and recognize the stuff that's not you.

In school, what were some of the non-conducting courses you took that have been most valuable to your conducting career?

Going to a small liberal arts college—as I did—is not the way one would think of doing to pursue a conducting career. And for years, I'd kick myself wondering why I didn't get my act together and apply to a conservatory. But as my career has progressed, the fact that I didn't go to conservatory for my undergraduate degree has been really important to the longevity of my career. From political science to art history to learning how to write and express oneself—all these courses have found their way into my work regularly. You have to interface with so many different types of people (musicians, junior and senior staff members, stagehands, even custodial crew, board members, patrons), and you have to be able to speak and appreciate where they're coming from and what they're bringing to this entire *Philharmonic* family. So, I can't stress enough the advantage of a wide swath of knowledge.

Speaking of relating to all those different folks, how did you learn the ropes?

I think it was just my upbringing. My dad was very influential, saying you must always treat everybody with the utmost respect. That was also part of the whole Pierre Monteux/Charles Bruck experience, too: "Your musicians are not just cogs in the wheel" (No. 12 of "The List"). As associate conductor of the

Cincinnati Symphony and for ten years with the Cincinnati Pops, every year we would have a student conductor from the College Conservatory of Music as a conducting assistant—a different one each year—and at the end of the year, I'd always give them the list of Pierre Monteux's rules for conductors. We called it "The List," and it was tradition to always talk about and refer to it.

Also, my teacher at University of Southern California, Daniel Lewis, used to say to us, "Damn it, it's a *we* thing!" And, "It's not what you want; it's what the music wants!" Adding to that, I would say it's not even what the composer wants; it's what the music wants. You know, sometimes you have composers who aren't able to express certain things, and you just know that their music is urging you to go a certain way to make it happen.

Is there anything you did not study in school that you now wish you had?

I would have wanted to jump in and learn more repertoire. At Pierre Monteux, we'd have these mammoth repertoire lists. You wouldn't know what you were going to conduct week to week, so every conductor had to have every single piece of repertoire ready. And when you get your first gig as an assistant at a symphony, you're just buying tons of scores and trying to learn them all; get all the Brahms symphonies, all the Beethoven symphonies, the last three Tchaikovskys, and all the Schumanns….and constantly digest all of them. You learn a work for the first time and congratulate yourself for doing it. Then you do it a second time, and you begin to understand what you didn't know before, and you do it a third time and you think, well, okay, maybe I have a clue with this piece. By the fifth, sixth, eighth, or ninth time, you realize you're really—finally!—doing it!

I should add here, speaking of the Monteux experience. Every year, they would do a final concert, almost a marathon in length. Every student conductor would do their piece, which were things like selections from Broadway musicals and waltzes. And Charles Bruck used to say that those pieces were like a conductor's etude. It's so fantastic with that repertoire, because in like ten minutes' time, you'll have maybe ten different tempo changes and a half dozen different meters, and each one has to flow seamlessly into the next. It's like an etude of transitions. It's the transitions where you earn your money, so to speak. So, once you establish the groove, then you can let the orchestra off on its own.

Do you always use a baton, and if not, why not and under what circumstances?

That's another Pierre Monteux thing: always use a baton! I find that with big orchestras, it's important for everyone to see what you're doing. But if I'm with the Hilton Head Symphony or Windsor Symphony when doing a Haydn symphony, I don't use it, because we're so closely packed together. I'm not so tied into doing one thing or another that I'm going to plan it out. If I'm not getting enough lyricism, for instance, I might try doing something else with or without the baton. Sometimes, even in rehearsal, you might put down the baton because you want to get a certain type of sound from the people around you.

Is your conducting approach any different in the recording studio?

When you're in the recording studio, it's not just you. You have a fantastic team around you: your producer (in the conducting profession, surround yourself with really good people!) should be like your best friend ever. When conducting in the studio, it'll kill you if you're over-thinking about all the little details, because it's your producer and your assistant in the booth who should be taking care of all those details. The conductor needs to be thinking about the overall scope, the flow, and the groove of things. And it's very important that with your very presence, you are making your musicians feel relaxed so they can do their best job.

How has your conducting technique or style changed since your earliest career days?

Well, in the early days, you're really into the music and you jump around a lot, but eventually you find yourself conducting less and putting more into less! The older I get, the more spare I am, and the more you know the repertoire, the more you can internalize the music and not have to show absolutely everything. So, you learn to trust your colleagues, and you know exactly what they need as well as what they don't need. You can save your grand gestures for the places where they're needed without having to spin your wheels the rest of the time.

Any basic guiding principles in developing programs for youth audiences?

1. Give them the good stuff. Beethoven, Tchaikovsky, Ellington, in not long excerpts, but good stuff!
2. Keep it upbeat. When talking, try to express as much as you can in as few words as possible. Give them just enough to hang their ears on.
3. You get so little rehearsal for these things, so it must be easy enough for the musicians to play well. Include some gnarly sections for yourself so that you can have the practice of conducting over and over again during the course of a week's worth of shows.
4. Make the extra audio-visual spectacles the exception, not the rule. If a kid's first experience is in a concert with dance or film, etc., then they're always going to expect that same level of stimulation. At a certain point, you have to engage their minds and imaginations, which can be done only by concentrating on listening.

Do you have a normal process for studying a score new to you?

Even before programming a piece, I'll already know it in some way, either from hearing a performance or recording of it. If a recording, I'll find as many recordings as I can just to hear what other people do. But at a certain time, then it's no recording, and I start listening to it in my own head. Often, I'll first look for the big phrases, learning it phrase by phrase, then putting the pieces back together. I like to sing it, finding where the melody is, progressing to bass line to rhythmic underpinning to countermelodies. Overall, starting with the broad approach, gradually working details, then putting it all back together again, back to broad!

What kinds of constraints have you been presented with, and how did you deal with them?

At the Windsor Symphony (a very small orchestra), in the financial collapse of 2008, we were decimated in terms of donor base and subscriptions. It was really tough, so I had to use a smaller and smaller orchestra. But it occurred to me that we were perfectly situated to do Haydn symphonies, and over my tenure there, we must have performed almost a third of all of them. After a while, we kicked Haydn ass! It was so much fun! The musicians loved it; we could do them inexpensively; we could explore them deeply musically. The fact that we had financial constraints gave us a real solid frame within which we could be totally creative. But being faced with having a small orchestra also meant that we could play in a lot of smaller venues, too, so we took the orchestra and went out there into the community. That allowed us to accompany a local arts school chorus or a French community choir, for instance. We didn't consider the situation a problem, but rather a challenge to which we had to find a creative solution that will further our goals and keep us moving forward.

What should the next generation of conductors know regarding leadership of an ensemble?

Be aware of the *Now*, but also aware of the *Past.* It's like knowing the works of the Past and their context so well, so you can make them relevant to the Now. That means you have to be *in* the Now, so you can make this repertoire speak to a generation that's hooked on YouTube and Instagram.

What are some of the chief responsibilities for today's music directors?

Remember that you're energizing lots of different people. Not just musicians, but your staff, your board, and patrons, to get them energized through music. And your programming shouldn't even be just year-to-year, but over a big chunk of time. You need to know what that story is over time but also how you're going to build your orchestra technically and musically. Find the right piece for your orchestra at the right time in its trajectory. Also, wherever you are, celebrate what's local—culture, artists, ideas, and themes.

Who do you depend on as colleagues other than the orchestra musicians?

My most important colleague is my wife! When we were new in Cincinnati, no one in the public knew who she was, so at my concerts she'd slip into the bathroom at intermission to hear the comments of the audience! Seriously, in Cincinnati, I bump into people around town, and I always ask them what they liked and didn't like about their experience at the Pops.

Personnel and operations managers and especially Librarians must be among your closest colleagues. And there will always be orchestra members who will be honest and give you the straight dope.

As far as executive directors are concerned, the role of that position is so much about bringing in the money these days, that the conductor needs to know what kind of programming will help the executive director do *his or her job*, or what will help the orchestra attain its goals.

What basic advice do you have for an aspiring conductor wanting to get into pops conducting?

There are those who say, you don't pick your career—your career picks you. Today, there are so many different types of ensembles needing leadership, that at a certain point in time, every emerging conductor needs to ask themselves what they want to do. Do they want the experience of being on stage in a tuxedo and getting adulation for doing a Mahler symphony, or do they just want to be around people and make them play better and help them play music together, more effectively, creating wonderful and unique experiences? It doesn't really matter what level you're at. For instance, if you've got an elementary school and you've got those kids fired up, what a great thrill that is! Everything today is so compartmentalized, and there's this feeling that you have to do this, that, and the other, but it's really just about making people play great together. Over time, one discovers that there's a certain calling, and that's where you go. You learn to love it and embrace it because it is so amazing that any of us has this opportunity to do what we're doing.

Emerging conductors should expect to become very familiar with the canon of the Great American Songbook—that's the foundation for pops, because the songbook has tunes in practically every style. There's a whole lot of American musical styles, and you have to know what they are—ragtime, big band swing compared to a 1920s swing, compared to Texas swing, a bluegrass lilt, or country-western, jazz, blues, Broadway, and all their sub-genres. They all have their own style, and you have to immerse yourself in those styles. American conductors? Know your music! Know your bebop artists, your early Dixieland pioneers, your great jazz vocalists, the great songwriters, and their great interpreters. This is our music!

What should emerging conductors ALWAYS and NEVER do?

ALWAYS be super-prepared; be super-grateful! Be appreciative and grateful to your orchestra, to your board, your staff members, and to the composers whom you are serving. Be humble! We are in service to the music.

NEVER: It's never about me, always about *we*.

46

Yohei Sato

My first acquaintance with Yohei Sato was a number of years ago at the Boston Conservatory, where I had been recently appointed as director of orchestral activities. Yohei had been an instrumental undergraduate major, and requested that I take him on as a graduate conducting major in the program we had just initiated at the Conservatory. I agreed. Yohei became my first-ever conducting graduate, and has continued an amazing and successful string of entrepreneurial conducting and teaching projects. Furthermore, in this series of interviews, he represents a younger generation of musicians who pursue new, non-traditional career paths. For that very reason, Yohei's work putting on a charity concert for orphans from the recent Japanese Tohoku earthquake disaster—not in Japan, but in the Czech Republic!—I find very impressive. Additionally, Yohei believes so much in music education as well that he founded the still-continuing Youth & Muse international summer music festival based in both Boston and Chichibu, Japan. Most of my interview with Yohei, however, focused on the conductor's role in conducting for video games—an art form that's becoming ever more popular around the world.

With any of your conducting activity, what did you learn the "hard" way?

How to make connections, how to get an audition, how to develop professional skills to help open doors for my career.

Given all your successes to date, is there any aspect of your conducting activity that you wish you had been trained for in advance?

If I had had the chance to go to Symphony Hall, I would have gone to more rehearsals. You can learn so much just observing other orchestras and conductors.

What are the basics of conducting video game orchestras?

It's very similar to film, actually. Sometimes, we use a screen, sometimes not. Basically, the audience already knows the music so well, and I have to know the scene, or story line.

How do you learn the scene, or the music, in advance?

Sometimes, I go to YouTube, to see if someone is playing the game. But also, some video game music is old video game music that I had never played, but always knew from childhood. When I was younger, I would maybe go to a friend's house who was playing the game, or, at home we had many arcades, and it's very easy to pick up the music from those places. And usually, a video game score is the same format as any other piece. But sometimes, you have a rock band in the ensemble, and their music is generally not included in the score, except maybe with a basic cue line.

Who follows whom when you have a rock band?

If there is a drum, the drummer and I must always be connecting with each other. If there is no drum, then I conduct the same as I would any regular orchestral concert.

What does a normal rehearsal sequence look like?

Normally, two rehearsals plus dress rehearsal, and it's done. It's much easier to play together than, say, classical music, and usually, the players for video game are very good, so I can do more running through the repertoire. The first rehearsal usually is orchestra only, not including rock band, which has their own rehearsal before we put it together. Second rehearsal, it all comes together, with the rock band. Dress rehearsal, we add the screen.

What does a video game orchestra performance look like?

The performance usually has no intermission (maybe ninety minutes, total), and with various combinations of medleys. There can be anywhere from half-a-dozen to a dozen different pieces in the program, including a wide variety of games from earliest historical ones to very contemporary. Much of the music is complicated with mixed meters and changes of tempo.

What do you like most about performing video game music?

The audience is very different, often all standing, and when I play a melody that they recognize, many will shout their enthusiasm, much like a rock concert or an orchestral pops concert. It's exciting!

Since much video game music is contemporary, are you dealing much with composers as well?

Composers will come sometimes to rehearsal or the concert. Basically, they care more about tempo than anything else, because they're secure in their interpretation of what they composed.

Are you the center of attention at a video game concert?

No, it's either the screen, or the rock band, or the people who have solo parts.

Besides conducting, what other skills does a video game orchestra conductor need?

A good sense of entertainment. Also, going with the flow—sometimes, I can't even hear the orchestra, if the audience is responding so loud, and yet the music is continuing. And you must also be in the same mental groove as the creator.

Who else is involved?

There is usually a team of about half a dozen people: the producer, the sound engineer, the screen production team, and conductor usually travel as an entire team to produce the video game orchestra concert.

What is the most basic difference between conducting for video games and concert orchestra?

Basically, a video game is more entertainment. I have to show I am in the spirit of video game and enjoying the music. Also, I usually conduct with larger and less subtle gestures, with entertainment in mind. Game music concerts can have medleys for one game that consist of twenty or thirty different tunes or sections, with some extended or repeated according to the composer/arranger. So, there are many tempo and quality changes throughout. Because we play arrangements, I don't have to think much about tone color, as I would in classical music, because we can always adjust the arrangement itself. We also always have our sound amplified, so I don't have to think much about volume or dynamic variations. That's being taken care of by the sound engineer (who is the boss!).

So, how much musical freedom do you have when so many other people are involved?

I really care very much about the phrasing! The sound engineer doesn't change the balance so much; I change the balance, then the sound engineer can amplify as he wishes for the audience to hear. And while there is less responsibility involved with what I do, more than elsewhere, I have to rely on other people to do their job equally well.

How would you advise emerging conductors who want to enter the video game music field?

Most video game conductors today come from the pops field or maybe Hollywood studios. There is usually no click track to follow, so the conductor must know the tempos. Click tracks are starting to be used more often, so all players will follow the click-track to synch with the screen. That's more comfortable and normal for Hollywood conductors and musicians.

What advice do you have for the emerging conductor?

It is important that emerging conductors pay attention to learning the basic skills from their teacher while they're together. If you want to change anything to make it more "your" style, you have plenty of time to do that later! And most important as a beginning, you have to develop a very clear beat, and it has to look natural because it has to be *in* and *from* the music. The basic patterns have to be digested, so you can concentrate on the music.

Many emerging conductors these days don't have a job. Most everything I've done, I created on my own. When graduating from school, you risk losing all your connections and have to deal with a new teacher at the same time! After graduation, it would be helpful to have another year or two to learn professional skills and how to build a résumé.

The bottom line is, I just want to make music with my friends. This is very important for me, so any new idea I come up with is all about making connections. Networking and connecting with friends, teachers, conductors, and musicians is very helpful.

What would you advise emerging conductors should ALWAYS do and NEVER do?

ALWAYS remain confident, and ALWAYS study the score!
ALWAYS be mindful of time management, especially in rehearsal.
ALWAYS be respectful and nice with your colleagues, especially if you're also the one contracting them for your own projects!
NEVER imitate someone else, but be yourself!

47

Lalo Schifrin

Lalo Schifrin and I had a really stimulating conversation about conducting and his career in general. Often described as a Renaissance man, Lalo is a pianist, composer, and conductor, and he is very much at home performing and composing in all kinds of jazz, symphonic, and classical styles. Certainly, everyone knows him for having composed the theme to *Mission: Impossible*, but his career incredibly spans so many more experiences and successes. He's received a lifetime achievement award, has had a documentary film of his career produced, recorded a four-CD box *Lalo Schifrin: My Life in Music*, authored the book *Music Composition for Film and Television* (Berklee Press), and had a biography released recently. Whether he's composing a banjo or tuba concerto; performing jazz with orchestra, at the piano, on the podium; or scoring works for film and television, Lalo has done it all—not just well, but superbly. Speaking with him, I was in the presence of a man who—from his childhood days in Argentina, to his schooling at the Paris Conservatory, to his home in Los Angeles—has done and seen it all. The world of music is better for having Lalo's creativity and inventiveness amongst us.

From whom did you learn the basics of conducting, and what was it you learned?

My father was concertmaster of Buenos Aires Philharmonic Orchestra, and he would take me to rehearsals. I even met Arturo Toscanini there. There were three seasons there—one for symphony, one for ballet, one for opera. We lived very close to the theater, the Teatro Colón, and by attending, I realized music was not a joke if you wanted to become a professional.

I began musical study on the piano at the age of five, and my teacher was a friend of my father's, Enrique Barenboim, father of the conductor Daniel Barenboim. Music was the only atmosphere in the house. My father the violinist, his brother the cellist, and there was yet another brother, who also played violin. In addition, my mother had two brothers who also played, one on oboe and the other on violin. You can see, I didn't hear anything but music, so it was impossible to continue with any other profession, as everyone in my family was a musician.

Conducting for me came much later, but also in Buenos Aires, because I started to write music—chamber music and some piano solos with the accompaniment of a few instruments. One of my father's friends said, "How are we going to have this performed?" And he told me, "You have to try to conduct this, otherwise you are going to be in trouble."

There was a very good conductor, Mariano Drago, who trained the orchestra for the ballet or opera. He was amazing. He came from Yugoslavia, sometime maybe at the end of the nineteenth century. He knew a lot about conducting, and was more a teacher than a professional conductor, as he chose a career of preparing and training orchestras. So, without a printed book, he showed me all the indications of how to start, how to end, where to place the downbeat, the cutoffs, and all the other gestures.

Conducting is all about communication. Your talking—your communication—is all done with the gestures. The reason for this, of course, is to communicate to the orchestra what they have to do. So, not only the beginning and the ending together, but all the things in between (like ***sfz***, ***p***, *sub*.***f***, rallentando, accelerando), you learn because they are all gestures you must know. Whether with or without a baton, it is very important that the orchestra knows where all these things are.

Did you have other mentors besides Mr. Barenboim and Mr. Drago?

Of course, I was able to observe and admire so many great conductors who came to Buenos Aires. Maestros like Toscanini and Fritz Reiner. One who I really liked the most was Pierre Boulez. I attended a concert of his in New York City some time later, and I told him I knew he was a great composer but didn't know he was a great conductor, too. He said, "I only conduct in self-defense." His conducting was so clear—without a baton. He would conduct the most complex music (like Messiaen or Berio) from memory. But Boulez didn't interpret; he conducted the music as written.

Can you recall having learned anything about conducting on your own, the "hard" way?

Everything! For instance, if you want to be a medical doctor, you go to school and do your autopsies, but that doesn't mean you're a good doctor.

Do you always use a baton?

The baton is an extension of the arm. When the orchestra or choir is too large, they have to look at it. It's not an issue of ego, or it's not to show how macho you are. It's an extension of the hands used to communicate to the orchestra how to play.

Is the actual act of conducting different when on stage as opposed to a recording studio?

On the concert stage, conducting is not a question of ego, but rather a question of theatricality. In the recording, you don't need the gestures for creating theatricality. You do need the basic correct gestures, as I learned from Mariano Drago.

In your career, you have accomplished so much so far, but is there anything more you still want to do?

Thank you for saying I have accomplished much, but I don't think I've accomplished anything. Because, the more I'm doing, the more I realize how much I still have to do. And I'm doing it. I'm still composing, and I still practice piano.

For instance, I have just written a tuba concerto for Gene Pokorny, the tubist of the Chicago Symphony. Riccardo Muti has seen the score and wants to do it, but unfortunately, not until four years from now. Also, the Yamaha Foundation has commissioned me to write one hour of solo piano music for pianist Mirian Conti. The recording of that will be out very soon. And in France, there is an orchestra conducted by composer-conductor Jean-Michel Bernard recording an album called "*Jean-Michel Bernard Plays Lalo Schifrin*." And also, I have written a mandolin concerto for Vincent Beer-Demander, who is based in Paris. And I'm going to write more things as well, but I am superstitious, so I don't say I'm writing anything until I've actually finished it. On the other hand, I don't say I'm superstitious because it might bring me bad luck!

What are the basics an emerging conductor should know when conducting in the recording studio?

They should know the score first. That's the most important thing. You know, music is an art, but it also is an industry. And the administrators of orchestras, opera, and studios all want to save money. If the conductor takes too long to achieve a good result, it's going to cost more. So the conductor needs to learn how to be fast and efficient. Those who can do that are the most successful.

So much of your music is very rhythmic, often requiring a drum kit. When there is a drummer, what is the relationship you as a conductor have with that player?

Well, for instance, jazz. The drummer follows the conductor, but after you start, after you've given the tempo, then the drummer is the conductor. I am in front of the orchestra to make sure there are no mistakes in the notes, or in some of the attacks, which musicians can make. But in general, the drummer is the one who keeps the tempo.

Do you use a click track in the studio, when recording a film score?

Yes, of course, in the studio, because it's important to synchronize with the screen visuals. Usually, the composer is also the conductor, but if the composer wrote music very exact to the movie, yes, you should follow the click.

In the recording studio, who is the most important person besides the conductor?

The sound engineer.

You have said composers should study opera in order to understand the basic elements of drama. Do you think that is important for conductors, too?

Yes, opera is very important. Especially for composers who want to write music for movies. Opera was audio-visual entertainment before movies were invented. Movies are opera with new technology.

How would you advise an emerging conductor to become familiar with the wide variety of compositional genres such as your music represents?

You must study with a good teacher like I had (Mariano Drago) because there's no other solution. The only other solution would be to be self-taught, and that would lead to disaster. Sometimes, there are exceptions, of course. I don't want to make rules here by telling you this. But in general, I would say that you need to study the grammar of conducting.

Have you seen the movie *The Competition*? You know, I was musical director of the whole thing, and I also wrote some original music for the film. Of course, the most important music was that of the great masters—Prokofiev, Beethoven, Mozart. I did the conducting when we prerecorded some, and then we called "real" pianists also to prerecord, but the actors didn't know anything about it. So, Richard Dreyfuss came to the director, Joel Oliansky, and said, "I want to change the script to have an argument with the conductor (Sam Wanamaker). I want to show them I know conducting, I know music, and that would be a very good dramatic moment. Conflict is drama, so that would be very good." Oliansky came to me to ask my opinion of that, and I said that would be very dangerous. If a soloist provokes a conflict with the conductor, the conductor might kill him. But I went to the rehearsal to see what could be done, to see what the possibility of conflict might be, despite my own feelings. What I thought to do was for Wanamaker as conductor to introduce an incorrect rallentando in the final movement of the Beethoven concerto. If you look at the movie, you'll see that Dreyfuss tells Wanamaker there's no rallentando there. So later, Dreyfuss comes to me and says he would like to learn conducting, so he can show Wanamaker in the scene how to conduct that passage. "I'll pay you," he says. I told him it's still a ridiculous idea, but he insisted. So, I invited him to come to my house. I have two batons, one for him and one for me. The first lesson was how to start, giving a downbeat, how to prepare an orchestra.

From your observations of other conductors conducting your music, what key principles of conducting would you share with emerging conductors?

Well, as I told you, every gesture is important. What is the purpose of the conductor? The purpose is to have an orchestra or choir or both doing things clearly and together. We have to learn how to get to that purpose, so it's more complicated than we think it is. The result should also be very simple, which is very difficult to get, to start from something very complicated and make it look very easy. There are many conductors who don't have too many gestures. You know, for instance, Gustavo Dudamel, he's totally different from the European school because his gestures are very fluid. It often looks like he's floating, but the musicians of the Los Angeles Philharmonic say he's fantastic, and he's very simple to follow.

48

Madeline Smith

Madeline Smith may be the youngest woman conductor currently on Broadway. A graduate of Harvard University in music and classical civilizations, she is based in New York as music director, arranger, and conductor. Most of our discussion centered on her current work with the show *Waitress* (Diane Paulus, director). Reading this discussion, emerging conductors wanting to enter this field of conducting musicals will quickly see that what's required here is so much more than just conducting. Keyboard skills, orchestration, vocal coaching, and of course all manner of interpersonal creative relationships with others in the team probably become even more important than "conducting." That's probably why Madeline has done so well, having worked with artists such as César Alvarez, Bobby Lopez, Matthew Sklar, and Kristen Anderson-Lopez.

Is there anything you learned the "hard" way after leaving school?

I believe several skills are better acquired on the job than in a classroom. A lot of my work involves music notation software, which I only had a peripheral knowledge of when I graduated from college. Transcribing music is a very lucrative, door-opening skill. Someone always needs something done overnight! And several of my long-term projects started as transcription gigs that snowballed into arranging, accompanying, or even conducting the show.

Conducting technique: what comes for you easiest, or hardest, in the real world?

Natural for me is finding ways to be communicative with individual players. I can find people "in the crowd" well. What's hardest for me is the technical requirement of, say, a really drastic tempo change. If something large-scale and dramatic has to happen suddenly, I'm still learning how best to physicalize that.

When you mount the conductor's podium or seat, what's going through your mind?

If I'm in the focused, calm headspace I strive for, I'm thinking about the music. That sounds corny, but it can be hard to keep the other noise out of your head—having to earn money, being new to New York, being a freelancer, worrying if a show might close. But if in those rare, beautiful, cathartic three hours of performance you feel like this is what you were born to do, it's all worthwhile.

In your music theater realm, what is the most essential task for you as conductor?

A musical theater conductor is most essentially a clear-headed problem-solver who can balance musicianship with many other variables that live theater presents. For instance, in *Waitress*, the band is on stage, in costume, and it's also a piano-conductor book…so I'm playing my instrument, cueing the band via a talkback mic, and also giving some physical cues into a camera. And sometimes the band platform physically moves around the stage. You have to access some form of internal chill!

But does this allow you to get lost in the music?

You find moments. *Waitress* is played entirely to a click track, so there never is any inconsistency. At first, I found that incredibly frustrating and limiting—not so much because I couldn't pick the tempo, but because of how disorienting and non-musical it can feel to play with a metronome. At first, I thought, "It's only a six-piece band; can't we just play"? But I've grown to be more intentional in finding the musicality, despite the ever-present click.

How does "being intentional in finding the musicality" play out for you?

It's about staying present—staying connected enough to the music to remain both consistent and spontaneous.

Whence comes your musical satisfaction?

There's inherent satisfaction in performing a good show, which all types of musicians can relate to. What's interesting about musical theater is that the music director is often involved with the creation and development of the piece, and his/her fingerprints end up all over the final product. So, for me, my artistic fulfillment also comes from having done the vocal arrangements, orchestrations, and even assisting the composer with melody lines. I often have more at stake than just being the conductor or pianist for the show.

How would you prioritize these aspects of your conducting field: gestural technique, eyes, ears, psychology, brain (evaluation), non-podium skills?

Non-podium skills are of high priority in musical theater, because they often open doors into creative teams—being an arranger, orchestrator, pianist, coach, etc. For many music theater conductors, the actual conducting aspect is very much an on-the-job skill that is acquired from bosses and mentors.

Given all your successes to date, is there any aspect of your conducting activity that you wish you had been trained for in advance?

I wish I had taken a conducting technique or orchestral conducting technique class, in order to be more conversant with the beautiful art form that I observe when attending an orchestral concert. I also wish I had spent an afternoon with a great drummer, discussing groove and feel. That's a layer of musicality that isn't always obvious from notation. Bassists and drummers often know this, but keyboardists should too! And in musical theater, a music director's ability to play with a band is increasingly important.

Who are your heroes?

Mary-Mitchell Campbell [Broadway music director, conductor, and arranger] is a superb music director and orchestrator icon. The first time I watched her run a rehearsal was a breakthrough moment for me. In terms of leadership style and approach, I thought, "This is how to make people trust you and love you."

Another hero is Alex Lacamoire (music director, orchestrator, music supervisor of *Hamilton*). He has changed the game of what a music director is and can be. If I can be someone's Alex Lacamoire, as he is to Lin-Manuel Miranda, that's the epitome of music directing, to me.

In music theater, how much of the show itself is all about you (or not)?

It's *never* about you. Really! The music directors I admire the most are the ones who have done everything in preparation. They're all over the show creatively, but they fly under the radar and don't draw attention to themselves.

There's a fascinating trend emerging, in which user-friendly and accessible technology—even something as simple as the Voice Memo—is allowing far more musicians and songwriters to write musicals. This is changing the relationship of a music director to a composer. Yes, you might start working with a composer who already has a meticulous full score of his/her show, and your job is primarily interpretative, but you also might collaborate with a composer who's written a bunch of songs on guitar, and it's your job to shape it into a show. That type of relationship is more interesting to me, by far.

What, in your opinion, makes conducting music theater repertoire different from symphonic repertoire, in terms of actual technique?

Much of your interpretive work has to precede the rehearsal process entirely. Once you're in rehearsal, it's no longer about you discovering the music; it's about pulling everyone together. Symphonic conducting seems like such an entirely different journey from mine, as it seemingly has so little to do with keeping the beat or consistency and everything to do with the nuances of the music. As a music theater conductor, you are one member of a very large team, and once in performance mode, you must embrace the logistical responsibilities you have as well as the artistic and interpretive.

When baton conducting, I check in with the musicians often to make sure they're getting the visual information they need from me. I think musicians can be suspicious and can easily smell fear. "What do you need me to cue?" "How can I make this tempo shift easy?" are the attitudes I maintain. Admitting that you don't know all the answers is a great way to gain trust. It shows that you are there to serve them, not for your own ego.

Having the opportunity to conduct an orchestra while in college, I remember thinking that was about the best feeling anyone could ever feel. To feel like music is coming from your body—it's pure magic! I learned quickly, however, that an ensemble will only watch you and connect with your conducting if you make your movements meaningful.

What are the most important areas of collaboration you need to deal with?

I expected the most important collaboration to be with the director. But in the world of new musicals, collaboration with the composer comes first and foremost. You are the composer's advocate, representing him/her to the creative team (director, choreographer, etc.). At the same time, you can present ideas from the creative team to the composer and help work towards compromise.

Once a show is finally out of development and into a theater, the music director works closely with essentially every other department—sound, lights, costumes, etc. It's all about the *team*. I strive to be present and available for every production member. Everyone works better when they feel heard and valued.

What is the one piece of advice you would have for the emerging musical theater conductor?

Most theater music directors are pianists—not concert pianists necessarily, but adaptable, versatile pianists. I'd advise emerging conductors to cultivate piano skills like sight-reading, playing by ear, transposing in your head, reading lead sheets, and most importantly, accompanying singers with openness and sensitivity. These are the type of skills that open doors for music directing.

Anything else?

On Broadway and the larger theater world, there's no guarantee that any show will continue for any length of time. Put as many eggs in as many baskets as possible. Meet many people, and offer your musical abilities and skills to as many of them as possible. Try to diversify and have a finger in every pie.

What would you say to the next generation of conductors to NEVER (or ALWAYS) do?

NEVER say, "It wasn't my fault." It's only a waste of time and energy. Move the conversation forward. Artists can be sensitive and possessive about their work, and as soon as people get defensive and begin pointing blame on others, the creativity dries up.

ALWAYS listen. Be everyone's confidant and work towards a solution.

49

Thomas Wilkins

Thomas Wilkins represents a new breed of highly principled, conscientious, citizen-conductors wanting to make music to better society rather than for his own glorification. Entirely humble yet also extremely capable at conducting the best orchestras in America, Thomas exudes a comforting self-assurance and concern for those to whom he's speaking. Currently, Thomas is the music director of the Omaha Symphony and principal conductor of the Hollywood Bowl Orchestra. Additionally, he visits the Boston Symphony several times during the season where he conducts their youth concerts and other events. His earlier career found him conducting in Detroit, Chicago, Chattanooga, Richmond, and Tampa. He brings a socially conscious point of view to all that he does because he also represents an emerging generation of African-Americans entering the classical music world. My own conducting students have had an opportunity to observe and speak with Thomas. They come away very impressed with his dedication to his work and his embracing worldview.

What advice or teaching from earlier mentors has stuck with you even to this day?

At New England Conservatory, my teacher Richard Pittman was the most influential teacher I've had. He so required both artistic and musical integrity. He wouldn't mince words. In his mind, it was not enough to be charming; you had to do your homework and be prepared. In fact, you have to *over*-prepare for the test of conducting.

What non-conducting courses did you take in school that became most valuable to you in your career?

Diction for singers. I always knew I'd be working with singers and choruses. A conductor must know pronunciation. To this day, there are those who swear I am a singer, but it's only my knowledge of what's required of a singer.

Also, solfege.

Was there any course of study you wished you had taken?

If you're smart, you realize there's a lot you don't know. Your greatest competitor is ignorance. I wish I had taken more European history courses, learning more about great figures like Dostoyevsky and Tchaikovsky.

I also wish I had learned piano. At New England Conservatory, I was not allowed to graduate until I could play all the Bach chorales. So every morning, I arrived at school early to get a piano.

What about conducting a professional orchestra do you believe you learned the "hard" way?

That less is more. Knowing what "trust" means. How to talk less. Many emerging conductors *over*-conduct, somehow needing to prove they know the score. But music is greater than all of that.

Do you always use a baton?

My batons are of my own design; I have someone make them for me because I don't want to feel like I'm holding onto something. But for chorus rehearsals, I don't use a baton on purpose.

Do you think the baton can actually be expressive, or is it simply an extension of your arm?

Yes, it's supposed to be expressive. But the problem is that many conductors beat time so much that they're unaware of that ability. A conducting fundamental is clarity with your technique, which is less about the music-making. Just the nuts and bolts issue of clarity for the musicians. But our expressivity should be with the goal of knowing when to relinquish the power and control that a baton can force. We're trying to turn our players into better people, to take charge of their own musical moments. Otherwise, they become robots.

Do you consciously think about the independence of right and left hands?

It just comes naturally. In the early days, you had to think about how to communicate. But if you're spending your time thinking about your moves, you're not listening anymore. Kind of like a golf swing.

How has your conducting style changed since your earliest days?

I'm now much less fatigued. I find I can now conduct just with facial gestures.

How do you study a score from the beginning? Is there a usual method?

First, I go from macro to micro. I start with a macro view, trying to deepen my relationship with the music. I like to read it like a book, looking for density, a word, certain measures and movements, familiarizing myself with the work overall. I'll then do a structural/phrase analysis, a harmonic analysis. And I'll look at every measure individually, looking for doublings, orchestration habits, voicings, even seeking the composer's elements of surprise or clever sayings in the music. I'll then make decisions about character as the next-to-last step, searching for the composer's clues. And last, I'll spend time just looking at the score. You have to familiarize yourself with what's on the printed page, so you don't have to look down so often.

Have you found any obstacles come to you being African-American?

I don't know, really. One doesn't know about hiring decisions, but I'm not so naïve as to think there weren't some places where it either helped or hindered. But life's course is more about navigating rather than surviving. The obstacle course makes you stronger. You find ways to rebound when dealing with obstacles.

You are Music Director of the Omaha Symphony, a significant regional orchestra. What does the title "Music Director" mean to you and what activities are expected of you besides conducting?

The ancillary stuff takes a large chunk of time—cultivating friends, donors, and supporters. You're involved with speaking at the Rotary Club to playing a round of golf and everything in-between. There are also receptions, lunches, and long-range planning meetings. I have found that an orchestra's leadership has to get used to saying the same thing over and over. It's a huge part of the job. Educational outreach and community engagement are so important; you're creating stakeholders. It's not about creating donors, but rather getting into their lives—into a whole other world.

Describe the circumstances behind a particular constraint (whether programming, administrative, or musical) that was placed on you. How did you deal with it?

Mostly, it's the budget that's most prevalent. We will always have grand ideas, but we must put a season together as a team, in order to work around budget restraints. Often, the question comes up: why do we need high-caliber (i.e., expensive) soloists? It's our job to convince those who ask that it's all about raising the level of the orchestra. High-reputation soloists bring in an equally high musical standard that serves to provide additional stimulus and inspiration to the musicians in the orchestra. Also, the marketing people need to understand why we're doing certain repertoire, as they're the ones developing materials that describe the repertoire to the greater audience. And, the CEO need not be worried about risk of bankruptcy that less thoughtful repertoire choices might help create. As music director, I am aware of all these dynamics, so organizationally, we have to depend on each other. Sometimes there are personnel restraints, too, but my leadership motto is to get the best from the best, and the most from the least musically capable.

How is your conducting approach with the Hollywood Bowl different from the Omaha Symphony, if at all?

The Hollywood Bowl orchestra works much faster. There are no more than two rehearsals, but mostly only one rehearsal. The musicians in L.A. are accustomed to working fast and to making fast switches between styles. Another difference is that backstage, the Hollywood Bowl has almost a cast of thousands—there are so many elements to make comfortable. And as conductor, you become a kind of artist whisperer. But preparing for performance is exactly the same, whether in Hollywood or Omaha.

As for the Boston Symphony Young People's Concerts, what are your overriding principles and concepts for programming?

First, the programs are designed to teach the young audiences about living—creating music as a tool. The principles of how orchestration equals community, rhythm equals perseverance. I speak of common courtesy and minding our musical manners—being "more graceful to each other" as I demonstrate with Dvořák's Sixth Symphony. Or, how the Berlioz *Rakoczy March* may be a Hungarian tune, but it's in his (Berlioz') voice. This will make better human beings. The concerts are also about helping the teachers help their students, and how as a large community, we can work together: from families to classrooms to neighborhoods.

Second, musically speaking, I'm never worried about Beethoven's ability to take care of himself with the youth audience. I choose real repertoire, in this great symphony hall. The kids walk into the building, which is a powerful and beautiful example itself of art, so there's a real direct relationship in the hall with the music and the orchestra that can be fun. I am never afraid of repertoire that others might say is too difficult for an audience of young people.

Any general advice to musicians of the younger generation?

Listen to a lot of music. All music informs all of your music-making. Unfortunately, today, everything needs to be quick and instantaneous. Today's young musicians need to digest a lot of repertoire.

Any final words?

Technique! (Less is more.) Purpose!

What would you say emerging conductors should ALWAYS do and NEVER do?

ALWAYS understand there are real human beings in their ensembles; ALWAYS respect them. They are not subservient; they are your co-participators.

NEVER believe you are the most important.

50

John Williams

Having had the pleasure and honor of working with and covering for John Williams at the Boston Pops, this is one interview I just had to have. Obviously, John needs no introduction to anyone; we are all familiar with *Star Wars*, the George Lucas films; *Home Alone*; and *Harry Potter*. But it's been a real privilege to observe John conducting the Boston Pops in concert and in rehearsal, where his stellar combination of talents as a conductor comes through in spades: the ability to hear everything in the orchestra, to conduct (and play piano!) in any given style of artist or repertoire, to create such a warm and supportive atmosphere with all the musicians in the orchestra, and to always be at the top of his game. Rarely does one find an artist-musician of such caliber who also can conduct with an effective technique, a genuine relationship with his audience, and the complete cooperation and respect of his colleagues on stage. John came into conducting almost by default over the years, having had a major career already as a Juilliard-trained pianist. So, his notes on conducting technique come from one who's essentially self-taught from his own observations of others. Some really remarkable comments and perspectives in this interview!

How did you first get into professional conducting?

I never had any formal instruction at it, but as a composer starting conducting in self-defense!

Did you ever have any mentors or podium models in the early days?

The only podium models I had were those I worked for as a pianist. I found Alfred Newman and Victor Young as being—I thought—the most effective conductors. They were the ones we did our best for, somehow. It may have been their personalities or their charisma that connected with what technique they might have had. And I admired Bernard Herrmann very much, whose great aspiration was not to succeed as a composer but as a conductor. And, actually, we had trouble following Mr. Herrmann, and found ourselves looking down a lot, and listening to each other. But he had a Toscanini-like way of scolding, which after a while we didn't take too seriously, as it became kind of charming and curmudgeon-like. From a musical point of view, he was always convincing, but his stick technique was pretty terrible.

So, even in those early days you recognized that, though you were not yet a conductor yourself?

I think so. As a player, we do recognize that, and you learn to read the boss pretty quickly, you develop favorites also quickly, and others that seem to need your help as a player.

And somehow in that time you also realize some basic principles, such as the first beat goes down?

That's right, and also up high enough so players can see the beat, not down low as Mr. Herrmann would have done, while he was grumpily looking at his score.

Sounds inspirational!

They were all very interesting. Dmitri Tiomkin was a very flamboyant man, whose coattails waved in the wind as he did his windmill-like strokes with the baton. But he got exciting, charged performances also. I always felt that Alfred Newman was the best that we had by far, and was a wonderful accompanist with singers. Richard Rodgers—as Gershwin had earlier—admired him very much, and I think all of that came through as we played for him.

Was there ever an "Aha!" moment later on in your own conducting that you had not realized before?

When I went to Boston to do some pops concerts, I had had twenty-plus years of recording in studios with "studio ears," which to me means that we've listened to so many takes and analyzed them and really listened into the performance very deeply as we did in editorial sessions. When I first began conducting in public, I became a little disturbed that I couldn't stop and fix something because there was an audience there. And some of the vertical precision that you might insist on in recording might be a little lax here and there, and it might have been a result of stick technique or whatever. There are so many variables in performance. But for me, it's been a general evolution to whatever level I've been able to achieve of shaping performances with orchestra.

The other good fortune I've had is that I've always conducted musicians who were so exceptionally fine that to reach a point of getting some "luft" into performance is a very different experience than to conduct students, which I've never really done. Conducting at other levels, where you have to teach as well as interpret, is not an experience I've had. So, I've been assisted greatly by all the artists that are in front of me all the time. I can't say I've had a single eureka moment, but I have had an increased sense of security over the years so that I could relax on the podium and not have to drive too hard. If the body and the arms are relaxed and the eyes do their work, the performance seems to take shape much more comfortably and naturally. And that, I suppose, is the result of years of being on the podium, one way or another, that young people will have to find through experience themselves.

Do you recall your conducting style in your earliest days, and what has changed over the years?

Probably, I was much more tense in my arm, shoulders, and maybe even legs! But now, I *feel* much more comfortable. I've always felt that the art of conducting is very related to the act of breathing. While we talk about breathing with the music, I think it is part of how we move, and probably illustrates a lot to musicians who have to work with us. So, I'm not so much thinking about hands and arms as I am about imparting some kind of physiological balance. I also agree completely with other conductors who say they now find themselves much more economical in terms of their actual movement. I think several things happen: we discover we don't have to make exaggerated gestures (not to mention that as we become older, we're less capable of making exaggerations!). For example, I so much admire Bernard Haitink, who does so much with so little body movement.

How do you study a score?

I go immediately to the piano, and work it out in the best way that I can. I may not do especially well playing off the full score, but that's the way I study. I go measure-by-measure, as I'm more interested as a composer than a conductor at that point.

In an orchestral pops setting, how important is the relationship between the conductor and the drummer?

In my earliest experiences, which were in musicals with a full orchestra, the drums were not very prominent. If you listen to Frank Carlson and the great MGM musicals, you won't hear much drums. Over the years, the pattern has been to have the drums become more and more important. Getting into the rock era, you have some pretty heavy drumming going on, against an orchestra that was never conceived to have that in it. So, a lot of adjustments had to be made. But I don't think drummers should ever have the idea that they set the tempo. In jazz, the beat, the swing, is implied. We all understand where that is, and we don't have to support that by drumming. But so much has changed stylistically that it's very hard to generalize.

What are some of the basic differences to conducting in the recording studio vs. the concert stage?

Rehearsal techniques differ, with getting to details and issues of balance very quickly. I think there's more time to do that in rehearsal than in the recording studio. In a two-and-a-half hour rehearsal, you have to go through two hours of repertoire. When I began conducting at Boston Pops, I didn't want to start until the theater was completely quiet, which of course it never was. Somebody would pop a cork at a concert, and my impulse would be to stop immediately, because in a recording setting you had to have absolute silence before, during, and six to ten seconds afterwards. So, I was easily distracted by noise in live performance, which of course I got used to over time.

Also in recording—at least in film—we're usually dealing with two- to three-minute musical fragments or sections, which is more of a microscopic look at the materials than the longer musical line. Great differences in atmosphere, obviously; besides composer and performers, an audience brings a third big, psychological element. I don't think any of us are the same person as we are with 2,500 people behind us.

What would you advise to emerging conductors how to carry themselves on the podium?

Have confidence in the orchestra itself. If the orchestra gets the impression that the conductor is leaving to them to do what they know how to do, and the conductor does not project an insecurity in the orchestra, then we can impart confidence in the players by knowledge of the score, or empathy with all kinds of nuance that don't need to be articulated but instead can be shown so easily with a flick of the hand. Or, the choice of exactly the right word at exactly the right time—a simple word, preferably.

I wasn't around in the days of the great tyrannical maestros. The world has changed, and our whole ideas of behavior and civility are modified. People are not fired on the spot or railed against, as conductors so often used to do. To put it in a few words: confidence in the orchestra, showing the confidence in their ability to come through.

As a composer, what would you advise a conductor to be sure to do if s/he were to conduct a work of yours for the first time?

Listen. Avoid smothering. Release the sound, let it come forth.

What would you advise emerging composer/conductors conducting their own music?

I've always felt that every conductor should compose even a little music, if possible, and composers ought to learn at least a little conducting. One thing supports the other so much. For composers, some time on the podium will only help them as composers, their orchestrations, and so on.

Any final words of advice, whatever specific path they take?

I think if their conscientiousness is something that's nurtured through their careers, and if they love music enough, they will put up with all the vagaries of the music profession and they should succeed.

APPENDIX A. BIBLIOGRAPHY

Conducting

Bailey, Wayne and Brandt Payne. *Conducting: The Art of Communication*. Oxford: Oxford University Press, 2014.

Battisti, Frank L. *On Becoming a Conductor: Lessons and Meditations on the Art of Conducting*. Delray Beach, FL: Meredith Music Publications, 2007.

Bowen, José Antoni, editor. *The Cambridge Companion to Conducting*. Cambridge: Cambridge University Press, 2003.

Colson, John F. *Conducting and Rehearsing the Instrumental Music Ensemble: Scenarios, Priorities, Strategies, Essentials, and Repertoire*. Lanham, MD: Scarecrow Press, Inc., 2012.

Gibson, Mark. *The Beat Stops Here: Lessons on and off the Podium for Today's Conductor*. Oxford: Oxford University Press, 2017.

Green, Elizabeth A.H., and Mark Gibson. *The Modern Conductor*. New Jersey: Pearson Prentice Hall, 2004.

Harris, Frederick, Jr. *Conducting with Feeling*. Delray Beach, FL: Meredith Music Publications, 2001.

Hunsberger, Donald and Roy E. Ernst. *The Art of Conducting, Second Edition*. New York: McGraw-Hill, Inc., 1992.

Jacobson, Bernard. *Conductors on Conducting*. Frenchtown, NJ: Columbia Publishing Co., 1979.

Jordan, James. *Conducting Technique Etudes: Laban-Based Etudes for Class or Individual Practice*. Chicago: GIA Publications, Inc., 2013.

Labuta, Joseph A. and Wendy K. Matthews. *Basic Conducting Techniques, 7th Edition*. London: Routledge/Taylor & Francis Group, 2017.

Lisk, Edward S. *Lyrical Conducting: A New Dimension in Expressive Musicianship*. Delray Beach, FL: Meredith Music Publications, 2013.

Maiello, Anthony. *Conducting Nuances: Little Things Mean a Lot*. Chicago: GIA Publications, Inc., 2007.

Maiello, Anthony. *Conducting: A Hands-On Approach*. Van Nuys, CA: Alfred Music, 1996.

Malko, Nicolai. *The Conductor and His Baton: Fundamentals of the Technic of Conducting*. Wilhelm Hansen, Copenhagen, 1950.

Mauceri, John. *Maestros and Their Music: The Art and Alchemy of Conducting.* New York: Alfred Knopf, 2017.

McElheran, Brock. *Conducting Technique: for Beginners and Professionals.* Oxford: Oxford University Press, 2004.

Meier, Gustav. *The Score, the Orchestra, and the Conductor.* Oxford: Oxford University Press, 2009.

Miller, Michael. *The Complete Idiot's Guide to Conducting Music.* New York: Alpha Books, Penguin Group, 2012.

Murakami, Haruki, and Seiji Ozawa. *Absolutely on Music: Conversations with Seiji Ozawa.* New York: Random House, 2016.

Nierenberg, Roger. *Maestro: A Surprising Story About Leading by Listening.* London: Penguin Group, 2009.

Phillips, Kenneth H. *Basic Techniques of Conducting.* New York: Oxford University Press, 1997.

Rudolf, Max. *The Grammar of Conducting: A Practical Guide to Baton Technique and Orchestral Interpretation.* New York: Schirmer Books, Macmillan Publishing, 1980.

Schifrin, Lalo, Richard Palmer, ed. *Mission Impossible: My Life in Music.* Toronto: The Scarecrow Press, 2008.

Schuller, Gunther. *The Compleat Conductor.* Oxford: Oxford University Press, 1997.

Schwiebert, Jerald and Dustin Barr. *Expressive Conducting: Movement and Performance Theory for Conductors.* New York: Routledge, 2018.

Seaman, Christopher. *Inside Conducting.* Rochester: University of Rochester, 2013.

Slatkin, Leonard. *Conducting Business: Unveiling the Mystery Behind the Maestro.* Milwaukee: Amadeus Press, 2012.

Stotter, Douglas. *Methods and Materials for Conducting.* Chicago: GIA Publications, 2006.

Thakar, Markand. *On the Principles and Practice of Conducting.* Rochester: University of Rochester Press, 2016.

Trotter, William R. *Priest of Music: The Life of Dimitri Mitropoulos.* Portland: Amadeus Press, 2003.

Tunstall, Tricia. *Changing Lives: Gustavo Dudamel, El Sistema, and the Transformative Power of Music.* New York: W.W. Norton & Company, 2012.

Wagner, Richard. *Wagner on Conducting.* New York: Dover Publications, 1989.

Watkins, John. *The Art of the Conductor: The Definitive Guide to Music Conducting Skills, Terms and Techniques.* New York: iUniverse, 2007.

Whitwell, David. *Psychological Problems in Conducting.* Austin, TX: Whitwell Books, 2016.

Wittry, Diane. *Beyond the Baton: What Every Conductor Needs to Know.* Oxford: Oxford University Press, 2011.

Leadership

Chopra, Deepak. *The Soul of Leadership: Unlocking Your Potential for Greatness.* New York: Harmony Books, 2010.

Covey, Stephen R. *Principle: Centered Leadership.* New York: Simon and Schuster, 1992.

De Pree, Max. *Leadership Is an Art.* New York: The Crown Publishing Group, 2004.

Dethmer, Jim, Diana Chapman, and Kaley Warner Klemp. *The 15 Commitments of Conscious Leadership: A New Paradigm for Sustainable Success.* Chicago: Conscious Leadership Group, 2015.

Drucker, Peter F. *The Effective Executive: The Definitive Guide to Getting the Right Things Done,* 50th Anniversary Edition. New York: Harper Collins Publishers, 2017.

Greenleaf, Robert K. *Servant Leadership: A Journey into the Nature of Legitimate Power & Greatness,* 25th Anniversary Edition. Mahwah, NJ: Paulist Press, 2002.

Hackman, J. Richard. *Leading Teams—Setting the Stage for Great Performances.* Boston: Harvard Business School Press, 2002.

Heider, John. *The Tao of Leadership: Leadership Strategies for a New Age.* New York: Bantam Books, 1986.

Hunter, James C. *The Servant: A Simple Story about the True Essence of Leadership.* New York: Crown Business, 2012.

Lautzenheiser, Tim. *Leadership: Vision, Commitment, Action.* Chicago: GIA Publications, Inc., 2006.

Levi, Daniel. *Group Dynamics for Teams.* Thousand Oaks, CA: Sage Publications Inc., 2011

Loeb, Marshall, and Stephen Kindel. *Leadership for Dummies.* Indianapolis, IN: Wiley Publishing Inc., 1999.

Marrin, Dr. John. *Leadership for Dummies.* Chichester, West Sussex, England: John Wiley and Sons, Ltd., 2011.

Patterson, Kerry, Joseph Grenny, Ron McMillan, and Al Switzler. *Crucial Conversations: Tools for Talking When Stakes Are High.* New York: McGraw Hill, 2012.

Rath, Tom and Barry Conchie. *Strengths Based Leadership: Great Leaders, Teams, and Why People Follow.* New York: Gallup Press, 2008.

Scoullar, James. *The Three Levels of Leadership.* Oxford: Management Books 2000 Ltd., 2016.

Wallace, David. *Engaging the Concert Audience: A Musician's Guide to Interactive Performance.* Boston: Berklee Press, 2018.

Walters, J. Donald. *The Art of Leadership: A Practical Guide for People in Positions of Responsibility.* New York: MJF Books, 1987.

Wheelan, Susan A. *Creating Effective Teams: A Guide for Members and Leaders.* Thousand Oaks, CA: Sage Publications, Inc., 2010.

Wis, Ramona M. *The Conductor as Leader: Principles of Leadership Applied to Life on the Podium.* Chicago: GIA Publications, Inc., 2007.

Music: General and Reference

Adler, Samuel. *The Study of Orchestration.* New York: W.W. Norton & Company, Inc., 2002.

Bernstein, Leonard. *Findings.* New York: Anchor, 1993.

Boldrey, Richard. *Guide to Operatic Roles and Arias.* Seattle, WA: Diction for Singers, 2010.

Boulez, Pierre. *Notes of an Apprenticeship.* New York: Alfred A. Knopf, 1968.

Daniels, David. *Orchestral Music: A Handbook.* Lanham MD: Scarecrow Press, 2005.

Eaton, Quaintance. *Opera Production I: A Handbook.* New York: Da Capo Press, 1974.

— *Opera Production II: A Handbook.* Minneapolis: University of Minnesota Press, 1974.

Girsberger, Russ, and Laurie Lake. *The Music Performance Library: A Practical Guide for Orchestra, Band, and Opera Librarians.* Delray Beach, FL: Meredith Music, 2011.

Girsberger, Russ, and Laurie Lake. *Insights and Essays on the Music Performance Library.* Galesville, MD: Meredith Music Publications, Inc., 2012.

Girsberger, Russ. *A Manual for the Performance Library.* Lanham, MD: Scarecrow Press, 2006.

Girsberger, Russ. *A Practical Guide to Percussion Terminology.* Ft. Lauderdale, FL: Meredith Music Publications, 1998.

Green, Elizabeth A. H. *Orchestral Bowings and Routines.* American String Teachers Association, 1990.

Grun, Bernard. *The Timetables of History: A Horizontal Linkage of People and Events.* New York: Simon and Schuster, 1982.

Kjelland, James. *Orchestral Bowing: Style and Function; Textbook.* Van Nuys, CA: Alfred Music Publishing Co., Inc., 2004.

— *Orchestral Bowing: Style and Function; Workbook.* Van Nuys, CA: Alfred Music Publishing Co., Inc., 2004.

Klickstein, Gerald. *The Musician's Way: A Guide to Practice, Performance, and Wellness.* Oxford: Oxford University Press, 2009.

Leinsdorf, Erich. *The Composer's Advocate: A Radical Orthodoxy for Musicians.* New Haven, CT: Yale University Press, 1982.

Manning, Lucy. *Orchestral "Pops" Music: A Handbook.* Lanham, MD: Scarecrow Press, Inc., 2009.

Meyer, Dirk. *Chamber Orchestra & Ensemble Repertoire: A Catalog of Modern Music.* Lanham, MD: Scarecrow Press, Inc., 2011.

Naughtin, Matthew. *Ballet Music: A Handbook.* Lanham, MD: Rowman & Littlefield, 2014.

Yaffé, John, and David Daniels. *Arias, Ensembles, & Choruses.* Lanham, MD: Scarecrow Press, Inc., 2012.

Movement

Billingham, Lisa A. *The Complete Conductor's Guide to Laban Movement Theory.* Chicago: GIA Publications, Inc., 2009.

Dawley, Nancy, Neil Schapera, and Vivien Schapera. *Guided Lessons for Students of the Alexander Technique.* Cincinnati: Four Winds Press, 2010.

Gelb, Michael J. *Body Learning: An Introduction to the Alexander Technique.* New York: Henry Holt & Co., 1996.

Jordan, James. *The Conductor's Gesture: A Practical Application of Rudolf von Laban's Movement Language.* Chicago: GIA Publications, Inc., 2011.

Teaching

Hanh, Thich Nhat, and Katherine Weare. *Happy Teachers Change the World.* Berkeley, CA: Parallax Press, 2017.

Lautzenheiser, Tim. *The Joy of Inspired Teaching.* Chicago: GIA Publications, Inc., 1993.

Lautzenheiser, Tim. *The Art of Successful Teaching: A Blend of Content & Context.* Chicago: GIA Publications, 1992.

Life

Amodeo, John. *The Authentic Heart: An Eightfold Path to Midlife Love.* Hoboken, NJ: John Wiley & Sons, 2001.

Babiak, Paul, and Robert D. Hare. *Snakes in Suits: When Psychopaths Go to Work.* New York: Harper Collins Publishers, 2006.

Barks, Coleman. *The Essential Rumi.* New York: HarperCollins Publishers, 2004.

Cameron, Julia. *The Artist's Way: A Spiritual Path to Higher Creativity,* 25th Anniversary Edition. New York: TarcherPerigee (Penguin Random House), 2016.

Carnegie, Dale. *How to Win Friends and Influence People.* New York: Simon & Schuster, 2009.

Covey, Stephen R. *The 7 Habits of Highly Effective People: Powerful Lessons in Personal Change.* New York: Simon & Schuster, 1989.

Csikszentmihalyi, Mihaly. *Creativity: Flow and the Psychology of Discovery and Invention.* New York: Harper Perennial, 1997.

Dimitrius, Jo-Ellan and Wendy Patrick Mazzarella. *Reading People: How to Understand People and Predict Their Behavior—Anytime, Anyplace.* New York: Ballantine Books, 2008.

Frankl, Victor E. *Man's Search for Meaning.* New York: Beacon Press, 2006.

Goffman, Erving. *The Presentation of Self in Everyday Life.* New York: Anchor Books/ Random House, 1959.

Hanh, Thich Nhat. *Inside the Now: Meditations on Time.* Berkeley, CA: Parallax Press, 2015.

Kushner, Malcolm. *Public Speaking for Dummies.* Hoboken, NJ: Wiley Publishing, Inc., 2004.

Patterson, Kerry, Joseph Grenny, Ron McMillan, and Al Switzler. *Crucial Conversations: Tools for Talking When Stakes Are High.* New York: McGraw-Hill, 2012.

Paul, Richard, and Linda Elder. *Critical Thinking: Concepts and Tools.* The Foundation for Critical Thinking. www.criticalthinking.org/files/Concepts_Tools.pdf (accessed July 3, 2019).

Ruiz, Don Miguel, and Janet Mills. *The Voice of Knowledge: A Practical Guide to Inner Peace.* San Rafael, CA: Amber-Allen Publishing, 2004.

Ruiz, Don Miguel. *The Four Agreements: A Practical Guide to Personal Freedom.* San Rafael, CA: Amber-Allen Publishing, 1997.

APPENDIX B. INSTRUMENT NAMES IN ENGLISH, GERMAN, FRENCH, AND ITALIAN

English	*German*	*French*	*Italian*
Piccolo (Picc, Pc.)	Kleine Flöte (Kl.Fl.)	Petite flûte (Pte fl)	Ottavino (Ott)
Flute (Fl)	Flöte	Flûte	Flauto
Alto Flute (Alt.Fl)	Altflöte	Flûte en sol	Flauto contralto
Oboe (Ob)	Oboe, Hoboe (Hob)	Hautbois (Hautb)	Oboe
English horn (E.H., Eh)	Englisches Horn	Cor anglais (Cor angl)	Corno Inglese (C.i.)
Clarinet (Cl, Clar)	Klarinette (Kl)	Clarinette	Clarinetto
Bass Clarinet (B.Cl)	Bassklarinette	Clarinette basse (Cl.b.)	Clarinetto basso
Basset horn	Bassetthorn	Cor de basset	Corno di bassetto
Saxophone (Sax)	Saxophon	Saxophone	Sassofono
Bassoon (Bsn)	Fagott (Fag, Fg)	Basson	Fagotto
Contrabassoon (C-Bsn)	Kontrafagott (K-Fag)	Contrebasson	Contrafagotto
French horn (Hn)	Horn	Cor	Corno
Trumpet (Tpt)	Trompete	Trompette	Tromba
Trombone (Trb)	Posaune (Pos)	Trombone	Trombone
Baritone (Bar), Euphonium (Euph)	Baryton, Euphonion	Baryton	Bombarda
Tuba (Tba)	Basstuba (Btba)	Tuba basse	Tuba di basso
Xylophone (Xyl)	Xylophon	Xylophone	Silofono
Marimba (Mar)	Marimbaphon	Marimba	Marimba
Vibraphone (Vibe)	Vibraphon	Vibraphone	Vibrafono
Bells	Glockenspiel (Glock)	Jeu de timbres (J.de t)	Campanelli (Cmplli)
Chimes (Chm)	Glocken (Glkn)	Jeu de cloches (J. de cl)	Campane (Cmpne)
Crotales (Crot)	Zimbeln (Zimb)	Crotales	Crotali
Timpani (Timp)	Pauken (Pauk)	Timbales (Timb)	Timpani
Cymbals (Cym)	Becken (Beck)	Cymbales	Piatti (Ptti)
Anvil (Anv)	Amboss	Enclume	Incudine
Woodblocks (Wblk, W.Bl.)	Holzblöcke (Hlzblk)	Blocs de bois	Blocci di legno cinese
Snare Drum (S.Dr.)	Kleine Trommel (Kl.Tr.)	Caisse Claire (C.Claire)	Tamburo (Tam)
Bass Drum (B.Dr.)	Grosse Trommel	Grosse caisse	Gran cassa
Piano	Klavier	Piano	Pianoforte
Harpsichord (Hpscd)	Cembalo (Cemb)	Clavecin	Cembalo
Synthesizer (Synth)	Synthesizer	Synthétiseur	Sintetizzatore
Organ	Orgel	Orgue	Organo
Harp	Harfe	Harpe	Arpa
Guitar (Gtr)	Gitarre	Guitare	Chitarra
Violin (Vln)	Geige	Violon	Violino
Viola (Vla)	Bratsche (Br)	Alto	Viola
Cello (Vc, Vcl)	Violoncello	Violoncelle	Violoncello
Double Bass (DB)	Kontrabass (Kb)	Contrebasse	Contrabasso
Woodwinds	Holzbläser	Bois	Fiati
Brass	Blechinstrumente	Instruments de cuivre	Stromenti d'ottone
Percussion	Schlagzeug	Percussion	Percussione
Strings	Streicher	Instruments à cordes	Il strumenti a corda

INDEX

Note: Page numbers in *italics* indicate photographs

C

D

E

F

G

H

I

J

K

L

M

N

O

P

ABOUT THE AUTHOR

Photo by Alice Gebura

Bruce Hangen is artistic director and conductor of the Orchestra of Indian Hill and director of orchestral activities and professor of conducting at the Boston Conservatory at Berklee, Boston, Massachusetts. Formerly music director of the Portland (Maine) and Omaha Symphony Orchestras, Hangen also was the founder and conductor of the Portland (Maine) Opera Repertory Theatre, and has held titled positions with the orchestras of Denver, Kansas City, Utah, Syracuse, and Buffalo. Guest conducting has taken him throughout North America as well as Taiwan and Japan. Known for his organizational leadership, musical versatility, and creative programming, Hangen also has conducted pops concerts extensively, including a twenty-year relationship with the Boston Pops Orchestra, for whom he was principal pops guest conductor. He also held the title of the Boston Symphony's Germeshausen Family Youth Concerts Conductor's Chair. For twelve years, Hangen was music director of the Omaha (Nebraska) Symphony. Under his direction, the Omaha Symphony achieved recognition for its significantly expanded program offerings, including the nationally acclaimed "West Meets West," a celebration of the Native American, conceived and conducted by Hangen. His influence extended far beyond the Midwest, too, in establishing a sister-orchestra relationship between the Omaha Symphony and the Orchestra of Shizuoka, Japan. Before taking the Omaha Symphony Music Directorship, Hangen was music director and conductor of the Portland (Maine) Symphony and associate conductor of the Denver Symphony. A graduate of the Eastman School of Music, Hangen was also a conducting fellow at the Berkshire Music Center at Tanglewood, where his conducting teachers included Gunther Schuller, Seiji Ozawa, Leonard Bernstein, Michael Tilson Thomas, Stanislaw Skrowaczewski, Bruno Maderna, and Joseph Silverstein.

STRINGS/ROOTS MUSIC

BERKLEE HARP
Chords, Styles, and Improvisation for Pedal and Lever Harp
by Felice Pomeranz
00144263 Book/Online Audio $19.99

BEYOND BLUEGRASS
Beyond Bluegrass Banjo
by Dave Hollander and Matt Glaser
50449610 Book/CD $19.99
Beyond Bluegrass Mandolin
by John McGann and Matt Glaser
50449609 Book/CD $19.99
Bluegrass Fiddle and Beyond
by Matt Glaser
50449602 Book/CD $19.99

EXPLORING CLASSICAL MANDOLIN
by August Watters
00125040 Book/Online Media $19.99

THE IRISH CELLO BOOK
by Liz Davis Maxfield
50449652 Book/Online Audio $24.99

JAZZ UKULELE
by Abe Lagrimas, Jr.
00121624 Book/Online Audio $19.99

BERKLEE PRACTICE METHOD

GET YOUR BAND TOGETHER
With additional volumes for other instruments, plus a teacher's guide.
Bass
by Rich Appleman, John Repucci and the Berklee Faculty
50449427 Book/CD $16.99
Drum Set
by Ron Savage, Casey Scheuerell and the Berklee Faculty
50449429 Book/CD $14.95
Guitar
by Larry Baione and the Berklee Faculty
50449426 Book/CD $16.99
Keyboard
by Russell Hoffmann, Paul Schmeling and the Berklee Faculty
50449428 Book/Online Audio $14.99

WELLNESS

MANAGE YOUR STRESS AND PAIN THROUGH MUSIC
by Dr. Suzanne B. Hanser and Dr. Susan E. Mandel
50449592 Book/CD $29.99

MUSICIAN'S YOGA
by Mia Olson
50449587 Book $17.99

THE NEW MUSIC THERAPIST'S HANDBOOK – 3RD EDITION
by Dr. Suzanne B. Hanser
00279325 Book $29.99

AUTOBIOGRAPHY

LEARNING TO LISTEN: THE JAZZ JOURNEY OF GARY BURTON
by Gary Burton
00117798 Book $27.99

HAL•LEONARD®

Prices subject to change without notice. Visit your local music dealer or bookstore, or go to **www.berkleepress.com**

MUSIC THEORY/EAR TRAINING/ IMPROVISATION

BEGINNING EAR TRAINING
by Gilson Schachnik
50449548 Book/Online Audio $16.99

THE BERKLEE BOOK OF JAZZ HARMONY
by Joe Mulholland & Tom Hojnacki
00113755 Book/Online Audio $27.50

BERKLEE MUSIC THEORY – 2ND ED.
by Paul Schmeling
Rhythm, Scales Intervals
50449615 Book/Online Audio $24.99
Harmony
50449616 Book/Online Audio $22.99

IMPROVISATION FOR CLASSICAL MUSICIANS
by Eugene Friesen with Wendy M. Friesen
50449637 Book/CD $24.99

REHARMONIZATION TECHNIQUES
by Randy Felts
50449496 Book $29.99

MUSIC BUSINESS

ENGAGING THE CONCERT AUDIENCE
by David Wallace
00244532 Book/Online Media $16.99

HOW TO GET A JOB IN THE MUSIC INDUSTRY – 3RD EDITION
by Keith Hatschek with Breanne Beseda
00130699 Book $27.99

MAKING MUSIC MAKE MONEY
by Eric Beall
50448009 Book $27.99

MUSIC LAW IN THE DIGITAL AGE – 2ND EDITION
by Allen Bargfrede
00148196 Book $19.99

MUSIC MARKETING
by Mike King
50449588 Book $24.99

PROJECT MANAGEMENT FOR MUSICIANS
by Jonathan Feist
50449659 Book $27.99

THE SELF-PROMOTING MUSICIAN – 3RD EDITION
by Peter Spellman
00119607 Book $24.99

MUSIC PRODUCTION & ENGINEERING

AUDIO MASTERING
by Jonathan Wyner
50449581 Book/CD $29.99

AUDIO POST PRODUCTION
by Mark Cross
50449627 Book $19.99

THE SINGER-SONGWRITER'S GUIDE TO RECORDING IN THE HOME STUDIO
by Shane Adams
00148211 Book $16.99

UNDERSTANDING AUDIO – 2ND EDITION
by Daniel M. Thompson
00148197 Book $24.99

SONGWRITING, COMPOSING, ARRANGING

ARRANGING FOR HORNS
by Jerry Gates
00121625 Book/Online Audio $19.99

BEGINNING SONGWRITING
by Andrea Stolpe with Jan Stolpe
00138503 Book/Online Audio $19.99

BERKLEE CONTEMPORARY MUSIC NOTATION
by Jonathan Feist
00202547 Book $17.99

COMPLETE GUIDE TO FILM SCORING – 2ND ED.
by Richard Davis
50449607 .... $29.99

CONTEMPORARY COUNTERPOINT: THEORY & APPLICATION
by Beth Denisch
00147050 Book/Online Audio $22.99

THE CRAFT OF SONGWRITING
by Scarlet Keys
00159283 Book/Online Audio $19.99

JAZZ COMPOSITION
by Ted Pease
50448000 Book/Online Audio $39.99

MELODY IN SONGWRITING
by Jack Perricone
50449419 Book $24.99

MODERN JAZZ VOICINGS
by Ted Pease and Ken Pullig
50449485 Book/Online Audio $24.99

MUSIC COMPOSITION FOR FILM AND TELEVISION
by Lalo Schifrin
50449604 Book $34.99

MUSIC NOTATION
Preparing Scores and Parts
by Matthew Nicholl and Richard Grudzinski
50449540 Book $16.99

MUSIC NOTATION
Theory and Technique for Music Notation
by Mark McGrain
50449399 Book $24.95

POPULAR LYRIC WRITING
by Andrea Stolpe
50449553 Book $15.99

SONGWRITING: ESSENTIAL GUIDE
Lyric and Form Structure
by Pat Pattison
50481582 Book $16.99
Rhyming
by Pat Pattison
00124366 2nd Ed. Book $17.99

SONGWRITING IN PRACTICE
by Mark Simos
00244545 Book $16.99

SONGWRITING STRATEGIES
by Mark Simos
50449621 Book $24.99

THE SONGWRITER'S WORKSHOP
Harmony
by Jimmy Kachulis
50449519 Book/Online Audio $29.99
Melody
by Jimmy Kachulis
50449518 Book/Online Audio $24.99

0819
309

LEARN MUSIC ONLINE WITH BERKLEE
Study with Berklee's world-renowned faculty and gain the professional credentials needed to advance your career in music.
• Online Bachelor of Professional Studies Degree
• Multi-Course Certificate Programs
• Interactive Online Courses
• Free Massive Open Online Courses (MOOCs)
PROGRAMS IN
Music Production
Guitar
Music Theory, Harmony, and Ear Training
Songwriting
Music Business
Voice
Piano and Keyboard
Arranging
Bass
Orchestration
Drums
Music History and Liberal Arts
Music for Film, TV, and Games
Improvisation
Berklee Online
1-866-BERKLEE
Learn more at online.berklee.edu